Show Town

Show Town

Theater and Culture in the Pacific Northwest
1890–1920

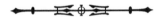

Holly George

UNIVERSITY OF OKLAHOMA PRESS : NORMAN

This book is published with the generous assistance of The Kerr Foundation, Inc.

Library of Congress Cataloging-in-Publication Data

Names: George, Holly, 1978– author.
Title: Show town : theater and culture in the Pacific Northwest, 1890–1920 / Holly George.
Description: Norman : University of Oklahoma Press, [2016] | Includes bibliographical references and index.
Identifiers: LCCN 2016009722 | ISBN 978-0-8061-5435-0 (hardcover) ISBN 978-0-8061-9219-2 (paperback) Subjects: LCSH: Theater—Washington (State)—Spokane—History—20th
century. | Theater—Washington (State)—Spokane—History—19th century. | Theater and society—Washington (State)—Spokane.
Classification: LCC PN2277.S66 G46 2016 | DDC 792.09797/37—dc23
LC record available at https://lccn.loc.gov/2016009722

The paper in this book meets the guidelines for permanence and durability of the Committee on Production Guidelines for Book Longevity of the Council on Library Resources, Inc. ∞

Contents

Illustrations

Tables

Acknowledgments

This work began as a question about the connection between boosterism and the arts in the urban West. From that question to this book, I have benefited from the remarkable support of friends, teachers, and systems throughout the West. Sara Early and Kim McKaig of *Pacific Northwest Quarterly* have taught me too much to list. The staff of the University of Washington (UW) libraries—especially Gary Lundell in Special Collections—were enormously helpful as were the staffs of the following libraries: Washington State University (WSU) Spokane, Eastern Washington University (EWU), the Spokane Public Library (SPL), the Las Vegas–Clark County Library District, and the Utah State Library. Jane Davey, Rose Krause, and Anna Harbine at the Northwest Museum of Arts and Culture (the MAC) deserve special mention, as does Riva Dean at the SPL. At one point while I was studying at UW, teaching adjunct at EWU, working part-time at WSU Spokane, and interning at the MAC, I was practically a ward of the State of Washington. Thank you, Washington. I learned so much from my friends at UW, Wendi Lindquist, Tim Wright, and Chris Herbert. Thank you to Judith Van Dongen, who translated old Dutch business records for me. Jeff Nichols generously shared his research on variety theaters in Salt Lake City. Kent Powell, Brad Westwood, Jed Rogers, and the incomparable Lisa Buckmiller, as well as other colleagues at the Utah State Historical Society, gave me a great deal of encouragement. Thank you also to Chris Hansen for last-minute architectural advice, and to Bruce Hevly, Margaret O'Mara, Barry Witham, and two anonymous readers who all helped to shape this study with their knowledge and insight. Carl Abbott's reading and suggestions (not to mention his scholarship) were invaluable. I owe Bob McPherson a big thank you for helping me finally get this project out the door. David Wrobel's kindness gave me the courage to send my manuscript to the University of Oklahoma Press. The support of Kathleen Kelly of OU Press has done much for this project. And then there's John Findlay—the ideal teacher and mentor, if you ask me. John's brilliant questions, generosity, and knowledge shaped this work in many ways. Thank you. Stephen and Tanya Buck, my parents, cannot be praised enough. Their dedication to their beliefs and to each other changed the course of our family. Finally, Rick George, my beloved husband, has sacrificed more than I care to think about in support of my goals. Darling, I owe you a pie.

Show Town

Introduction

Spokane and the Stage

Marinus Crommelin had been in Spokane, Washington, for only five weeks on an October evening in 1901, but he already knew that the girls there expected fellows to treat them to the "theater now and then, the outing for the Americans and especially the people of Spokane." The Dutch youth started his efforts at making female friends by taking a certain Miss Roy to watch "Hermann the Great" and other vaudevillians at the posh Auditorium Theater. By early December, theater ranked high in Crommelin's list of fixed expenses—a fact his mother did not appreciate.[1] But in Spokane, theater ranked high in many people's priorities.

Spokanites loved theater. They prided themselves on living in a "good show town," and from roughly 1890 to 1920 theirs was a lively, at times recognized, theatrical scene. How, then, did the professional stage relate to Spokane's image and identity as a city? How did theater help or hinder the efforts of Spokanites to advertise their home in the American West? How did the business of theater connect Spokane to national and international markets? How did stage productions, which focused increasingly on female beauty after the Civil War, influence the opinions and behaviors of Spokanites about gender and sexuality?

From Spokane's origins in the 1870s, its people boosted the city relentlessly. The Victorians defined culture as Culture—those manifestations of the highest white human endeavors, such as visual arts, literature, and music—and civic promoters paraded whatever emblems of culture they could to demonstrate their advancement.[2] Throughout the United States, theaters joined the mansions and Mozart clubs that boosters bragged of in their pamphlets. In the late nineteenth

A 1908 panoramic view of Spokane, Washington, likely from the southeast. Note the fine homes, ponderosa pines, and business district in the background. Haines Photograph Company. Courtesy Library of Congress, 2007662943.

and early twentieth centuries, however, theatrical genres included not only the drama and opera patronized by elite audiences but also far more plebeian forms, such as variety theater. Thus a local theater scene could prove a blessing or an embarrassment for publicists. Middle-class Spokanites cited access to high-toned "road shows" as evidence of the city's cultural refinement and economic maturity. But Spokane also had a notorious theatrical underworld, with variety houses that felt anything but genteel. The city's theaters could make the community seem like a center of art and learning (at least in print) or like an unfinished, uninhibited mining town (and that not in print).

Just so, Spokane's theaters tell us much about its place within the United States, both geographically and economically, at the turn of the century. Spokane acted as the urban hub of an area of the Pacific Northwest that contemporaries called the Inland Empire, whose economy was built on the resource-extractive industries of mining, agriculture, and logging. These industries gave Spokane its foundation, but they also made it vulnerable. Like much of the North American West, the city was a "resource colony" for the East, and Spokanites depended on European and eastern investors and systems for their prosperity.[3] Furthermore, those extractive industries required a cheap, seasonal labor force. Itinerant laborers—

mostly male, mostly unattached—filled that need. At the end of a stint in the mines, forests, or fields, thousands of workingmen flocked to Spokane, where they spent their pay on riotous entertainments. There was a reason the city's downtown felt like the Wild West. The issues of western vulnerability and western imagery became major elements in the business of and debates about theater in Spokane.

Finally, the years when professional theater flourished in Spokane were also years of great social change in America, when the prevailing ethos shifted from the Victorian insistence on self-control to the "modern" search for self-fulfillment. Much of this involved an evolution in the behavior of women, in public discussion of sexuality, and in the boundaries of interaction between men and women. Genres across the theatrical spectrum fed into this change. In Spokane, the stage galvanized debate about gender ideals within that slippery, heterogeneous group called the middle class. This is not to say that Spokanites of other classes did not attend or talk about the stage. Working people kept the city's variety theaters alive with their patronage. However, the ideals that underwent change were generally those of middle America. What is more (and more frustrating for the historian), most extant records about Spokane's theatrical experience come from middle-class sources. The city's gentry surely contributed to Spokane's theatrical life, but such individuals were often only one generation removed—if that—from humbler circumstances. Consequently, middle-class Spokanites are the main actors in this study.

All of these subjects pertain to Spokane's image as a city. In this book theater—its business and content—is used to understand social relations and cultural norms, outside connections, and urban identity in Spokane from 1890 to 1920. Theater provided Spokanites with both a source of metropolitan pride and a degree of western rawness. It affected and reflected their concepts of propriety and showed the difficulty of cultivating connections with outside capital and influences. The current work elucidates two not unrelated trends: the shift from Victorian to modern values and the effects of market relationships.

Boosterism, Urban Hierarchies, and Culture

Cities played a critical role in the Euro-American settlement of the West, their development often preceding (or at least coinciding with) non-urban growth. But not every western town prospered or survived. As cities and towns became integrated into an increasingly market-driven nation, they vied for control of the resources—in politics, transportation, economic development, and population— that would allow them to command "watersheds of urban allegiance."[4] Each new settlement wanted to become the entrepôt that its hinterland looked to for services and leadership. Yet even regional hubs required investment from truly powerful metropolises like New York City or London; local boosters knew this and courted capital from the international system of cities.[5]

Beyond a sense of civic pride, town builders competed so heavily with one another because they often had a vested interest in a town's success. Many a western settlement existed as a neatly platted map long before it thrived as an actual city—if that indeed ever happened. These paper towns were filled with lots available for sale, lots that land speculators bought cheap and hoped to sell dear as they convinced settlers this was the investment chance of a lifetime. The speculator and his colleague the civic booster were central figures in this key aspect of western settlement, and their grandiose language pervaded western advertising and newspapers. Boosting and speculation defined settlement in the Pacific Northwest as much as anywhere. As Carlos Schwantes notes, "townsite gambling became an epidemic, a regional vice. The amount of money and energy that promoters spent in describing the resources, capabilities, and wonders of the Pacific Northwest was prodigious," as chambers of commerce, railroads, and local immigration boards sponsored a deluge of publicity.[6]

Urban promotion begs the question of urban identity. Which images, what arguments did that publicity contain? First, boosters advertised their towns as the place nature itself had chosen for prominence, but even as they boasted of climate, waterways, soil, mineral resources, and a host of other natural advantages, they also informed their audiences of a town's more human achievements: its culture. If the boosters could be trusted, clubs, academies, and opera houses graced (or would, someday) the tree-lined streets of countless western towns. The culture described in brochures and articles was derived from the styles and forms of culture in the East, which in turn had descended from those in Europe.

Ballyhoo aside, westerners established cultural institutions early, frequently, and for a number of reasons. Settlers often wanted to prove that their new little town could uphold eastern standards of civilization and respectability; they wanted family and associates to know that theirs was a decent place where decent people lived, not an outpost in the wilderness. Certain people and cities could take this to another level and use culture (such as museums, musical organizations, architecture, or expositions) to demonstrate that they were not only respectable but on par with the East in terms of wealth and position. In other words, such people consumed as Thorstein Veblen theorized they did: conspicuously, to establish their social status.[7] San Francisco's nouveaux riches, for example, self-consciously built gorgeous homes and hotels as a symbol to the world that the Bay city had transitioned "from a raw mining camp and disordered boom-town to an established, civilized city."[8] This phrase describes Spokane's cultural history well, its anxieties and its pride. Accordingly, civic promotion and identity help us understand how cultural endeavors like professional theater influenced the development of western cities.

The Evolution of the American Stage

Our story spans from 1890 to 1920, but cultural and social trends from earlier decades bear heavily on it. Middle-class Spokanites cultivated certain theatrical genres for their prestige and scorned others for their infamy. Social class was key to the connotations surrounding theatrical genres, as the bifurcated history of nineteenth-century American culture establishes. Separately, the development of show business affected what Spokane's theatergoers could watch and circumscribed their ability to control the artistic face of the city.

The Cultural Divide, 1820s–1890s

The American theater changed markedly from early to the late nineteenth century. During the early republic and Jacksonian eras, theater-going was a cross-class affair with a rowdy feel. Performances were as variegated as audiences. Americans of this era did not designate certain playwrights, composers, or art forms as "high" or "low." Rather, as Lawrence Levine has demonstrated, Shakespeare himself provided the most popular of entertainments, and the Bard's work often appeared alongside farce and animal tricks.[9]

Then, during the mid- to late 1840s, audiences started to fracture along class lines. Impresarios eager for an expanded market began courting "respectable" women by insisting on well-behaved audiences and sanitized shows.[10] Houses began focusing on "legitimate" theater—plays without variety acts, burlesque, or musical comedy—and kept dramatic bills pure of popular diversions. By 1860 the "noisy, dirty, disgusting, and vulgar" had largely been expunged from bourgeois theater.[11]

As theaters cleaned up, they joined a program for establishing middle-class Victorian respectability and reinforcing upper-class prestige.[12] The division in theater was part of a larger cultural split, where the arbiters of gentility designated certain forms and artists as Art—those that edified, refined, and educated—and condemned the rest as "lowbrow" drivel, merely amusing.[13] Meanwhile, working-class diversions took their own route; such entertainments included the penny press; freak, medicine, and tent shows; and blackface minstrelsy.[14] Entrepreneurs learned to play to either one crowd or the other. It became clear, one critic noted, that amusements now separated on the basis of a "division of labor."[15]

A popular form of great importance to this work is variety theater. Nationally, variety flourished from around the Civil War to the 1890s.

An evening at a variety house included short acts presented by a resident troupe, ready access to alcohol, and critically, the company of attractive young waitresses. As Robert Allen notes about variety's cousin, the concert saloon, these theaters celebrated everything purged from proper houses: blue material, drinking, and a rollicking atmosphere.[16] Further, men formed the bulk of patrons; women attended these shows at the risk of their reputation. If legitimate rested atop the theatrical hierarchy, gilding people and communities with the gleam of high culture, then variety could do the opposite.

The Form and Business of the Theater

Just as American audiences evolved throughout the nineteenth century, so too did the business of troupes and booking change. For much of the 1800s, resident stock companies dominated the legitimate stage. After the Civil War, touring repertory companies flourished. Late in the century, a new system arose: the traveling combination company or "road show." As their name indicated, road shows existed because of an expanding transcontinental railroad system. Combination troupes focused on one play, generally originated in New York City, and toured throughout the United States. Railroads were the lifeblood of road shows, and booking was their bane. Local managers arrived in New York City every June and haggled with producers for next season's lineup. Not infrequently, companies and managers signed multiple and conflicting contracts, leaving each other without a show or without a house.[17]

Theatrical circuits soon developed as an answer to this complicated situation. Some theaters in the 1870s began scheduling attractions cooperatively, creating small regional circuits that were appreciated by the traveling companies for their simplicity. As local circuits grew in the 1880s, booking agencies in New York City opened to work with them. During this era of business conglomeration, the next step seemed logical. In 1896 three partnerships joined their concerns into one super-agency: the Theatrical Syndicate. Together, six men controlled many of the nation's first-class theaters as well as the smaller houses and markets that the troupes depended on for financial success. Moreover, "the trust" mandated that, if a town had a syndicate theater, attractions could only play in that house. Under these conditions, independent theaters struggled to secure top Broadway stars, and companies could easily fail if they were operating outside the syndicate.[18]

Many actors and managers hated the syndicate, but they resisted the organization at their peril. As the century turned, new conglomerates and agencies arose to combat the trust. Especially spirited fights came from the Shubert brothers and a group of Pacific Northwest theatrical managers. In the meantime, circuits and booking trusts had developed for popular-priced legitimate theater and vaudeville. All of these business innovations and circumstances had a tremendous impact on Spokane's theatrical scene.[19]

The City and the Stage in a New Century

Historians agree that American social mores at the turn of the twentieth century shifted markedly, from so-called Victorian to modern values. At the heart of American Victorianism lay a dichotomy between things uplifting, which must be cultivated, and things base, which must be controlled. During the nineteenth century white, middle-class Americans generally endorsed an ethic of thrift, piety, delayed gratification, and a strictly controlled body (especially of its animal-like sexuality). Of course these values represented an ideal, not the reality of everyday behavior. Still, many Americans encouraged their sons to develop an unyielding "character" that would facilitate success in a competitive world. Women and girls, meanwhile, were to remain passionless and cloistered within the home.[20]

Victorianism began to erode in the 1890s when, as T. J. Jackson Lears notes, "many yearned to smash the glass and breathe freely— to experience 'real life' in all its intensity."[21] The forces that challenged this predominant culture included the experiences of Civil War and westward migration, a dissatisfaction with liberal Protestantism, a fear that modern industrial life had become too easy, intellectual and scientific developments that challenged Victorian tenets, an influx of immigrants, and the growth of cities. Through their participation in such "frontier" amusements as variety theaters and gambling joints, working-class Spokanites and other westerners were at the forefront of so-called modern indulgence. By the first decades of the twentieth century, Victorianism was gradually being replaced by a celebration of leisure, spending, and individual fulfillment; a desire to integrate the "animal" and "divine" elements that the Victorians had worked so hard to keep separate; and an expanding public role for women.

Mass commercial entertainments such as amusement parks, dance halls, ice cream parlors, nickelodeons, and vaudeville theaters reflected and fed this evolution of values. These amusements relaxed social boundaries and brought once private activities into the public sphere, just as they popularized styles from working-class, immigrant, African American, and demimonde cultures. The stage joined other entertainments in setting trends and changing minds. For instance, actors and actresses had long remained outside polite society, their public and itinerant lives at odds with the elevated domesticity of the nineteenth-century middle class. But when Americans began to chafe against the strictures of Victorian morality and industrialization, the life of a performer began to seem free and fun. Actresses especially offered other women an example of apparent glamor and independence.[22]

Meanwhile, theatrical genres at all levels of the cultural hierarchy pushed the boundaries of propriety. Serious "problem plays" such as Henrik Ibsen's *Ghosts* or Clyde Fitch's *Sapho* forced discussion about marriage, the place of women, and the double standard. Musical comedies and spectaculars—often viewed on the same provincial stages as legitimate dramas but considered less refined or artistic—changed standards in another way. Around the mid-nineteenth century, American theater began glorifying the visual rather than the verbal.[23] By the 1900s once-scandalous "leg shows" were common, and frothy extravaganzas built around feminine beauty filled the middle-brow stage. Such displays led to an increasing fascination with actresses and to reconsideration of what female modesty entailed.

During this era a genre with a tremendous cultural impact arose: vaudeville. In the late 1880s Tony Pastor, B. F. Keith, and other impresarios realized the money-making potential of affordable entertainments that were safe for the entire family. They presented lineups that, like the naughty old variety theaters, featured a string of unrelated acts and a low price. Unlike variety theaters, vaudeville houses were self-consciously free of alcohol and innuendo.[24]

While managers capitalized on a scrubbed-clean image, many vaudevillians "skirted the edges of indecency."[25] Performers like Eva Tanguay, who was known as the "I Don't Care" Girl, made sly challenges to genteel propriety, while slapstick and ethnic comedians brought big-city, immigrant humor to the farthest reaches of the United States. The genius of vaudeville lay not only in its Sunday-school reputation (however inaccurate) but also in its format. With shows throughout the day, vaudeville catered to urban life; patrons could drop in at lunch, after work, or in the midst of a shopping excursion. Finally, vaudeville emerged during an era of geographical connections, becoming a premier expression of modern, mass America: cheap, urban, popular, unintellectual but harmless, and tailored to a host of tastes.[26]

The accessibility of vaudeville raises one final point about turn-of-the-century American theater: how transportation systems and urban growth nurtured it. To paraphrase Benjamin McArthur, it was no accident that vaudeville, musical comedies, boilerplate melodramas, legitimate, and other live entertainments flourished in this era. They did so because America was becoming a nation of cities, where commercial amusements augmented or replaced home-based recreation as urbanites sought respite from industrial life.[27] That shows originated in metropolises and were made available—via the railroad—to hamlets and cities across the United States meant they spread urban style and ideals. When audiences in places such as Spokane (or the hinterland surrounding it) watched an Ibsen drama, a girlie Florence Ziegfeld show, or a vaudeville slapstick, they came away having been at least introduced to new ideas about gender, sexual relations, and manners.

A Show Town in the Provinces

The history of the professional stage in Spokane largely mirrored the path of the city itself: small but self-consciously striving in the 1880s; bolstered by boomtown money—and riven with class conflict—in the 1890s; dynamic throughout the 1900s, though increasingly controlled by outside financing; and falling into shabby gentility in the 1910s. To use a different comparison, professional entertainment in the inland city looked like a roller-coaster, lifted and dropped by the momentum of external forces. This study of Spokane as a show town follows the course of its professional theater from the late 1880s to 1920, using the stage to understand a tangle of concepts, including urban promotion, identity, and hierarchies; municipal reform politics; class relations; gender identity; and broad cultural change.

Chapter 1 tells the story of the Auditorium Theater, a monument to boosterism and new money that set the standard for polite Spokane, exploring the ambitions of Spokane's privileged classes (people made wealthy through mining and real estate gambles), the efforts of a frontier town to brand itself as culturally advanced, and how such attempts fed into Spokane's campaign to position itself above rival towns. The Auditorium's history must be understood within the contexts of both a speculation-frenzied West—where town-builders glorified whatever assets they could to attract settlers and market connections—and late Victorian concepts of cultural proprieties and hierarchies. For Spokane had plenty of other institutions (theaters, in fact) that offended nineteenth-century sensibilities, even as they benefited local merchants.

Mines, farms, and lumber camps: these things made Spokane. The extractive industries that buttressed the city's economy employed thousands of wage laborers on a seasonal basis. Spokane was the big city and rail center of the Inland Northwest, so those workers, most of whom were young men, passed their between-job furloughs there, resting, romancing, drinking, and spending. Among the establishments most attractive to workingmen were variety theaters: naughty, rollicking, and profitable.

The variety houses enriched those shopkeepers whose sights were set on fleecing hired hands, but they thwarted the broader ambitions of people trying—for reasons of ideals or investments—to promote Spokane as a respectable "home city." From the late 1880s to 1908, variety theaters proved a source of perennial discord in a city attempting to define itself. Those years of discord provide a particular opportunity to explore how Spokanites dealt with images of their city and with cultural change. To those people for whom varieties signaled barbarism and malaise, *modernity* meant using public policy to expunge savage entertainments from their city's social life. Variety theaters form the topic of chapters 2 and 3.

Capitalism fostered the conditions that led to Spokane's trade in variety theaters, but market and geographical networks also influenced the city's "respectable" stage, as chapter 4 establishes. The mechanisms that made Spokane a resource colony to the East—a supplier of wood, grain, and silver—also made it a place that theater moguls could incorporate into their empires. Further, just as Spokane by the early twentieth century was ever more implicated in big business and high finance, nationwide the professional stage was increasingly consolidated and monopolized. This reminded smaller cities and businesses of their low place in the pecking order. Geography and urban position were key, because the theatrical trusts originated in New York City and operated via railroad-facilitated circuits. Showmen in Spokane and the Northwest became involved—at times deeply, at times to their own detriment—in the fight against these big city trusts. In the end, Spokanites dealt with both the windfalls and the vulnerability that came from being on the receiving end of corporate decisions.

Finally, chapter 5 is an examination of the meeting point of civic identity, geography, and morality in Spokane throughout the 1900s and 1910s. Even as Spokanites fought over variety theaters, they attended racy, raucous shows at legitimate and vaudeville houses. Spokanites perceived such risqué theater to have originated in Paris and New York at the peril of their own city, and indeed, traveling productions appeared in Spokane through the instrumentality of physical and financial networks emanating from regional and national metropolises. Spokane's enjoyment of daring theater occurred amidst a broad cultural shift from Victorian to twentieth-century values. Despite their protestations, local theatergoers financially supported shows that pushed forward social change, and after their initial hesitation many Spokanites adopted the styles promoted onstage.

As the relationships among urban identity, cultural change, and market connections are elucidated in this study, several lines of thought emerge, which include the histories of cities, reform, and culture in the American West—as well as American cultural history, especially as it pertains to gender and the shift from Victorian to modern ideals. Western urban history, in the nineteenth and early twentieth centuries, forms the starting point for this project.[28] The setting of the American West matters tremendously, for the differences of western life played a significant role in the cultural development of Spokane and the Inland Northwest.

A growing number of historians have written sophisticated analyses of American theater, culture, and gender during this era. Just so, studies of cultural hierarchy, late Victorian malaise, gender identity within the cultural marketplace, and mass commercial amusements have become numerous and rich within the past three decades.[29] Yet such research focuses almost exclusively on the eastern United States and New York. Further, though a smattering of scholars and enthusiasts have written about theater in the West, this subject has not received the same coverage as it has for the eastern context. And studies of the stage in the Northwest only rarely go beyond chronicling and local color.[30] These represent missed opportunities, for the stage can help historians understand broader concepts such as civic promotion, political reform, gender identity, shifting values, social class, and the connections between geography, capitalism, and culture. General research on turn-of-the-century culture in the West compared to the East is less spotty than study of theater but still meager. This scholarship tends to concern literature, tourism, architecture, expositions, or homegrown efforts to enjoy the blessings of civilization, rather than a sustained and long-term industry like professional theater.[31]

It would be new enough to place studies of vaudeville, amusement parks, and showgirls in the American West. The western context matters, for institutions developed differently there than in the East, the nation's cultural center. But more must be done than simply move the story west. The insights of western urban history (market connections, regional insecurities, speculative town-building), combined with those of turn-of-the-century cultural history (specifically, gender identity and shifting values), teach us much about the West and about American life in this era. We learn how politics, business, and reform mingled with culture; how westerners dealt with outside ideas, including images of themselves; how they manipulated culture to promote their region; and how the instruments of capitalism and technology were used to both disseminate information and gather the West into the national marketplace.

In this book we explore the transition from Victorian to twentieth-century values in the context of the inland American West, a region where cultural change unfolded differently than elsewhere. Because of the western setting, a host of influences fed into the inland West's cultural experience and transition: the late-nineteenth-century boosterism that, in order to attract outside attention and investment, magnified any scrap of "respectable" art and tried to disown anything that smacked of "western" abandon; the demographic imbalance that initially pushed the market to favor disreputable amusements and thus belied the boosters' claims; the region's role as a resource colony for the East, which fostered both the early preponderance of young men and the continuing local dependence on outside infrastructure and investment for first-class entertainment; and the ongoing self-consciousness that led art aficionados to qualify so many of their opinions and enjoyments in relation to those of the East. These aspects of the Inland Northwest's cultural development meant that, even as its people grew along with other Americans to favor "self-realization" over Victorian self-control in the early twentieth century, they did so in a fundamentally different setting.

CHAPTER ONE

Theater and Boosterism in Late Victorian Spokane

In 1889 the *Spokane Globe* described the residents of Spokane, Washington, as "refined, intellectual and energetic," people who "would add luster to the most cultured court of the period" and whose urbanity sprang, from among other things, their love of the stage.[1] The *Globe's* deployment of culture for civic promotion was hardly uncommon, either in Spokane or elsewhere in the West, and for a good reason: a city's clubs, churches, schools, or theaters marked it as a place that fit within established white middle-class America. Thus white middle-class Spokanites made cultural claims part of the steady stream of ballyhoo they produced; when Spokane's white middle-class people boasted of their refinement, they were telling other Americans that respectable Victorians could live there. In late-century Spokane, legitimate theater symbolized the boosting efforts of the city's middle and upper class.

Young Spokane's promotional use of the stage culminated with the 1890 opening of the Auditorium, a facility built by local nouveaux riches and openly acknowledged as an advertisement for the city.[2] Yet, if the Auditorium embodied elite Spokane's attempts to market the town to potential residents and investors, the theater also demonstrated the difficultly of the city's relationship with the very groups its people tried to attract. First, though affluent Spokanites sought the validation of highbrow culture by building and patronizing the Auditorium, they did not walk the line of Victorian propriety—showing, instead, a proclivity for the light and the naughty. Upper-class Spokanites sponsored the derivative art that lent them a patina of culture—but apparently did not particularly like it. They at once aped and rejected the culture prescribed by eastern, Victorian critics. With this judgment of the canon, Spokanites expressed their distance from both the East and from the values of the nineteenth century.

The Auditorium of the 1890s illustrated a second aspect of Spokane's connection to outside forces. The theater was conceived and built by local men, but they did not finance it. Rather, it was one of many Spokane properties heavily mortgaged to an investment bank. When the Panic of 1893 occurred, the Inland Northwest could not resist the malaise. Spokane crashed hard, and the Auditorium was repossessed by European capitalists. Late-nineteenth-century networks of transportation, communication, and commerce facilitated upper-class Spokane's enjoyment of the arts but also made the city a financial house of cards. All told, the story of the Auditorium demonstrates the many factors that complicated Spokane's relationship with eastern and European society: factors that included a desire to conform to Victorian standards even as these standards lost currency throughout the United States, the reality of Spokane's arriviste upper-class and its preference for "middle-brow" theater, and finally, the economic and cultural difficulties Spokanites faced as they tried to transplant eastern art into a raw western environment.

Joining the Cultural Order

Spokane began its urban career as did many American towns: inconspicuous, but ambitious nonetheless. Native Americans for years had used the area near the falls of the Spokane River as a gathering place, and a fur trading post known as the Spokane House existed in the region in the early nineteenth century. Still, as late as the 1860s, there was little indication of the site's future use. This changed in 1873, when a pair of Oregon speculators bought a claim near the falls because they had heard the Northern Pacific Railroad might pass through there. But things remained quiet for years. Finally, in 1879, news that the Northern Pacific's Pend Oreille division would indeed be built led to burgeoning settlement in the region. By 1880 Spokane Falls (as it was known until 1891) had a population of 350, putting it well behind local rivals such as Dayton (996) and belying its claims to be the natural place for metropolitan growth.[3]

When growth occurred, it did so largely because of the decisions of powerful entities and financiers.[4] From 1881 to 1892 Spokane enjoyed its first rush of development as its economic foundations were laid. The importance of railroads in this process cannot be overemphasized. The first big event of the decade took place in 1881 when the Northern Pacific arrived. This watershed moment could have easily not occurred if the company had based its route on a different river; Spokane would have then remained geographically isolated until the 1890s. As it was, Spokane was only a small town on a rail line, competing with other small towns for what prizes it could.[5]

The second key event stretched from 1882 to 1885, when mineral discoveries in the Idaho panhandle allowed Spokane to become an outfitting point for the lucrative rush. But again, Spokane's victory here was not a fait accompli, for although Spokanites stocked mining supplies and perfected a byzantine method for reaching the diggings, theirs was neither the closest nor the solitary gateway to the Coeur d'Alenes. Then in 1886, an eastern capitalist named Daniel Chase Corbin concluded that a rail line through the Idaho mines meant profit. Luckily for Spokane, timing and legalities made the Washington site the outlet for Corbin's road. The story illustrates well how mining and railroads interacted to Spokane's benefit. As further mineral deposits were discovered in the Inland Northwest in the 1880s—and roads were built to them—Spokane became a mining headquarters.

Railroad development placed another major stone in Spokane's economic foundation: agriculture. As with other aspects of the city's growth, attracting the farm market required plenty of competition and promotion. When a competing railroad threatened to siphon away the business of Palouse farmers, Corbin built the Spokane and Palouse Line (1886–1888). With that Spokane became the Palouse's supply and distribution point. By 1888 rail lines stretched east, west, and south from Spokane, connecting northwestern mines and farms with eastern markets. In 1892 the city became part of another transcontinental line when property holders gladly supplied James J. Hill with the free right-of-way that guaranteed Spokane a spot on the Great Northern. Spokane was "railroad made."[6] The rail building of the 1880s and 1890s realigned transportation corridors—and thus urban influence—away from Lewiston and Walla Walla and made Spokane the largest railroad hub between Minneapolis and Seattle.[7]

The 1880s were heady years for Spokane. Its population mush-roomed from 350 (1880) to 1,169 (1885) to 19,922 (1890), a nearly 6,000 percent increase. Haphazard, often sloppy, development accompanied the boom. Spokane was a jumble of unpaved streets, false front shops, and ponderosa pines. But the boomtown had pretensions—many of them. Spokanites aggressively advertised their town from the start, recognizing that they had to attract settlers, investors, and business to keep the good times coming.[8] An 1888 account, for instance, compared Spokane's prospects to those of Minneapolis, advising readers that "those who buy in the primary stage of successful towns are the ones who reap the largest rewards." The following year, the local board of trade sponsored a pamphlet that waxed eloquent about "the commercial and manufacturing advantages of the city" and proudly displayed its few fine homes and buildings.[9]

An important aspect of such civic promotion was a demonstration that Spokane fit a certain cultural order, that this rough new town belonged to the white, educated, and respectable world of mainstream America. Respectability, in other words, was an important asset in attracting settlers and investors. For this reason and others, prominent Spokanites pushed forward a small but ambitious cultural life in the 1880s.[10] Theater joined the list of attainments Spokanites bragged about during the decade, though their claims were obviously threadbare. The genres at the top of the cultural hierarchy, legitimate and grand opera, came to town only through the concerted action of Spokane's "better element." When large productions played in Spokane, they did so once the railroad had made the trip convenient and then as one-night stands—signaling that even if Spokanites considered themselves to be devotees of the stage, the market did not justify risking much on their town.

The theatrical highlights of 1880s Spokane demonstrate how towns used culture against each other. Consider the February 1887 appearance of the Emma Abbott opera company. Securing a troupe of this caliber required an advance subscription of $1,000, which local elites gladly contributed. Abbott threw Spokane into a dither: nearly every business closed in the diva's honor, and people waded through ankle-deep mud to meet her.[11] Yet the show took place in a drafty frame hall that its builder "had the great nerve [to call] 'Joy's Opera House.'"[12] When the company traveled on to Walla Walla, the level of local identity wrapped up in the affair became obvious. In Spokane Abbott performed Michael Balfe's opera *Bohemian Girl*; in Walla Walla she presented lighter fare. The *Spokane Falls Review* seized on this fact as proof of Spokane's cultural (and hence overall) superiority.[13] A Walla Walla newspaper rebutted that *Bohemian Girl* was grand, too grand for a "Punch and Judy" venue like Joy's Opera House and a pup like Spokane. Spokane dismissed the insult and instead reflected on its progress, but Walla Walla had a point: one month after Abbott's appearance, Joy's was converted from an "opera house" to an agricultural implement store.[14]

Walla Walla's sarcasm reflected a deeper injury. Positioned near the Columbia River, Walla Walla had served as a major inland trading center for years. With the regional advent of the railroad, the Columbia lost some of its primacy as a transportation route, as did Walla Walla. By 1887 Spokane stood poised to wrest control of lucrative trading routes from Walla Walla, and in the upcoming years Spokane shot ahead of its erstwhile rival.[15] The Emma Abbott scrimmage, then, reflected how aspiring western towns connected cultural hierarchy with civic identity and used it as another tool to gain dominance.[16]

After this Spokanites only amplified their efforts to put their town on the artistic map. In the summer of 1887 with Joy's Opera House having renounced show business, those of a cultural and civic mind scrambled to find a site for another large opera company. Their answer was a canvas tent lit by two borrowed street lamps.[17] These circumstances embarrassed the booming town and were corrected with the November 1887 opening of the Falls City Opera House. As the top stories of a business block, the new hall was still crude, but it allowed Spokane to enjoy legitimate drama with more regularity and sophistication.[18]

Almost as important, the Falls City Opera House—its name imbued with local pride—gave Spokane bragging rights. *Spokane Falls Illustrated*, an 1889 pamphlet published under the auspices of the board of trade, boasted that Spokane had "ever retained" the honor among professional thespians of being a "'good show town.'" The best shows from the best companies, the brochure continued, were exhibited "to the criticism of intelligent and art-loving audiences."[19] In other words, cramped and inconvenient though it was, the Falls City Opera House served as another feather in the cap of the boosters eager to mark Spokane as a place of finish and grace—where one could live and invest.

Shakespeare, Cannon, Beethoven, and Browne

Whatever theatrical venues Spokane had by the end of the 1880s, the situation changed on August 4, 1889, when fire destroyed thirty-two square blocks of downtown Spokane, including the new opera house.[20] The city's residents responded to the disaster with vigor but also in a way that showed their speculative and derivative bent. After the initial devastation, Spokanites used the disaster as an opportunity to remake their city in a finer fashion: haphazard wooden buildings yielded to brick, and the town's already lively real estate market skyrocketed.[21] Spokane's rebuilding set off an over-heated real estate boom and by 1892, more than a million dollars had been invested in new buildings. But the hundreds of new houses and business blocks did not take on just any form. No. Spokanites wanted their reborn home to look metropolitan and eastern and therefore modeled it on powerful American cities, specifically Chicago. In this city of mud streets, a visiting Dutch banker remarked that he had never seen a place with such overwhelming buildings, prompting him to ask whether local leaders had been a touch excessive.[22]

Spokane's first citizens had much impetus to reconstruct their city. On one hand, with an increasing concentration of railroads in the late 1880s, Spokane was becoming the regional hub its promoters dreamed of.[23] Economic expansion meant both a developing local gentry and growing investment by Spokane's stakeholders, groups concerned with the image their city projected and the amenities it offered. On the other hand, few could describe the months that followed the fire as refined. Amid the tents that popped up in the ruined downtown were those of Jacob "Dutch Jake" Goetz and Harry Baer, partners who kept their notorious gambling resort more than alive throughout that cold winter. Such considerations surely played into the decision to make Spokane a more attractive, more culturally advanced, place.[24]

A celebrated feature of the reborn Spokane was a structure already under construction when the fire broke out, the Auditorium Theater.[25] Initially referred to as the "new" or "grand" opera house, the Auditorium became a symbol of civic progress and social status, serving notice that this rich little city had arrived. Like their theater, the Auditorium's owners—Anthony M. Cannon and John J. Browne—were emblematic of Spokane's economic development. Both men hailed from the Midwest, Cannon looking for his main chance from Kansas to Los Angeles, Browne studying and practicing law; they likely met in Portland, Oregon.[26]

These "live-wire promoters" came to Spokane in the 1870s, purchased much real estate, and quickly became dealers in the kind of speculative transactions that had made (and unmade) fortunes throughout the West. Their names strewn throughout town—Browne's Addition, Cannon's Addition, Cannon's Block, Browne Street—the two men were able to capitalize on the mineral rushes, political plums, and railroad business that caused 1880s Spokane to boom so fabulously. By 1889 Browne and Cannon had decided that a beautiful theater could only enhance the town's image and that they would bankroll it.[27]

As with cultural endeavors throughout the United States, the Auditorium borrowed its form and style from theaters in older areas. This derivative aspect was intentional for it signaled that Spokane belonged to the world of established respectability. The Pacific Northwest, at this point, had fresh examples of highbrow theaters. Harry C. Hayward, Spokane's theater manager since 1887, returned in November 1889 from a tour of trend-setting opera houses in three of the region's top cities, Tacoma, Portland, and San Francisco. That Hayward visited these theaters during the Auditorium's construction was no coincidence, for Spokane's city fathers intended their house to be as grand as anything in the United States. Accordingly, Cannon and Browne patterned the Auditorium not on a Portland or a Tacoma house but, rather, on New York City's Broadway, "with many additional

The Auditorium Theater, a pressed-brick Victorian commercial-style building. A gilded statue of Thalia topped the central tower. The L-shaped structure, seen here from Main and Post, consisted of two wings. The wing pictured here housed businesses and ran along Post Street. Theatergoers entered at the northern corner through a long lobby corridor that led to the theater proper. The Auditorium was built in part as an advertisement for Spokane; through its location in a business block, the venue was physically tied to commerce as well. Courtesy Northwest Room, Spokane Public Library.

improvements."[28] The boosters' desire to cement Spokane's place in the cultural and urban hierarchy becomes clear with a story often told about the Auditorium: on discovering that a Chicago theater had the largest stage in the nation, Browne and Cannon ordered their builders to make the Auditorium's stage wider and deeper by one foot.[29]

A neighboring mountain supplied the granite that became the Auditorium building. Nearly every detail of design and embellishment in the theater, however—architecture, brass work, scenery, draperies, curtains, carpets, carpentry, chairs, chandeliers, tiling, frescoes, wainscoting—came from Chicago or New York.[30] Altogether, the Auditorium's borrowed nature points to Spokane's imitation of accepted external aesthetics, to the young city's dependence on outside markets and transportation systems for its existence, and to its self-conscious use of things cultural to remake Spokane in the image of Victorian America.

The Auditorium's opening in September 1890 marked an apex in elite Spokane's self-regard, as both a class and a city. In the early 1890s Spokane's wealthy citizens included men such as James N. Glover and F. Rockwood Moore, enriched through real estate, banking, and commercial ventures, and D. C. Corbin, who built the first railroad to the mines in the Coeur d'Alenes. As a group some two hundred well-heeled families dominated the city's social, political, and economic life in these years. Although often of solid midwestern roots, the "four hundred" were also nouveaux riches who "exalted the formal" and took pains to observe the latest in eastern and European fashions—an effort that required long and frequent travel to the centers of style.[31] With the Auditorium, where the proscenium boxes formed the hall's "main ornament," they at last had a setting handsome enough for all the opulence new money could buy.[32]

The theater's inaugural night provided a singular opportunity for the high society of the Inland Northwest to flaunt its wealth. Days before the opening on September 16, Hayward auctioned off private boxes and dress circle seats for the evening; in an era when one dollar purchased a premium theatrical ticket, the highest bid came in at $360. When the gala arrived, Spokane rejoiced not only in the Auditorium's appearance but also in the carriage-borne audience's style. The *Spokane Falls Review* remarked that "all the wealth, beauty and fashion of Eastern Washington and Northern Idaho was represented [creating] the most brilliant audience that has ever been assembled on the North Pacific coast [and a] metropolitan air that was very impressive."[33] (The Carleton Opera Company's performance of *Nanon* was obviously less interesting to both spectators and reviewers than the house and the audience.) The most marked exultation of self and class occurred in the Auditorium's foyer: along with stained-glass windows of the muses, Shakespeare, and Beethoven was a depiction of A. M. Cannon and J. J. Browne.

Another stained-glass window in the entryway, bearing the words "Spokane Falls," further communicated the Auditorium's role as a carefully chosen emblem of civic pride. Spokanites wanted to prove their city's accomplishments and its adherence to eastern standards. For more than a decade the Auditorium provided one of the foremost vehicles in that effort. On the theater's opening, local newspapers were quick to emphasize its superiority to anything in the Northwest and its equality to anything in the nation. Certainly Spokane deserved such a showplace (its gorgeous appointments described ad infinitum), for the city, like the theater, "must have the best and it is needless to say that it has just what it wanted." Was Spokane a parvenu city, not twenty years old, not quite the peer of its counterparts? No matter. It could now boast of a theater "unrivaled in the northwest," decorated in the finest taste by the finest craftsmen in America, patterned after the Broadway of New York City, and costing $400,000.[34] Spokane could now enjoy highbrow theater in a palatial facility. Spokane had arrived.[35]

And where had it arrived? For its builders and contemporaries, the Auditorium certified that Spokane could be counted among America's finished, "civilized," and emphatically white metropolises and not its coarse Wild West. These people described the Auditorium and Spokane in terms that specifically marked them as places belonging in the upper tiers of the Victorian hierarchy, a designation that called for a suppression of things supposedly base and untamed (including peoples, personal behavior, and cultural expressions) and an apotheosizing of the delicate. For example, the *Spokane Falls Review* noted that the Auditorium's interior design, while beautiful, was never "pronounced or loud."[36] There was, in other words, nothing vulgar about it.

That Spokane's promoters saw their city as a triumph over savagery became evident in an opinion column published immediately after the Auditorium's debut. In it, the *Chronicle* explained how right the pioneers of Spokane were to congratulate themselves as they enjoyed their gala evening. Had not the same eyes that soaked in the beauty of the Auditorium witnessed, only a few years ago, "the song and dance of the Indians" on Spokane's prairies? Where once sat the "grim homes of the savage" now stood the "palatial business houses and the beautiful homes of refined and educated civilization. All around about us are the substantial evidences of material progress"—and this, moreover, in a city that had burned to the ground only one year earlier. Surely such a place could only prosper. The opera night proved this was true as "it brought together under one roof the people whose combined efforts have made the city the wonder of the age." Spokane's handsome homes and businesses may once have surprised commentators around the nation, the *Chronicle* remarked, "but no more wonder—no more surprise": to a people with "so much of refinement, intellect and business capacity," anything was possible. The rapid growth could only continue. The *Chronicle* made clear the connections among cultural hierarchy, civic pride, and race as it reflected how the "axe of civilization" had replaced Native structures and art forms with those of Europe and the East.[37]

Three years later, the Auditorium's orchestra expanded this depiction of evolutionary progress through cultural expressions. The occasion was a staged musical history of Spokane from 1877 to 1893 led by the ensemble's conductor, Fred Hoppe, and presented at the 1893 Chicago World's Fair. Every element of the show, from costumes to instrumentation, pressed the argument that elite Spokanites had conquered both Natives and uncouth whites. The show began with the orchestra dressed in buckskin and performing an "Indian war whoop" on tuba and bass drum. Next came a musical depiction of Indian festivities, interrupted by the arrival of the U.S. cavalry and the consequent bloodshed. The annihilation of Natives left Spokane open to white settlers, who relished the sound of a single

A stereopticon view of the Auditorium's interior. The theater was decorated in earth-tone tints of terracotta, green, pink, and sky blue, creating a light-filled effect. Ten private boxes, five on each side of the high proscenium arch, were the main embellishments of the hall, which had a seating capacity of 1,750. The eastern firm of J. B. McElfatrick designed the Auditorium; Spokane's German-born Herman Preusse was the supervising architect. Northwest Museum of Arts and Culture/Eastern Washington State Historical Society, Spokane, Washington, L94-24.192.

fiddle playing "good old New England tunes." A round of vignettes then illustrated Spokane's (ostensibly concluded) Wild West days: a saloon with the laughably "grand orchestra" of two fiddlers, gunfights, and a slain "Chinaman"; dance houses with meager musical ensembles and homely dance steps; and a variety show complete with song-and-dance men and an acrobat. Then came the advent of Art: the "First Legitimate Theater" performance of a "Heavy Tragedian" at Joy's Opera House; the first fireman's ball, accompanied by the "full grand orchestra" of five instruments; a true "grand ball" graced by "Spokane's Four Hundred" and French music; and topping all this grandeur, a performance by the complete Auditorium orchestra.[38]

This illustration of the "progress of music in the West" took place within a highly stratified context. By the late nineteenth century, professional symphony orchestras had joined legitimate drama and serious opera at the sacrosanct tip of the cultural pyramid. Things such as variety performances and light music, meanwhile, were dismissed as tasteless mass amusement. The styles of immigrants, racial minorities, and demimondaines were lowlier still. Hoppe's musical history—with its crescendo of instruments and progression from Native to frontier to canonical entertainments—communicated that civilization had arrived and was flourishing in eastern Washington. Significantly, despite their western setting, Hoppe's musical evolution and the *Chronicle* editorial purposely rejected markers of westernness: Indians, gunfights, and dance halls represented precisely the cultural world "highbrow" Spokanites wanted to distance themselves from.[39]

Hoppe and his colleagues, it seems, protested a bit too loudly. Recall that, after Spokane's 1889 fire, one of the first businesses to spring back to life was Goetz and Baer's boisterous gambling pavilion. Such establishments more than continued after the city's reconstruction and included variety theaters that were the quintessence of the unfettered West. Likewise, the Auditorium's position within 1890s Spokane betrayed the city's mixed nature: though the seven-story building formed an imposing landmark, it was located in the northeast corner of downtown and off the major thoroughfare of Riverside Avenue. Indeed, the Auditorium sat but two blocks from the infamous Stockholm and Coeur d'Alene resorts, which enjoyed more central locations within the business district. Not even the Auditorium's inaugural performance remained free of boorishness. Although the *Spokane Falls Review* congratulated "the gallery" (an epithet for those who sat in a theater's cheapest section) on refraining from its "wonted exuberance" that evening, one incident could not be ignored: during the opera's romantic climax, an "audacious [gallery] god" pulled an imaginary champagne cork and set the whole audience laughing.[40]

Spokane's upper crust did not want their home to look like this: a mining camp where Art was mocked and wild amusements reigned. This sentiment adds much meaning to Hoppe's history of Spokane, performed not only at the world's fair but also at "nearly every city of importance" en route to Chicago. Spokanites were plugging their city by insisting that they had progressed beyond the frontier and had at least approached the top of the Victorian cultural structure.[41]

"Solid on Shakespeare"

Throughout the 1890s the Auditorium dominated Spokane's legitimate theatrical scene. Indeed, for most of the decade, it *was* the scene. Experiments in "popular-priced" legitimate theater struggled, likely because of the combined sway of the Auditorium and the variety houses. This created an unmistakable relationship between theatergoing, social class, and respectability. If Spokanites wanted to see a professional show, they could either risk their reputations at a variety theater or pay the high cost of an Auditorium ticket. Most middle- and working-class people could not enjoy the Auditorium with any kind of regularity, if at all, and so for years the theater remained an expression of upper-class fancies.[42]

Wealthy Spokanites—or at least those people who could pay for a ticket—took a mixed view of high art. On one hand, civic leaders tried to make Spokane look and feel like a polished eastern metropolis by championing external or derivative culture.[43] Further, some of Spokane's residents genuinely loved theater and yearned for the art they had left behind. On the other hand, many arriviste Spokanites apparently wanted the form and validation of highbrow culture, not its substance: to wit, low and middlebrow genres like comic spectaculars generally fared better at the Auditorium than the serious stuff favored by critics. That local blockbusters sometimes hinted at the racially or sexually risqué concerned Spokane's pundits. Why, then, did the city's theatergoers not embrace high art more fully? Perhaps living in the far West had changed them; perhaps the social origins of parvenu Spokanites meant they had little previous exposure to high art; maybe they would have never liked opera. Whatever the case, the people for whom the Auditorium was built only toyed with the late Victorian canon.

Westerners reproduced culture for manifold reasons. A man could be both a real estate speculator, who knew the value of a good public image, and a lover of art. J. J. Browne was such a man. Browne and his family filled their letters to each other with discussions of the stage. These letters teach us that Spokane's isolated gentry remained connected to theatrical trends through modern systems of transportation and communication. Because of Browne's financial success, his family could subscribe to publications that discussed the stage. They could visit cultural centers such as New York and Chicago and take full advantage of the Auditorium and its predecessors. J. J. and Anna Stratton Browne, during their frequent trips to the East, attended the latest theatrical productions and watched stars such as Edwin Booth. At home in the Northwest their children had regular access to the stage and "enjoyed it hugely."[44] In short, theatergoing formed an important part of the family's life. Money and railroads enabled other wealthy Spokanites to be familiar with high culture. Together, the city's rich families formed a social group that could be conversant in the latest theatrical news because they had seen the same troupes and shows, often together, in New York or Chicago.[45]

Other Spokanites nurtured local theater because they dearly missed eastern culture. Mrs. S. R. Flynn, for instance, remarked that the theater programs Anna Browne sent from New York "almost made [her] homesick."[46] Flynn acted as caretaker to the Browne children when their parents traveled, and she relished her excursions with them to Spokane theaters.

Mary Willis Dwight's story was more poignant. The daughter and wife of two successful real estate developers, Dwight belonged to

A youthful image of Anna Stratton Browne, the wife of J. J. Browne, one of early Spokane's foremost promoters. The photographer's stamp is from Warren, Ohio. Courtesy Northwest Room, Spokane Public Library.

the "four hundred." But socializing with the upper crust of a frontier town was hardly her ambition. The New Englander possessed a fine singing voice and had studied at the Boston Conservatory. As her daughter put it, Dwight "was all ready for grand opera in Germany, [but] Father convinced her to stay out here in Spokane." No wonder, for the father (Daniel H. Dwight) earned a healthy living off his real estate dealings and became a leading Spokane politician. Mary Willis Dwight, meanwhile, contented herself with amateur *Mikado* productions and Cultus Club musicales.[47]

If the Brownes, Flynns, and Dwights add nuance to the picture of 1890s highbrow theatergoing in Spokane, altogether that image is one of fair-weather interest. Public voices like the *Chronicle* may have professed Spokane's refinement, but the mixed success of legitimate theater and grand opera indicate otherwise. During the 1890s, especially before the mid-decade depression, upper-class Spokanites used the Auditorium as a tool for personal and civic promotion, as evidence of their cultivation and respectability.

The Victorian canon provided the baseline for elite culture in Spokane. Philosophically, that canon was guided by a desire to separate the human from the animal. Good Victorians viewed art as an instrument of morality and education that could convey truths and uplift humanity. But only a certain kind of art could do this, and by the late nineteenth century it was overwhelmingly European, professional, and exclusive. Critics exalted continental work (German symphonies, Italian operas, and English plays) and pooh-poohed American or American-inspired culture (such as blackface minstrelsy or even Antonin Dvorák's *New World Symphony*) as silly, worthless, or worse. This occurred within a competitive social climate, where upwardly mobile Americans used the many facets of cultural life—dress, etiquette, arts, foodways, speech, home decor—to propel themselves ever higher.[48]

Certain Spokanites had reasons aplenty to prove the quality of their upper-class credentials. Not only did their city need promotion in order to grow, they needed culture to sanctify their money. The city's self-made barons rejoiced in the talents of Kirtland K. Cutter, the architect of European-style mansions that graced the South Hill and Browne's Addition; their wives made the most correct of social calls, while their daughters bought Parisian wardrobes. Perhaps of all their emblems of prestige, the Auditorium pleased 1890s Spokanites the most. As Bruce Wasserman notes, "the Auditorium symbolized the cultural sophistication that the society people felt their city had attained."[49]

Besides its physical splendor, the Auditorium had another asset that gave Spokane cachet. Harry Hayward was a Londoner whose jobs on and off the stage had taken him around the world since his early teens. He came to Spokane in 1881 as a railroad clerk and as soon as he could started securing entertainments for the little town. Hayward managed Spokane's mish-mash of legitimate theaters throughout the 1880s, then he presided over the Auditorium from 1890 to 1911. Enterprising and peripatetic, Hayward yet maintained "a polish and courtesy most attractive."[50] Spokanites fully appreciated that with his English manners, evening dress, and insistence on a well-behaved audience, Hayward completed the Auditorium's air of wealth and class.[51] Just as they published any outside compliment of the Auditorium, so too did city newspapers applaud the respect visitors and theater people had for Hayward.[52] The man and the theater advertised the city.

Throughout the 1890s much promotion of the city's cultural affairs came specifically through the daily *Chronicle*. Not incidentally, for the majority of the decade the evening newspaper belonged to Spokane's foremost cultural booster—J. J. Browne.[53] The *Chronicle* extolled the city's every artistic triumph, claiming that Spokane was "solid on Shakespeare" or that its opera lovers were "legion."[54] At times, the *Chronicle*'s remarks assumed the spirit of interurban rivalry so prominent in the Northwest. In 1897, for example, Fanny Davenport could only stop in a few cities en route from Chicago to San Francisco. When the English actress chose Spokane instead of Seattle and Tacoma, the *Chronicle* declared Spokane "the Favored City of the Northwest."[55]

At other times, the newspaper separated taste along class lines: only some of Spokane's residents, it suggested, distinguished the city with their urbanity. A pointed 1890 article reminded theatergoers that, though actors accepted the gallery's applause, the accolades they sought came from the expensive floor seats for, "As a rule, a gallery audience is neither artistically intelligent nor critical and cannot appreciate the finer points of an actor's efforts."[56] Likewise, in response to Thomas Keene's 1891 visit, the *Chronicle* attributed approval of such masters to the European travel made "by the very class to which the legitimate drama must cater in order to succeed."[57] The newspaper remarked that, though the masses might demand "inferior dramas or variety entertainments" and though "a large percent of our population have lost the power of appreciating . . . the classic or heroic," Keene's grateful Spokane audience testified "to the hundreds in our city who are educated to and capable of appreciating the higher arts."[58]

Yet the *Chronicle* tried to pass the knowledge that led to taste on to its readers. In a markedly Victorian fashion, the newspaper insisted that culture be didactic. In 1899, for instance, the *Chronicle* reprinted a series of home study courses, telling young men that if they would forsake "dime novels, idle gossip, and silly amusements" in honor of these courses, they could obtain a decent education. Prepared by "leading educators," the articles began with analyses of Shakespeare, Moliere, and other dramatists.[59]

Allen S. Cook's introduction to Shakespeare illustrates the high-toned approach the courses took toward the stage. Cook's Shakespeare was an ideal Victorian who glorified civic virtues, disparaged lawlessness, and never misled morally. Indeed (the Yale University professor wrote), Shakespeare's readers could perceive his interest in upholding "the moral order of the world . . . and how he lashes those who are guilty of any attempt to subvert this moral order, while he bestows honors . . . upon those who are concerned in maintaining it." Thus the *Chronicle* provided Inland Northwesterners with a textbook Victorian interpretation of Shakespeare as uplifting and orderly.[60]

In its theatrical reviews and announcements, the *Chronicle* followed a similar line of thought. Anticipating "Two Nights of True Art" with Richard Mansfield, the newspaper quoted the Chicago critic Amy Leslie who argued that the actor's purpose was to teach his audiences and never to "grovel for public favor." Mansfield "is for art most pure," Leslie wrote, and possessed a brain "so spiritual, so exalted" that his disappointments came from "sillies."[61] As with the Shakespeare analysis, then, the *Chronicle* wanted its readers to understand that the value of "true art" had nothing to do with popularity. Notably, these two perceptions of the stage came from metropolitan authorities. In its own theatrical writing, the *Chronicle* made certain to distinguish classic art from mediocre entertainment.

This was the message of a tepid 1898 review of Nellie Melba in Giuseppe Verdi's *La Traviata*. The reporter was willing to forgive the choice of productions because the Inland Northwest rarely received opera companies, let alone ones headed by Melba. Yes, *Traviata* hardly represented "the best of Italian opera," or "even the best of Verdi, who is always nearer the 'catchy' order than other writers," but after all, Spokane had seen Melba: "it would be ungrateful . . . to regret that we did not hear Rossini's music."[62] In the context of the late nineteenth century when culture was intensely hierarchical and connoisseurs took pride in art that was as esoteric as it was edifying, the *Chronicle*'s disdain for Verdi's "catchy" melodies was meant to demonstrate that some Spokanites knew what made art good.

Dilettantes

But congratulate, chastise, and instruct though it might, the *Chronicle* could only paper over the reality that, collectively, upper-class Spokanites had a middling regard for the Victorian canon. To begin with, the infatuation with the Auditorium concerned appearances as much as substance; that is to say, the city's wealthy theatergoers were dilettantes. The September 1891 appearance of Sarah Bernhardt demonstrates this well: before the performance the elite flaunted their ability to watch a world-famous actress in the highest of style, but afterward they dismissed Bernhardt because they could not understand her.

The Bernhardt engagement belonged to Spokane's upper crust from the outset. Getting the French actress to the Northwest was no easy task—Bernhardt required a three-thousand-dollar guarantee—but rich Spokanites willingly contributed to the subscription fund that ensured her visit. After Hayward had auctioned off the best seats and boxes, the general prices (from one to five dollars) put Bernhardt's performance of Victorien Sardou's *La Tosca* outside the reach of even middle-class people.[63] Adelaide Sutton Gilbert, the wife of Northern Pacific Railroad division superintendent, told her parents that "We did not make any plans to see Bernhardt supposing tickets would be 5 dollars." (Several days later, Gilbert accentuated the Auditorium's exclusivity by remarking that "We don't go to entertainments unless we have complementaries.")[64]

Reportage preceding the engagement both enhanced its connection with money and portrayed Spokane as a city adequate to host the "divine Sarah." Three days before the performance, the *Chronicle* devoted two columns to the whirl of preparations taking place in a downtown dressmaker's shop. Sprinkled with French and laden with details of fabric and cuts, the article made local society belles sound like cosmopolitan princesses. The *Spokane Review,* meanwhile, manifested its civic pride by mocking the people in Butte, Montana, who would next see Bernhardt as rubes who would need a few "local gags" mixed in to enjoy the show. When the big event finally arrived, city newspapers outdid themselves with descriptions of the glamor that filled the Auditorium. Like the theater's opening a year before, Bernhardt's appearance provided Spokane with a chance to advertise its new and growing wealth.[65]

Then came *La Tosca* itself. Bernhardt performed strictly in French, and though Spokanites professed a familiarity with the story, many in the audience heard Sardou's play in a language they did not understand. They responded in a manner "downright cold," hardly applauding for two-thirds of the show, then filing out of the house visibly deflated and "halfway glad that the agony was over."[66] From one angle, these Spokanites were poseurs, who tossed out words like "demoseilles" and "décolleté" in anticipation of the French actress but would themselves have benefited from "local gags." Their educations had left them unprepared to appreciate the tragedienne, a fact few of them admitted, claiming instead Bernhardt experienced an off-night or ascribing the failed evening to her manager. From another perspective, elite Spokanites were pragmatists who paid for and expected good entertainment, receiving in its place a performance that humbled and disappointed them. Either way, boasts that Spokane was a center of culture and learning fell short on this occasion.[67]

It was not, however, on this occasion alone that the Auditorium crowd spurned the late Victorian canon. Despite knowing which genres and artists received high marks (Browne's *Chronicle* certainly strove to inculcate the city with taste), those people who could afford Auditorium tickets routinely demonstrated their preference for the light and "catchy" over the deep and refined. In one of its many anxious appraisals of local aesthetics, the *Chronicle* hinted at these tastes when it said that next to Shakespearean drama and grand opera, Spokane theatergoers enjoyed "beautiful sights" and entertainments that would take their breath away with laughter.[68] The newspaper indulged in a bit of wishful thinking here. In his study of 1890s Spokane, Wasserman tabulated professional performances at the Auditorium from 1890 to 1893 and found farce-comedy to have been the most popular genre at the theater—and overwhelmingly so. After farce came melodramas, spectaculars, and contemporary dramas. Whatever city boosters may have said, classics and opera ranked at the numerical bottom of the city's entertainment choices.[69]

Instead, Auditorium audiences wanted beauty and humor: extravaganzas and comedies full of attractive costumes, scenery, and girls. Evidence of Spokane's inclination toward fluff abounded. For example, many a newspaper column praising high culture came on the heels of advertisements and reviews for productions like *A Turkish Bath*, "entirely devoid of plot."[70] Hayward sometimes offered these crowd pleasers at popular prices, but they usually cost dearly, with gallery seats starting at fifty cents. Further, the content of the many light shows cycling through the Auditorium often resembled the farce, vaudeville, and minstrelsy playing at Spokane's variety theaters, if on the "three carloads of scenery" scale. The city's elite not only supported these productions financially, they at times became actively involved in them.[71] All told, prominent Spokanites preferred the kind of silly (even titillating) amusement anathema to Victorian critics trying to exalt the mind and suppress the body; they simply did so in a setting more plush than their popular-price neighbors.

The predominance of froth over substance at the Auditorium did not result from a lack of touring highbrow companies; rather, it came from the choices of the ticket buyers. As the new century approached, light shows drew consistently large houses while the classics and particularly opera failed to do so.[72] By the late 1890s, what the *Chronicle* called "idiocies and indecencies" subsidized more artistic productions and kept the Auditorium open. They also contributed to the newspaper's budget, since the *Chronicle* was not above running paid advertisements for shows it later condemned. Significantly, the declining attendance for high-toned performances occurred at a time of renewed prosperity for the Inland Northwest. By the close of the 1890s, the region was climbing out of the depression, while several mining booms had enriched Spokane itself. Affluent Spokanites could afford grand opera but they apparently did not want it.[73]

If—within the logic of nineteenth-century cultural and urban hierarchies—Spokane's support of highbrow theater made it a worthier (and potentially wealthier) place than its rivals, then its neglect of such art degraded the city. The *Chronicle* applied this logic and reacted accordingly. At the close of the 1897–1898 season, the editors became incensed at the lopsided Auditorium houses and ran several articles scolding the city for its taste. The newspaper laid the blame squarely at the feet of Spokanites, who compelled Hayward to schedule "noisy mediocrities" and caused the theater to take a loss on the "artistic and instructive": "a sad commentary upon the culture and refinement of the public." The *Chronicle* would not let Spokanites forget how these choices reflected on their city, telling them that the Auditorium's box-office evidence was "disgraceful in a city where a degree of intellectuality somewhat higher than on the Bowery is supposed to obtain."[74]

And the *Chronicle* dealt in hierarchies. After the final show in June 1898, the newspaper ranked the season's attractions according to their merits. At the top of its list, the *Chronicle* placed plays that were not particularly classic, but which it deemed well acted and wholesome, like the American family comedy *The Hoosier Doctor*.[75] What, then, did the newspaper find offensive? Productions either too plebeian or too prurient in their appeal: "mechanical melodrama," "noisy farce," and "thinly veiled exhibitions of depravity."[76]

Consider Lincoln J. Carter's *The Heart of Chicago*, which topped the Auditorium's receipts that season. Carter's blood-and-thunder melodramas used innovative stage effects to draw crowds. In *The*

Heart of Chicago, he depicted the city's 1871 fire by setting off pyro-
technics behind painted scrims; another climactic moment manipulated lighting and perspective to suggest a train at the precipice's
edge.[77] Unlike the Spokanites who packed the Auditorium from
dress circle to gallery, the *Chronicle* did not appreciate these novelties.
Instead, it consistently described Carter's production as fireworks—
not a play. In its disdain for *The Heart of Chicago*, the *Chronicle* echoed
the opinion of other Victorian critics who dismissed any mass-
produced or mechanized cultural form (such as a pianola, lithograph, or camera) as fake.[78]

   Another aspect of the *Chronicle*'s commentary on Carter's production showed how Spokanites dealt in hierarchies: the newspaper
remarked that *The Heart of Chicago* had a cast composed of "as poor
a lot of cheap people as could be gathered together, even in Chicago."[79] Respectable Spokane's opinion of major metropolises cut
two ways. When trying to make their hometown look like a big city,
Spokanites purposefully imitated and imported fashions from the
East and Europe, especially New York City and Chicago. But when
the culture, politics, or people from those places felt too fast, Spokanites claimed the high ground by painting the great cities as wellsprings of immorality that could contaminate an unheeding Northwest. Hence the *Chronicle*'s rebuke to local theatergoers for not rising
above the "intellectuality" of New York's working-class Bowery.

   At the end of the 1897–1898 season, the *Chronicle* confirmed the
geography of its criticism by leveling its sharpest invective against
two farces that brought the debauchery of New York café society to
the Inland Northwest.[80] These farces not only played in late-century
Spokane, they played to full, well-heeled Auditorium houses. Instead
of providing purely Victorian edification (try though Hayward and
the *Chronicle* might to educate their fellow citizens), the Auditorium
had become a place where Spokane's ostensibly highbrow and certainly wealthy upper class could enjoy the pleasures of the masses in
style. Those pleasures clearly violated the Victorian repression of the
body by edging ever nearer to things sexual, a trend that became
pronounced in the next century.

   The mass entertainments enjoyed by upper-class Spokane also
transgressed the Victorian racial hierarchy, which connected biology

to depravity and condemned African American culture as both wicked and inane. In the 1890s white Spokanites stepped toward black culture with their enthusiasm for the cakewalk. Southern slaves had created the cakewalk as a celebratory dance that used high-kneed struts and exaggerated movement to mock the solemnity of the master class. The dance spread from plantations to minstrelsy in the latter half of the nineteenth century and became a national fad in the 1890s. Although the theatrical cakewalk did not always retain a subversive meaning, it did remain connected to the supposed abandon of black culture.[81]

Spokanites could learn of and participate in the cakewalk craze because the Auditorium frequently booked touring minstrel shows. Despite its widespread performance, minstrelsy suggested racial promiscuity. Advance reviews for an 1896 mixed-race Primrose and West production, for example, traded on the promise of a "genuine southern cake walk" and "darkey sports" but also assured theatergoers that this was "wholesome minstrel entertainment" with blacks largely confined to musical ensembles.[82]

When the Auditorium offered a program featuring a "grand cakewalk" in 1895, the racial and sexual danger connected to the performance was equally obvious—and equally skirted around. That February, "the very best of local colored talent" participated in the cakewalk portion of the Criterion Quartette's *The South in Slavery* for the benefit of the African Methodist Episcopal Church in Spokane.[83] The benefit had another important feature: a panel of cakewalk judges that included some of the city's most prominent white men. But the event still required sanitizing. The *Chronicle* vowed that the judges were "all, all honorable men" and advertised a matinée for "ladies and school children" with "practically the same" program as the main performance. Yet it also noted the difficulty those honorable men would have in choosing the cakewalk winner from among the "pretty, graceful," and *black* young dancers. Well might the Auditorium alter the show for matrons and infants.[84]

If Spokane's theatergoers liked the cakewalk in 1895, they loved it in 1899, one year after the dance's popularity had skyrocketed with the Broadway opening of *Clorindy, the Origin of the Cakewalk*. And by 1899 Auditorium patrons had only continued their pattern of

flocking to alleged mediocrities and ignoring art. Nance O'Neil, a
star of the legitimate stage, brought three dramas to Spokane that
April, but the city's theatergoers paid meager attention to them. The
Chronicle reacted by berating audiences for their decisions and wring-
ing its hands at the state of the city's taste. Of the popular forms
Spokanites chose above O'Neil, the infectious, unmistakably racial
cakewalk offended the newspaper the most.[85]

Perhaps the *Chronicle* had cause for concern: that champion of
the "instructive and ennobling" watched as those who could afford
the Auditorium put their financial weight behind the racial danger
of cakewalks, the growing innuendo of farce-comedies, and the
pure spectacle of shows like *The Heart of Chicago*. With the help of
Auditorium ticket buyers, these light-hearted, popular, and (contemporary critics would argue) lowbrow genres were eclipsing the opera
and legitimate for which Browne and Cannon had built their theater.
Whatever the city's cultural commentators might say, and however
they might exhort, affluent Spokanites had only a waffling commitment to Victorian artistic values.

Toward the Twentieth Century

Evidence outside the Auditorium's box office and the *Chronicle*'s
drama column testifies of Spokane's shifting ideals. To begin with,
Spokanites' patronage of the theater demonstrated their drift away
from the mores of past generations: theatergoing was not a regular
experience for the bulk of nineteenth-century Americans. Many had
long regarded the stage as a corrupting, almost pagan, influence.
This attitude persisted among the small-town and the pious into the
late 1800s, despite the growth of theatrical circuits. The Methodist
Episcopal Church, for instance, banned theater and other amusements in 1877 and refused to repeal the decision until 1924. Though
the Methodist leadership took an extreme position, some Spokanites likewise condemned the theater as immoral.[86]

Furthermore, until the century's close, most Americans rarely
took their fun in commercial venues. Instead, they enjoyed the Sunday
School picnics, union balls, and parlor games of their own creation.
But by the final years of the nineteenth century, Americans—especially in cities—increasingly relaxed at dance halls, ice cream parlors,

amusement parks, and theaters. The very language used by turn-of-the-century Americans distanced them from the preceding "rural mainstream": the latter's communication steeped in religiosity and providential certainties, the former's attention directed more to acquisition, individual fulfillment, and worldly entertainment.[87]

The Browne family papers illuminate this difference between the self-denial of nineteenth-century Victorians and the gradual shift made by their children to twentieth-century values. J. J. Browne's grandmother-in-law, Anna M. Stratton, spent her waning years in Browne's Spokane home. There she kept a daily record of household activities and, particularly, her own spirituality. Stratton made occasional visits to the Auditorium, but she remained aloof from the Brownes' constant theatergoing. Stratton's journal conveys a sense that she lived almost in a separate cultural world than her extended family—their opera box and cross-continental travel versus her sewing basket and Bible study.[88]

In contrast, in the letters he wrote from across the nation, Browne made certain his children appreciated the theater. During an 1890 visit to New York City, for instance, Browne watched several productions and asked his daughters, Alta May and Irma, to learn about the stars he had just seen.[89] Ten years later, Browne communicated his love of the stage to a third daughter, Hazel, remarking on the treat she had in watching a performance by Henry Irving, "now generally considered the greatest living actor." Years before, Browne had seen Irving and believed then he was the "finest actor" he had ever seen, with the exception of Edwin Booth. He closed his letter noting that it was "a very great privilege and very instructive to hear such actors, and I am very glad you have had the opportunity."[90] Consider the implications of these admonitions. Here, a community pillar, son-in-law to a reverend, recommended that his children learn more about an institution still condemned by the Methodist Church. And this advice was given to his daughters, those creatures whom past generations would have kept pure by keeping them from the stage.[91]

If late-century Spokanites demonstrated their budding modernity by attending shows at the Auditorium (and not those most acclaimed), their enthusiasm for the actors themselves also evinced an evolution in values. Just as "respectable" Americans often disparaged the stage, so too did they condemn players as being outside the pale: touring demanded itinerancy, which marked nineteenth-century actors as "vagabonds" in an era that exalted the home. Moreover, the transparency of a performer's personal life made the private public in a manner that was uncomfortable to Victorians. For these reasons, the cream of American society showed actors to the figurative and actual back door. Not so in Spokane, where the wealthy tripped over themselves to welcome visiting performers, feting them in the best homes and hotels.[92]

In his study of actors vis-à-vis society, Benjamin McArthur argues that players were pivotal figures in the shift from the Victorian quest for self-discipline to the celebration of individual freedom. Specifically, the apparently unfettered life of actors appealed to Americans as they pushed against the constraints of industrial and late Victorian life. Stage performers, moreover, symbolized an important cultural realignment: ministers and socialites (among others) dictated proprieties and protocols for much of the nineteenth century. As these groups lost some of their power in the new century, another kind of trend-setter took their place—the celebrity.[93]

With their enthusiasm for touring stars, affluent Spokanites put themselves on the edge of this development. Yet having come from or visited the East, these people would have known that the best of American society looked askance at actors. Why, then, give actors their highest respect? This question has multiple answers. First, many of Spokane's elite began life more humbly, and their taste had at times an upstart tinge. Living in a place as remote as Spokane could have only added parochialism to this mix.[94] Likewise, their far-flung location left Spokanites hungry for the metropolitan glamor that actors represented. Finally, notably, life in the West may have changed Spokanites altogether—a consideration that explains, to an extent, why the wealth of 1890s Spokane took such a meager view of Victorianism.

The historian Lewis O. Saum attributes the evolving attitudes of nineteenth-century Americans (from almost puritanical to almost modern) to two events: the Civil War and westward migration. To everyday people, Saum maintains, the war and the West meant

separation, confusion, suffering, boredom, adventure, and opportunity, involving a break from regular life that deeply changed Americans' behavior. In the West, Americans encountered unsettled conditions, skewed gender ratios (with men predominant), the fast
lifestyle of mining camps and boomtowns, and a "ruthless pursuit
of private gain." Emigrants could never entirely succeed in repli-
cating the manners of the East in such an environment; at times,
westerners did not even want to resume the somber ways of their
past. Thus the growth of a "loose-jointed, easy-going" style.[95]

These were certainly the circumstances in Spokane, a city born
of real estate speculation, mining booms, and promotional schemes,
where exquisite buildings like the Auditorium shared muddy streets
with saloons and honky-tonks. As Spokane ballooned at the turn
of the century, it retained this mixed character: itinerant workingmen flowed in and out of the city, the once lowly became millionaires, brothels proliferated, while the civic-minded campaigned for
a home-centered city, and nouveaux riches continued to build fabulous mansions. Many Spokanites apparently cared more for the
trappings of eastern culture than for its substance. At the same time
their acceptance of such a "loose-jointed" style of living presaged
the coming century's focus on individual freedom. In other words—
though some residents of the West saw frontier behavior as the very
opposite of modernity—western culture eased the path of twentieth-
century attitudes.[96]

The work of Gunther Barth casts further light on the decisions
of wealthy Spokanites. His study of nineteenth-century San Francisco
and Denver includes an analysis of their "culture for the moment."
Barth argues that people in these cities chose the illusion, rather
than the substance, of art—the "gaudy-conventional hodge podge"
that was at once shoddy and fancy. The point was to promote city
and self, not to create solid cultural institutions.[97] This pertains, again,
to Spokanites, people who elected to be highbrow for the moment:
receiving Sarah Bernhardt and Nellie Melba because they could
and because it looked refined to do so but rejecting the art of those
grand dames because they did not understand the truly difficult,
they found it tiresome and inapplicable to their western lives, or
they simply preferred cakewalks and fireworks.

Outside Culture

By the 1890s, then, Spokane's comfortable classes had done much
to imitate and import high culture from the East. They had not,
however, displayed a firm commitment to the Victorianism that
prescribed such culture. The Auditorium Theater, built in 1890,
was especially emblematic of Spokane's half-hearted relationship
with the canon dictated by outside authorities. That showplace symbolized another critical aspect of Spokane's relationship with external
people and trends: economics. Spokanites depended for their wealth
on capital, markets, and transportation systems not of their own
making and largely out of their control.[98] The precariousness of that
arrangement became evident in mid-1893, when a national financial panic sent Spokane into dangerous territory and stripped local
men of some of their dearest prizes, including the Auditorium.

The story began four years earlier, after the 1889 fire that destroyed
so much of downtown Spokane. In a flurry of civic pride Spokanites
declared that their city would arise from the fire bigger and better
than before. And it did, at a price. Before 1889 Inland Northwesterners had dealt with a Dutch investment firm called the Northwestern and Pacific Hypotheek Bank. In order to rebuild, Spokane
borrowed heavily from the Hypotheek Bank, which by the end of
1892 had loaned more than $4.8 million on urban properties.[99]

Then came the Panic of 1893, when a burst railroad bubble and a
precipitous drop in the gold supply conspired to plunge the United
States into depression. Institutions and fortunes throughout the
nation failed in the panic, a contagion from which Spokane was
hardly immune. Indeed, as the distress spread to the Northwest, it
soon became evident that many leading Spokanites had badly overextended themselves. Misfortune consumed not only residents of
the city, but also farmers throughout the Inland Empire.[100] It was,
as Nelson Durham wrote in 1912, a time of "gloom and disaster, of
crashing banks and crippled industry, of riotous demonstrations
and counter organization for law and order," the memory of which
haunted its survivors.[101]

A. M. Cannon—millionaire, founder, and investor—found himself
in particular trouble. After the 1889 fire Browne's "white-bearded"
colleague continued speculating in the manner that had launched

his fortune. But when the panic hit, the reality was that Cannon had invested in shaky ventures, spread his resources too thin, and trusted too much in his eastern creditors—hardly an enviable position to be in amid crisis. Chief among his mistakes was the use of deposits to build a structure not unlike the Auditorium in its derivative grandeur: a marble bank of "Grecian style and proportions." Cannon's financial affairs failed examination, and on June 5, 1893, his Bank of Spokane Falls failed to open.[102]

That institution's insolvency touched off a panic within Spokane that resulted in a number of bank runs and closures during the summer of 1893. Spokane's dependency on outside resources and the town's vulnerability to outside events became painfully clear that summer, when local banks could not meet their obligations mainly because of their distance from cash reserves in Portland or New York. Conversely, the city's hopes rebounded on news that reinforcement had arrived. Likewise, the *Chronicle* tried to cheer its readers by remarking that powerful metropolitan creditors trusted that Spokane could pay its bills—which it could not.[103] Seven of the city's ten banks succumbed to the panic, taking with them the most prominent of Spokanites.[104] Among the casualties was the Browne National Bank, which suspended operations and could only repay creditors to 13 percent, the balance of obligations met from Browne's own pocketbook. Cannon, meanwhile, lost his fortune (and his wife) in 1893. The now ostracized old man left for Brazil to do what he had always done, seek prosperity in a new field. He died penniless in a New York hotel two years later.[105]

With both of the Auditorium's owners on the rocks, the theater could not remain in their hands. Rather, at some point during the crisis, the Auditorium passed into the possession of its actual owner, the Hypotheek Bank.[106] That European creditor's name meant "mortgage," and surely, Spokane was mortgaged. With the Panic of 1893, the foolishness of the city's building spree—financed at 8 and 10 percent interest—became evident as one-quarter of Spokane became the property of Hypotheek Bank.[107] The foreclosures included the city's loveliest and most profitable downtown buildings: banks, apartments, business blocks, variety theaters, and the Auditorium. Thenceforth, the manager Harry Hayward worked for and settled accounts with a truly external organization, not those pioneers whose monument had seemed so solid only three years earlier.[108] If the Auditorium's shows proved the fickleness of upper-class Spokane, its brick-and-mortar realities demonstrated the risks Spokanites took when they tried to be high rollers at the world's gaming table.

Legitimate theater in late-century Spokane represented well the attempts made to promote the young city. When Fred Hoppe staged a musical, and intensely hierarchical, history of Spokane; when newspapermen rumbled with their Walla Walla counterparts over theatrical superiority; when society people prepared—physically—to watch Sarah Bernhardt, they all sent a message to the world that Spokane conformed to the standards of high-toned America. But theater at the city's best venue, the Auditorium, demonstrated much more about elite Spokane's regard for Victorian art. Despite knowing the standards of outside critics, Spokanites did not much care for them. Indeed, Spokane's entire relationship to external forces was a difficult one, a fact that became obvious with the Panic of 1893 and the repossession of the Auditorium. If a clash of values, a difficulty in controlling behavior, messages, and events accompanied the Auditorium's fin de siècle career, these same elements dominated the debate about Spokane's variety theaters.

CHAPTER TWO

Variety Theater, Politics, and Pragmatism

The year was 1894, and a young William Brady was sinking to his lowest point: performing melodramas in one of the saloon-theater combinations known as variety theaters that peppered the wide-open West. At this theater in Portland, Oregon, "purely ornamental girls" amused a loud male audience with variety routines from eight in the evening to midnight. After midnight, the girls entertained the men on a closer basis, cajoling them into the purchase of beer and companionship. Brady often kept the melodrama coming until five in the morning, but the real show was in the house with bouncers, fistfights, and girls struggling to escape drunken embraces. It was, as Brady observed, no place for a convention of Sunday School superintendents.[1]

Scenes every bit as wild occurred regularly in Spokane, the city James J. Hill called the "'worst old hole' in the West."[2] This was not quite the image of their community that local promoters wanted the world to see. Yet Spokane's livelihood came in large part from resource-extractive industries, especially mining, agriculture, and logging. The town's boosters knew that. They wanted that. But there was a rub: those industries required a labor force that was generally composed of unattached and mobile men, eager for entertainment after months in the woods, diggings, and fields. Spokane sold entertainment, and plenty of it, in a red light district centered on the area where Howard Street met the river and the railroad tracks. From the late 1880s till at least the First World War, the district was a carnival of saloons, brothels, lodging houses, gambling joints, dance halls, and variety theaters—a neighborhood at once lucrative and despised.

Lucrative, because those red lights attracted migrant workingmen to Spokane, where they spent money not only at theaters and brothels but also at clothing stores and cafeterias. Despised, because wild downtown nights belied the boosters' claims that Spokane was a cultured hometown. The variety theaters became emblematic of these competing hopes, and from the early 1890s until 1908 Spokanites engaged in an almost constant struggle with each other over the fate of the varieties. Although the theaters were patronized by and associated with the working class, this was largely a contest between elements of the middle and upper classes.

On one hand ministers, newspapermen, and others longed for Spokane to be the ideal city described in their brochures with churches, homes, and highbrow culture (notably, the Auditorium). These reformers imagined Victorian America as a kind of moral map and strove to place Spokane within its borders. The variety theaters thwarted this effort to ensure Spokane's spot within the civilized world because they made it feel like places middle-class reformers despised: either a corrupt metropolis or, especially, an outpost in the Wild West. On the other hand, what shopkeepers and showmen wanted from Spokane was a return on their investments. If that meant sidestepping law, propriety, and religion, cornerstones of their civilization, so be it. At the heart of the variety theater debate, then, were different expectations of what a city should yield, of what urban life meant: respectability or profit.

The variety theater fights exposed a related struggle—the transition from Victorian to "modern" values—taking place around the turn of the century. Throughout the 1890s Spokanites chose business over propriety by allowing the varieties to exist and to thrive. In so doing, they passed a pragmatic judgment on nineteenth-century norms. In contrast to more conscious and articulated rebellions against Victorianism, this was a prolonged and workaday rejection of morality by the bottom line.[3] Ironically, this decision came from the bourgeoisie, the very class of people who had benefited from the Victorian code throughout the century.

These decisions and contests became political for the fundamental reason that Victorians used government to organize what was permissible; variety theaters, for instance, could only operate legally

through municipal licenses. There were three episodes, in particular, during the 1890s when the variety theater question became
entangled in local politics. The first occurred in the mid-1890s,
during a high tide of depression and Populism; the final two took
place at the end of the decade as the economy and conservatives
regained ground. The variety theater fights of the 1890s symbolize
both the battle between prescribed values and business realities and
the ambivalence of Spokanites about the character of their city and
its place within America's moral and geographic order.

The Trouble with Variety Theaters

The sins committed by American theaters in the early 1800s included
not only rowdiness, rudeness, and alcohol but also an air of sexual
permissiveness, to the extent that a house generally reserved its third
tier for prostitutes and johns.[4] Around the 1840s impresarios began
to make theaters safe for children and "respectable" women by
expunging these guilty pleasures, but the market for them hardly
disappeared, and a new kind of theater developed: the concert saloon,
predecessor to variety theaters and a reverse image of the bourgeois
theater. By the mid-1850s concert saloons and the related "free and
easies" had a firm hold in New York City. The venues served as male
social centers and attracted customers through bawdy entertainment, drink and tobacco, and girls in short dresses, where men of
all classes came for "the lowest kind of amusement."[5]

The appeal of concert saloons came only partially from the stage.
Many of the resorts made their money through food, drinks, and
gambling, but girls formed the real attraction. Here, notoriously,
"waiter girls" flirted, hustled drinks on commission, and—sometimes—sold their bodies. Not all the waitresses prostituted themselves,
but female sexuality was unquestionably part of the show. Even the
geography of a concert saloon recalled prostitution: their third tiers
generally housed a number of private curtained boxes, where the barmaids drummed up alcohol sales with the promise of their company.
The young women, short skirts, and curtained chambers of concert
saloons did not go unnoticed. Upstanding citizens rallied against such
"Bacchus and Phallus worship" in New York City, San Francisco, and
elsewhere, but with only varying levels of success. Sex still sold.[6]

Showmen approached this dilemma with the old solution of cleaning up a bit and adopting a pretentious style. Concert saloons now became concert rooms, concert gardens, music halls, and finally, variety theaters. At ornately named houses, men could still find drinks and girls, but with a smaller dose of vulgarity. By the 1870s and 1880s variety theaters had earned a broader appeal and a slightly cleaner reputation, though they still catered to men intent on worldly pleasure. It was at this point that the format came to Spokane, where the city's many varieties offered onstage entertainments and in-house atmospheres similar to those of their national counterparts. At the Spokane venues, resident and itinerant performers presented song and dance routines; short farces, topical plays, ethnic comedies, or even comic operas; and novelties such as magic tricks, prize fights, and aerial acts. Most of the varieties employed brass bands that accompanied the artists and advertised the theater by playing on the street. At times the content on stage became lewd, but in general their shows were neither more mindless nor more offensive than much of what played at the Auditorium.[7]

What offended Victorians was the drinking, gambling, and titillation available at the varieties; these elements distinguished the venues from their more respectable counterparts and made them places no woman could attend without ruining her reputation. Middle-class Spokanites had additional complaints against the resorts. Critically, outside of New York City, variety theaters flourished in cities and towns that functioned as trading centers or whose resource-centered economies demanded a workforce of unattached men: places like Spokane. The residents of Cincinnati, Kansas City, and Fort Worth, for example, wrestled with the same questions of variety theater reform as did middle-class Spokanites. Yet, unlike these places, Spokane's later founding and later function as a resource colony meant that its "rowdy" period began at the tail end of the nineteenth century, a point when earlier frontiers had ostensibly joined the wider cultural order. Spokane thus appeared "wild and woolly" at a time when older cities, even those with variety theaters in their pasts, seemed more staid.[8]

Variety theaters could hardly be ignored in Spokane. Their location within the town—adjacent to city hall and near valuable, visible

real estate—made the theaters difficult to miss. In Spokane, as elsewhere in the West, showmen established large and well-equipped
varieties much in advance of legitimate theaters. It must have galled
early Spokanites that variety theaters thrived while local society
watched highbrow drama in a tent. The growing town had several
variety theaters by the mid-1880s, the most celebrated of which
was the Theater Comique, a venue firmly connected to the liquor
business. When fire destroyed Spokane in August 1889, the Comique
had only existed for a few months, yet it had strength enough to
reopen that December with a stage that was 142 feet deep and scenery
painted by a Chicago expert. In contrast, respectable theatergoers
were compelled to watch what shows they could at Concordia Hall,
a singing club with a capacity of 250 souls and a stage of 25 feet.[9]

With the 1890 opening of the Auditorium, affluent Spokanites
no longer worried about taking their entertainment in choral clubs
and warehouses, but they still worried about theater. Attempts to
reform the variety houses began in the early 1890s and formed part
of a larger drive against vice. As Carlos Schwantes notes, during the
1880s and 1890s Pacific Northwestern cities witnessed multiple
campaigns against saloons, cigarettes, prostitution, and Sabbath-day
commerce. Saloons especially disturbed middle-class crusaders, who
viewed them as a breeding ground for prostitution, lawlessness, and
corruption. But if liquor was dangerous, liquor plus women was dyna-
mite. Consequently, ministers, editors, and politicians led regular
attacks against variety theaters during the closing decades of the nineteenth century in Seattle, Tacoma, and other northwestern cities.[10]

So it was in Spokane, where politics, business, and boosterism
made an explosive mix and where tactical realities often trumped
moral ideals. Concerted drives against variety theaters began in 1890,
failed, and sputtered back to life again in 1893. Local authorities
certainly created regulations aimed at taming or closing the theaters but enforcing such laws proved more difficult. Throughout the
1890s, the attempts of reformers meant little compared with the
variety managers' ability to draw profits and flout the city ordinances
aimed against them. In 1893 the local press particularly connected
the impresarios' disregard for the law to politics.[11] Well might the
newspapers infer that electoral politics fed into the controversy over

variety theaters. From the 1890s to 1908 politicians and partisans
on either side of the variety theater question manipulated the issue
to their benefit. One could almost bet that, as another election
season approached, someone in Spokane would voice an opinion
about the theaters.

Municipal Politics and Urban Priorities, 1895

The political, business, and class elements of the variety theater debate
became especially intense during the mid-1890s, and for good cause:
Spokane's economic underpinnings made it a site of class tensions,
which were exacerbated by the Panic of 1893. The public debate
reflected and fed this charged social atmosphere, where miners from
the Kootenays and the Coeur d'Alenes, farmhands from the Big Bend,
and lumberjacks from inland forests poured into Spokane on a
seasonal basis.[12] In the evocative words of one lumberjack, Spokane
was the "big eddy," where a fellow could come for a quick turn in
the city's stores, flophouses, employment agencies, and brothels
before whirling back into the river of temporary jobs.[13]

If Spokane provided an important stop in the seasonal flow of
work, the "blanket stiffs"—or rather, their money—mattered a great
deal to Spokane's economy. The city's business people clearly profited
from the constant influx of laborers on holiday. Merchants outfitted
with them with the boots, tools, and clothing needed for another
round of work. Saloon keepers, lodging house operators, and impresarios provided so-called floating workers with a home base. Prostitutes sold them another kind of home comfort. Some of the city's
most visible, well-placed people enjoyed tremendous gain from the
market (legitimate and otherwise) tailored to itinerant laborers. The
trouble was that many of the establishments that attracted hired
hands to Spokane, such as its notorious variety theaters, were less
likely to attract the "right" sorts of settlers.[14] City boosters wanted
Spokane to serve as the central city of the Inland Empire; they wanted
the business that came from miners, hired hands, and lumberjacks.
They did not want their city to feel like a mining camp.

Yet by 1893 Spokane was in no position to turn away business.
From 1893 to 1897 depression gripped the United States, and the
Northwest was not immune from national troubles. In Spokane the
volatile combination of panicked depositors and inadequate bank

reserves touched off years of "misery and insolvency"; railroad monopolies and exploitative shipping rates added to the region's burdens.
Consequently, farmers, laborers, and some businessmen united in
the mid-1890s to make eastern Washington and Spokane itself a
stronghold of Populism, a political movement that celebrated the
"producers" of wealth (such as farmers and laborers) and called for
government intervention in the economy. Meanwhile, Spokane also
became a center of labor radicalism, and within the city, labor activism
and Populist fervor were closely related. By this point, the region had
already experienced intense class struggle; class-conscious political
movements like Populism, therefore, struck a nerve in the city.[15]

Variety theaters were connected to all of these issues. They attracted
workingmen to Spokane, which benefited shopkeepers. At the same
time, in the eyes of reformers, the varieties presented two sticky
problems. First, they increased the raucous (some would say immoral)
atmosphere of downtown Spokane. Second, they supposedly fostered
an environment wherein politicians could pander to and manipulate the "floating vote" of migratory workers. The economic and
social troubles of the mid-1890s forced these issues to a head, as
the variety theater question made Spokanites—including elected
officials, newspapermen, ministers, showmen, and thousands of
laborers—choose between revenues and respectability.

Like other boomtown newspapers, the *Spokesman-Review* had a
vested interest in the success of its town. Part of achieving that success was an appearance of propriety and culture, and the newspaper's top men considered their publication a guardian of public
morals and an important player in municipal politics. Usually in
alliance with middle-class citizen groups, throughout the 1890s the
paper regularly accused public officials of perpetuating corrupt ward-
and boss-based politics. The *Spokesman-Review* bundled variety theaters
into this system of corruption in part because of their patrons.
The Republican newspaper argued that as sites that welcomed
laborers (people whose votes, the *Spokesman-Review* suggested, could
be purchased), variety theaters served as centers of both sexual
and political immorality.[16]

The people who ran the varieties troubled the *Spokesman-Review*
as much as did the theaters' patrons and supposedly represented
the kind of jaded urban lifestyle that the newspaper and its allies

in no way wanted associated with Spokane. John W. Considine was the focus of the reformers' fury. Born in 1860s Chicago of an Irish father, Considine landed in Seattle in 1889. A teetotaler who never gambled but otherwise bore all the marks of the so-called sporting crowd, Considine knew how to make it in the urban underworld. In Seattle he managed the People's Theater, a skid road basement dedicated to "wine, women, and faro." When the 1893 financial disaster proved too much for his Seattle resort, he set up shop in Spokane in late 1894. Considine kept the name "People's Theater" for his new variety house and located it in the heart of Spokane's red light district, at 123 North Howard.[17]

The showman leased the venue from one of Spokane's most important and controversial firms, the partnership of Jacob Goetz ("Dutch Jake") and Harry Baer. Goetz and Baer were running a saloon in the Coeur d'Alenes when they struck it rich as some of the original discoverers of the Bunker Hill vein. Arriving in Spokane in the late 1880s, they used their Bunker Hill profits to build the deliciously ornate Frankfurt building, a four-story bar, theater, dance hall, and gambling resort—a sporting crowd answer to the Auditorium. But though the Frankfurt building and the Coeur d'Alene Company (as Goetz and Baer called their firm) played a tremendous role in the local economy, the company's trade in gambling, titillation, and luxury was certain to make waves in Spokane, despite its undeniable profits.[18]

In Considine, Goetz and Baer found a manager who could bring lucrative show business to Spokane. In January 1895 Baer explained that other downtown varieties "have had the attractions and they have been making all the money. . . . Now we have a chance with this show in our place to pull out. We have $250,000 invested here." Baer's statement revealed both Considine's skill as an impresario and, more important, the profits that a Spokane variety house could realize. The People's Theater presented standard 1890s fare (one advertisement announced an Irish comedy, a "sweet little singer," and twenty-four novelty artists), but Considine's house quickly raised the ire of solid Spokane.[19] The young man retained from Seattle a reputation for running a rowdy establishment, and this drew the eyes of ministers and councilmen to the People's Theater. Within weeks of its debut, Considine, Baer, and Goetz found themselves defending the theater in public forums.[20]

Chief among Considine's accusers were Protestant clergy and the city's Good Government Club, who worried that he was not merely a disreputable tough but also a man who brought with him a style of business and politics that would soil Spokane's reputation. The heart of the argument against Considine was his connection with boss politics and with larger cities that Spokanites painted as corrupt. During these years of unruly urbanization, Spokane's "better element" did not want such a connection made to their home. The *Spokesman-Review* quoted the *Seattle Post-Intelligencer*'s description of Considine as a "democratic war horse" with a sporting-crowd style (complete with tailored clothing, a diamond stud, and a "'cud' of gum"), the kind of man more than capable of manipulating primary elections. "He has evidently got his mind set on running a show in Spokane," the Seattle newspaper warned, "and may teach the council some of the tricks he learned in Chicago politics."[21] To ministers, good-government advocates, and newspapermen, then, Considine represented the wrong kind of politics—the kind with wards, bosses, and unwashed voters—and might bring that big-city taint to Spokane.[22]

The name of Considine's establishment, the People's Theater, indicated other elements of this public debate: class conflict and business interests. True to its name, the variety was cheap enough for common people to attend. Unlike the high-priced Auditorium, Spokane's variety houses asked for relatively low cover charges or for nothing at all, making their money instead from alcohol sales. Although men of means also attended local varieties, it was the workingmen who filled them. Furthermore, the variety theaters catered to laborers by offering (for ten cents admission) such productions as *Sawdust Arthur, or The Bogus Checks*, "the latest satire on mining life."[23] When discussing these theaters, the issue of social class could not be avoided.

The connection between social class and business interests became clear in the spring of 1895, when partisans on both sides of the fight rallied local opinion (see table 1 in the appendix). In late February clergymen circulated a petition asking the city council to prohibit all theaters and dance halls that in any way sold or distributed alcohol. Tellingly, the anti-theater petition found support in suburban and residential districts: most of Spokane's laboring class lived downtown.[24] Soon thereafter another group began campaigning on behalf of the variety theaters. Their document made explicit the connection between the laborers who frequented the variety shows and the shopkeepers who wanted their business. The petitioners objected especially to laws that arbitrarily interfered with the revenue of citizens who had invested in Spokane; they argued that the variety theaters enhanced the city's appeal for miners and others, which in turn brought business to the merchants. The Louvre's proprietor, for instance, reported that his theater enriched the city through its operating expenses, the activities of its employees, and crucially, the thousands of dollars spent by men from the diggings. A shoe dealer put it more bluntly when asked why the varieties should remain open: "I have miners' shoes in stock, and I want to sell them."[25]

That Spokane's business element stood behind the variety theaters was obvious. The *Spokesman-Review* reported that among the more than two thousand pro-theater signatures were those of all but five storekeepers on Riverside Avenue, the city's chief marketplace. The newspaper printed a sampling of the signatories, a list of four hundred names that included many community pillars and important concerns.[26] Those signatures represented not only an endorsement of the variety theaters but also a business-sense referendum on the Victorian code. Historians have detailed how, in the mid-nineteenth century, middle-class Americans embraced the so-called Victorian ethic of thrift, sobriety, hard work, and strictly controlled bodies. By attaching their names to the cause of the raucous and sensual variety theaters, Spokane's bourgeoisie were walking away from the norms of their class for most of a century, a signal that in this year of 1895, America stood at the brink of great social change.[27]

This was far from a simple affair. The loudest contestants during the 1895 debates, members of the middle and upper classes, remained ambivalent about less fortunate Spokanites and about their city's image. People who looked the same demographically might disagree about what amusements the working class should have access to. A well-connected lawyer named John Onderdonk, for example, protested the efforts to shut down the varieties, as he argued that those who could afford the Auditorium had no right to deny working people what little amusement they could find. Popular entertainments, the lawyer continued, could offer "the masses" a healthy alternative to the saloon. A. G. Wilson, a Unitarian pastor, did not agree. If Onderdonk counted little difference between variety shows and the farces playing at the Auditorium, Wilson saw varieties as the work of greedy managers, happy to satisfy to "mass" cravings for indecency. Both men viewed the "masses" from a paternalistic height, but Wilson added fear to the mix.[28]

The middle-class uncertainty about variety theaters extended to the image they gave Spokane. Merchants appreciated the attractiveness varieties lent to the town, but others complained that the theaters gave Spokane the reputation of either a decadent metropolis or a wide-open mining camp. The concern over both of these images in turn manifested the uncertainty of Spokanites regarding their position within the hierarchy of American cities and culture. When ministers denounced Considine before the city council, they did so in part by portraying him as a pander who used corrupt methods, redolent of Tammany Hall, to advance his business and political interests. From the 1890s to the 1910s middle-class Spokanites expressed their desire to be grandly urban in many ways, such as imitating the architecture of New York City and Chicago. Yet this group also exhibited much anxiety about the moral and municipal problems they associated with these metropolises. Thus when the reverends called Considine a vote-manipulating demagogue, they hinted at a pervasive concern that growth meant decay. Pro-theater partisans argued that the varieties gave Spokane a metropolitan feel, but this did little to convince reformers that Spokane could be at once respectable and home to the resorts.[29]

If certain people viewed Considine and his business as harbingers of big-city crime, others felt that variety theaters created quite the opposite problem for Spokane. They maintained that all the miners, beer, and barmaids—the "wild west hurrah business"—made their town look like the untamed setting of a dime novel.[30] While later generations capitalized on the American West's mythic abandon, many nineteenth-century westerners wanted nothing of it, seeking instead to distance themselves from the wide-open reputation that violated the essence of Victorian self-control.[31] In Spokane, that distancing had an economic motivation, for the variety theaters' westernness threatened the efforts to draw families to the Inland Northwest. One man reported that a relative had inquired if Spokane was an appropriate place to raise a family. "He, with many others" was "likely to come here," but only if the city moved against varieties.[32] Spokane's promoters were constantly courting the favorable attention of middle-class outsiders, and variety theaters did not serve their purposes well.

The disquiet regarding Spokane's image as either corrupt or wild reflected a broader distress over how the town and its people fit within the stratified world of late-nineteenth-century America. F. B. Cherington, for example, attempted to sway the city council by insisting that two of Spokane's regional competitors, Seattle and Tacoma, would not endure such disorderly variety theaters.[33] To people deeply involved in urban rivalries, this was a powerful argument. At the same time Spokanites tried to reconcile their desires for respectability with the city's economic and geographic realities, as when the *Spokesman-Review* stated that the theory that "vice and immorality are essential to the prosperity of a mining center has ceased to prevail" elsewhere, and must likewise end in Spokane.[34] In short, certain middle-class Spokanites worried how the city's livelihood and lifestyle made it appear to outsiders and how that appearance affected Spokane's place within regional and national hierarchies.

Throughout early 1895 Spokanites spent much time and ink debating the place of those theaters within their city. Finally, after three months of sermons, petitions, editorials, and seemingly endless meetings, the city's councilmen passed a measure policing variety theaters and prohibiting alcohol from their premises.[35] The forces of order, it seemed, had won the day (see table 2 in the appendix). Local businesspeople had made it clear that the protection of investments—not propriety—was their priority. Yet, backed by the authority of Spokane's legislative body, a specific vision of the city's future prevailed: the vision of the Ministerial Association and its allies of Spokane as a respectable Victorian hometown and emphatically not a corrupt city or a raucous mining camp.

Enter Horatio N. Belt. Like so many other Spokanites, Belt came from someplace else, skipping his way across the nation until he found success in the Northwest. Arriving in 1887, Belt focused on real estate and boosterism, an altogether common activity in the young boomtown. But he was not like every other man who plugged the Inland Empire. In the spring of 1894 Belt drew on a coalition of Populists, silver Republicans, prohibitionists, and Democrats to become the city's first Populist mayor and a key figure in Washington's Populist circles.[36] One year later Mayor Belt faced the ostensibly minor decision of whether to approve the city council's ordinance against variety theaters. The anti-theater camp felt certain that the prominent, prohibitionist, churchgoing Belt would sign the legislation into law.[37] He did not.

Belt served as a deacon at the Westminster Congregational Church, and he was also a Populist politician who courted the blue-collar vote. In the year since his May 1894 election, Belt had used his credibility with working people to guide Spokane through several moments of extraordinary social tension.[38] Belt's connection to the proletariat did not draw universal praise. When the Northwest Industrial Army—a contingent of unemployed laborers marching with Coxey's Army to bring attention to their plight—arrived in eastern Washington in 1894, conservative Spokane especially questioned "Brother Belt" and alleged that he had manipulated the "floating vote" of itinerant workers.[39] When Belt killed the variety theater ordinance in March 1895, such accusations quickly resurfaced. Belt's veto crystallized the class-based politics surrounding the varieties, making it clear that different segments of Spokane's population had competing hopes regarding the city's future and purpose.

For his part, Belt made a direct connection between the regulation of variety theaters and Populist reform. He did so by attempting to bring a signature Populist cause, the referendum, into the debate.[40] In a letter explaining his actions Belt noted that, though he respected the clergymen who endorsed the anti-theater proposition, he had an even deeper regard for the people as a whole. The mayor asked why a handful of councilmen should have the right to legislate away the happiness of thousands of people. Instead, Spokane's citizens should act in a "sovereign capacity at the polls" and shape the laws that governed them. Belt suggested that the matter of variety theaters be printed on the upcoming ballot, allowing the city fathers to understand the true will of the people and approach it with reverence.[41] By so doing, the mayor asserted that he, too, was a reformer, one oriented toward the common man.

Whatever Belt intended with his veto, that action made him a turncoat in the eyes of the Protestant ministers, conservative politicians, and the *Spokesman-Review*. On the Sunday following Belt's move, clerics throughout the city denounced him before large and eager audiences. While Spokanites had engaged in a lively conversation about Considine, Belt's veto electrified the city's public forums. The trouble was not simply that a pillar of the Congregational church had killed the variety theater ordinance; it was how, and through whom, Belt suggested resolving the dilemma. The mayor offended Spokane's conservative elements because of his appeal to the people and to methods of direct democracy, an approach that they felt constituted demagoguery and opened the door to "mob majorities." Given the success of the pro-theater petition, perhaps the ministers feared that Spokane's voters would keep the theaters open; clearly, they believed the referendum gave power to a dangerous crowd. The mayor's opponents further impugned him as one who placed power, favor, and cash before his conscience. They accused Belt of hiding his true motives behind an appeal to the popular will. Those ulterior purposes, the reformers insinuated, emanated from collusion between Belt and the theater and liquor interests. They conjured from Belt's decision the backroom dealings of a politician in league with Spokane's lowest elements.[42]

Belt vetoed the variety theater ordinance a short six weeks before municipal elections, which gave his enemies ground for further charges of corruption. The variety theater question joined a handful of other issues to create a campaign season that was socially charged, to say the least. These issues included the free coinage of silver (instead of a pure adherence to the gold standard) and the nativist ideals of the anti-Catholic American Protective Association (APA).[43] Like the varieties, these topics were germane to Inland Empire campaigning because of the region's reliance on silver mining and because of the workforce attracted by that industry. A three-way mayoral race reflected the tensions in the depression-burdened city: opposing Belt were Charles Hopkins, a Republican, and Walter France, a councilman who had voted against the varieties and was now running on the APA-affiliated "Citizens" ticket.[44] The city newspapers joined in the fight, with the Republican *Spokesman-Review* vehemently attacking Belt and the Democratic *Chronicle* eventually endorsing him. In this municipal fray, the variety theater question may not have formed an official part of any one platform, but it surely influenced the outcome of an election characterized by class struggle and mudslinging.

The *Spokesman-Review*, led by William Cowles and Nelson Durham, especially tried to portray Mayor Belt as corrupt and discounted by his own party. The Republican newspaper had an interest in Populist failure. It regularly reminded its readers of Considine's alleged dealings in machine politics and then declared that an "unholy alliance" existed "between the Sunday School nominee and the vaudeville showman." The morning after the city's Populist primary, which Belt won by a handy majority, the newspaper reported that Belt's defeated opponents had openly accused "Considine and his 'gang'" of packing the polls on the mayor's behalf. "Respectable men," disgruntled Populists reportedly remarked, had stepped aside and left the "variety theater crowd" to run the election.[45]

Throughout the election season, the *Spokesman-Review* printed many such accusations of a Belt-Considine cabal and plainly argued that the two men cultivated rotten ward politics. In late April the newspaper described how "Mayor Belt's forces"—led by Considine—rounded up votes: "'What John Considine can't do can't be done,' said one of Mayor Belt's admirers yesterday. 'Wait until election day and see the results in the Second ward.'"[46] With this comment the *Spokesman-Review* not only suggested that Belt and the variety theater men ran a political machine, it also connected such corruption to Spokane's working and "undesirable" classes. The second ward—or "de second ward," as the newspaper called it—was the jurisdiction that covered downtown Spokane with its railroad depots, boardinghouses, brothels, and saloons. It was largely this section that housed and entertained hosts of poor, wandering, or unattached working people.[47] Here, as police records testify, occurred the majority of Spokane's crimes: disorderly at Post Street; assault and battery on

Main; drunk on Howard; gambling, prostitution, larceny, vagrancy, lodging. Here, actors, addicts, laundrymen, miners, orphans, peddlers, and radicals lived, worked, and lounged. Here, in "de second ward," was the heart of Spokane's undesirable element.[48]

The social aspects of the election did not go without comment. Just as local ministers insisted that the pro-theater petition was padded with hobo signatures, so too did Belt's political enemies emphasize the supposed itinerancy of his supporters. The *Spokesman-Review* wrote that Belt had won downtown Spokane in the Populist primaries because, in several precincts, the count was triple the registered voters. How? Belt's ticket "was voted solidly by the floating vote," this in a city whose upstanding citizens frequently expressed distaste for and alarm over tramps. Accordingly, the *Spokesman-Review* connected the high number of voters registered in 1894, the year of Belt's initial victory, to a glutting of the books by the Northwestern Industrial Army. That publication did not mince words in its descriptions of the alleged ballot box stuffers, calling them gangs, minions, henchmen.[49]

The *Spokesman-Review* was fighting not only perceived corruption but also the very real force of Populism, which held a special attraction for the farmers and laborers of eastern Washington in the troubled mid-1890s. Populism also drew the region's attention by emphasizing the place of silver in the nation's money supply. Because the economy of eastern Washington was tied to silver production and because some Populists—notably Horatio Belt—focused their message on silver, Populist candidates carried Washington State elections in 1896.[50] Spokane's Republicans must have sensed the danger that Populism posed to them, for the *Spokesman-Review* made every attempt to expose splits within the People's party, paint Belt as unelectable, and demonstrate (in this town of boosters) how Populist victories would ruin Spokane's name.[51] At the same time, the newspaper steadily promoted Charles Hopkins, Republican and underdog. The *Spokesman-Review* tried to overturn the foremost pro-variety theater argument—that the resorts underpinned much of Spokane's retail market—by claiming that the GOP platform was the platform of business. It reported that merchants and businessmen were giving their support to Hopkins. "Beltism," the *Spokesman-Review* thundered, damaged "the business and commercial interests of this city."[52]

Two days before the election, the *Spokesman-Review* printed its harshest critique of Belt and Considine: "Votes Were Cheap." On the front page of the Sunday edition, the newspaper published testimonials and affidavits gathered from disaffected Populists. That evidence told a lurid tale of how, on the evening of the Populist primaries, Belt and Considine's henchmen had rounded up men from "the slums of the city," paid pennies for their votes, and "herded" them from poll to poll. Although it was Populist operatives who did the dirty work, always at the center of machinations stood one man, Considine: his employees the captains of the operation, his theater its headquarters, his "methods" its organizing force. Of course the showman could not pack polls alone; he needed voters willing to sell their franchise. That degradation, the *Spokesman-Review* argued, came from Spokane's lower-class and wandering men, who bartered their rights for a few cents.[53] In phrase after phrase—"slum politics," "dive politics," "rounders herding men," "human cattle"—the *Spokesman-Review* fastened political corruption to the city's poorest residents and its rowdiest district, the second ward.[54] Considine and the People's Theater were depicted as the heart of political corruption in Spokane, Belt's allegedly low-life constituency the body.

The *Spokesman-Review*'s accusations did not go unanswered. Two voices, J. J. Browne's Democratic *Chronicle* and the mayor himself, met the charges with recriminations of their own. For his part Belt dispensed briefly with the variety theater question, focused on the bread and butter of local Populism, and called the Republican Party a "combination" that had run Spokane "for years for its own selfish ends."[55] Although the *Chronicle* professed neutrality, it also rebutted images of Populist corruption and Republican ascendancy almost point by point.[56] For instance, Browne's newspaper reversed the *Spokesman-Review*'s rhetorical strategies by using terms like "ward-heelers" to describe the Republican operation, while it praised Belt's "business integrity."[57] Finally, immediately after the *Spokesman-Review* printed its exposé, the *Chronicle* shot back with its own collection of affidavits and testimonials that depicted the Republican newspaper's story as part of a plot designed to ruin Belt.[58]

Did the mayor conspire with the "vaudeville showman" to secure his position? Evidence from both sides is flawed, suggesting that either the Republicans or the Populists or both were up to something. More significant was the fact of Belt's substantial victory in May 1895.[59] After having endured the invective of conservative Spokane that unlikely champion of variety theaters enjoyed two more years as mayor, nearly became a gubernatorial candidate in 1896, and retained "great popularity" among the laboring class. Belt's election suggested that, even though Spokane's upper crust controlled much of the public discourse, the town's less substantial classes could still make their will felt. Like the pro–variety theater petition, Belt's triumphs signified that the majority of politically active Spokanites chose to put something—whether business sense or political principles—above middle-class morality and thus give their tacit support to the cultural change that the theaters represented.[60]

Within the Borders of Civilization, 1897–1899

Hard times and experimental politics formed the backdrop of Spokane's 1895 variety theater debate. Yet in the late 1890s, when the economic and political tides had turned, Spokanites continued to dispute the place of variety theaters in their city. The 1895 fight revealed the connection between electoral politics and varieties, but the disquiet surrounding those sites of working-class leisure concerned something deeper still: the ambivalence of Spokanites regarding their city's economic base and resulting image and the character of modern cities altogether.

The city's bourgeoisie had two competing economic interests with regards to the variety theaters. On the retail level, shopkeepers supported the varieties because they helped draw miners and lumberjacks into Spokane's stores. But on the larger scale of land speculation and city promotion, boosters worried how the downtown theaters affected Spokane's reputation as a maturing city. Even as Spokanites strove to create the "queen city" of the Inland Empire, some of their neighbors were not entirely convinced of the virtue of urban life. In 1897 and 1899 Howard Street theaters became the targets of two major anti-vice drives. As in 1895, these campaigns demonstrated that, though late-century Spokanites might worry about the image and influence of variety theaters, they ultimately placed profits above the sensibilities of moralists and promoters.

Spokane did well after recovering from the tumult and depression of the mid-1890s. The waning years of the century were ones of tremendous growth for the town—in population, built environment, and regional importance, as key economic drivers once again gathered momentum.[61] In 1896 and 1898, for instance, the Colville Indian reservation—rich in mineral deposits but previously off-limits—opened to prospectors, who rushed in for the spoils. As the nearest supply route and the home of mining investors, Spokane enjoyed a neat profit from the Colville rushes. These years also saw an increase in Spokane's importance as an agricultural distribution point. Because of expanding markets (and much advertising) Spokane became the entrepôt for the fertile orchards of the Inland Northwest. Not only did Spokane act as one of the foremost American shippers of fruit, by around 1903 it also supplied the needs of regional farmers—turning the successes of the Palouse and Big Bend areas into its own.[62]

With growth came the same problem that Spokane's boosters had faced in the early and mid-1890s: because the city was married to a resource-extractive economy, it was likewise bound to a transient male workforce. Renewed success meant more workers and more troublesome entertainments. The civic-minded lamented that mining gains had made Spokane a magnet for the "riff raff and scum of large cities," fast degenerating into the "most thoroughly wicked and demoralized town in the Northwest."[63] They recognized that laws aplenty existed to calm the varieties but that both police and public looked the other way (see table 3 in the appendix). This was so, in part, precisely because the red-light businessmen also knew their role in prosperity's return and wielded corresponding power.[64]

Nelson Durham's summary of 1897 Spokane neatly encapsulated the city's tensions and dichotomy: two U.S. senators now hailed from Spokane, the city's population continued to increase, and several capitalists were building mansions. But "fine residences" could not hide Spokane's wild downtown, and Durham admitted that lax law enforcement allowed an atmosphere of vice more daringly wide-open than at any period since the 1889 fire. Indeed, while at least four city ordinances, a new set of police rules, and a state law existed to regulate the variety theaters, their proprietors felt confident enough to parade brass bands and barmaids through the streets of an afternoon.[65] In such a setting, the stakes for cultural control were high.

The 1897 and 1899 anti-vice drives followed similar, even predictable, outlines: ministerial outrage, political promises, community debate, temporary victory, quiet failure. The sameness of these episodes points to how entrenched the resistance to reform was and how much Spokane's status quo and apparent future troubled some of its residents. The 1897 fight began early in the year, when clergymen involved in the 1895 affair took up arms again.[66] This time, the ministers had the incoming mayor, Dr. E. D. Olmsted, on their side. In support of Olmsted and reform, the city council recommended several existing ordinances that could tame the red light district—if enforced. Among these ordinances was a municipal "barmaid law" similar to those passed by Washington and other states that forbade women from working in any establishment that sold alcohol.[67]

Olmsted soon filed complaints against three variety theaters, likely on the basis of the local barmaid ordinance, and asked the council to revoke their licenses. Since licensing formed one of the city's major regulatory tools, the council's quick and unanimous revocation of the theaters' licenses seemed to auger moral reform. Meanwhile, at the People's Theater, news of the council's ruling against the varieties led to a packed house and a verbal duel between showmen and authorities. But propriety prevailed for a time, and throughout the summer of 1897 the varieties and dance halls remained closed. Then in late September the venues managed to get their licenses renewed, setting the stage for future contests about Spokane's identity.[68]

Between the bookends of outrage and failure, the public discourse about variety theaters focused intensely on the geographic meanings of respectability. Reformers worried that institutions like variety theaters marked Spokane—a fledgling city already associated with boom and bust industries—as outside the pale of civilization. The Reverend W. A. Spalding demanded that Spokanites recognize their home was "not a mining camp on the border of civilization." Likewise, a teacher named N. F. Coleman noted that Spokane had become a byword among easterners, a place whose wickedness could only be trumped by hell itself. Coleman's remark suggests that one of the great fears of the moralists was that decent people would not move there. As Spalding put it, "Spokane is bidding for permanency and respectability. . . . It is bidding for immigration of the best families, but these are not coming unless we have a clean city."[69]

The activists tried to prove that Spokane could exist, geographically and spiritually, within the larger moral order. The *Spokesman-Review* maintained that Spokane had all the requisites for prosperity and decorum. Yet physically and morally, it had a cancer—lower Howard Street—where "vice has been given such license . . . that the district has degenerated into a hotbed of immorality." That district, the newspaper insisted, threatened to make a hell-hole of what could be a placidly middle-class American city. This did not have to be. The *Spokesman-Review* offered the example of Denver: since the regulation of its variety theaters, the chief American mining entrepôt was no longer a den of wide-open vice. Spokane, too, could be a mining center and still be within the so-called borders of civilization. Spokane could have decency and profit.[70]

The *Chronicle* took a somewhat more pragmatic view of Spokane's moral map. In its editorial space the newspaper described a downtown already filled with businesses and unlikely to expand in the near future. Too much of that crowded district (some of its best land, in fact) was taken up by saloons, variety theaters, gambling joints, and dance halls that pushed "reputable" concerns to the margins. If Spokane must have such establishments in order to remain prosperous (suggesting that, indeed, it must), then they should at least be moved to "some less conspicuous" quarters. The *Chronicle*, in other words, hoped to realign the geography of morality within Spokane by partially purging vice from its most visible district.[71]

This geography of respectability could be applied within and without the city. The *Chronicle* also tried to convince its readers that Spokane and the Inland Northwest were hardly unruly outliers begging for inclusion within the borders of Victorian America but, rather, wellsprings of virtue. The newspaper warned the youth of the Palouse, for instance, that whatever isolation they might imagine to be their rural lot, nowhere was lonelier than a metropolis like

London or New York City; far better to stay close to home and enjoy pure, real sociality.[72] More pointedly, the *Chronicle* noted that "Even Paris, the gayest and wickedest city in the world, is in the throes of a moral crusade. . . . The good work first advocated by the *Chronicle* and later carried out by Mayor Olmsted and the city council is far reaching in its effects and influences."[73] Bluntly and ambitiously, Spokanites were attempting to redraw the map of civilization and put themselves squarely at its center.

Even as Spokane's reformers placed their city within the bounds of propriety, they also tried to convince their neighbors that Victorian ideals should matter more than money-making. Coleman insisted that, as the city grew physically and commercially, it had a responsibility also to serve as the region's "moral guide." Reverend Spalding approached the problem of business interests less diplomatically, recounting a conversation with "a German" who opposed the reform drive because it would reduce his rent profits. The cleric responded that he, too, had a tremendous investment he would not see ruined— his boy. Spalding concluded by noting his distaste for men who knew the importance of a wholesome urban environment, but who walked away from reform in honor of "selfish interests." Whereas Spalding and Coleman quietly acknowledged that Spokane did profit from vice, others maintained that the wild entertainment district now hindered the city's prosperity.[74]

Whatever people like Spalding argued, in 1897 they ultimately failed. Two years earlier Spokanites had brushed aside the distaste they felt for variety theaters in honor of the receipts from those venues, and in the fall of 1897 they made a similar decision. With little fanfare the city council reviewed the licenses of the Comique and Coeur d'Alene variety theaters. Police and councilmen reported that they had inspected the venues and found that private theater boxes had been removed. This brought them into compliance with a new city ordinance that set a curfew on theaters and forbade them from providing private boxes. With that the council approved the licenses, and the theaters began advertising again in the newspapers that had so recently condemned them. It is highly likely that, behind the scenes, the powerful saloon and theater lobby had reminded the city fathers of Howard Street's economic and political

The interior of the Coeur d'Alene theater, circa 1896. The theater's powerful owners, Jacob Goetz and Harry Baer, are at the bottom of the steps. Notice the promise of an "entire new show every week" and the masculine atmosphere. Northwest Museum of Arts and Culture/Eastern Washington State Historical Society, Spokane, Washington, L2003-14.659.

might, pressuring them to find a way to reopen the theaters. However much editors, ministers, and mayors championed morality, marketplace practicality once again won the day.[75]

Two more years passed, a new mayor took charge of Spokane, and the city delved once more into the variety theater debate. The context of the discussion had changed markedly since mid-decade. The green shoots of 1897 were developing into a florescence of economic and physical growth that continued for much of the following decade. Further, by 1899, voters in Spokane and throughout Washington had abandoned Populism and solidly returned to the

GOP.[76] The basic dilemma behind the variety theater question, however, remained the same. And if in 1897 Spokanites discussed the discordance between their desires for respectability and their desires for profit, in 1899 they raged about it.

The 1899 affair was so heated because it occurred during an event that embodied these conflicting ideals—the Northwest Industrial Exposition. The annual exposition began after the 1889 fire as a method of attracting attention to the natural wealth that came from Spokane's "tributary" regions. By 1899 the fair's promoters were boasting their best show yet, with large crowds and large returns. Some of the exposition's draw came from high-toned entertainments and customers, but Spokane's businessmen knew that if they did well during the fair they had the itinerant laborers to thank.[77] Among the businesses that most attracted those spenders were the Howard Street theaters. Spokanites had to decide—this time in dramatic fashion—if they wanted to gain immediate profits by serving the workingmen or if, during the fair, Spokane would appear to be a prim and bustling place that middle-class outsiders could appreciate.

As it roared along in 1899, Spokane felt ever less like that kind of staid hometown. Worse yet, to certain Spokanites the booming city did not even appear to belong within the American order. The *Spokesman-Review* reported that men back from the Klondike, that ultimate in Wild West abandon, considered Dutch Jake's Coeur d'Alene resort more raucously wicked than anything in Dawson City. Spokane's failure to live up to Victorian standards, its falling off the map of respectability, resulted largely from its rejection of a center-piece of civilized life—the law itself. At this point the body of variety theater regulations included not only several city ordinances and a state law but also two higher court decisions. Spokane's own geography symbolized this disregard for the rule of law: city hall and the Couer d'Alene resort were neighbors. Spokanites—including the civic authorities—knew how flagrantly illegal the variety theaters had become, but they also knew that a handful of ministers could not break up a force at least tacitly supported by so many businesspeople.[78]

In the waning days of his term in May 1899, a weary E. D. Olmsted admitted that he could not solve the theater problem. He then made a telling comment: he favored reform but only to the extent that the citizenry—especially the merchants—would support change.[79] Olmsted's voice of experience did not prevent the incoming mayor, J. M. Comstock, from insisting that the theaters comply with the law by the close of May 1899. Through an order to the police force, Comstock declared an end to curtained boxes and beer-peddling waitresses, for on his watch there would be "no winking at violation, no 'fixing it up' after arrest." When Comstock tried to impress his weight (and the weight of moral legislation) upon the public, however, Dutch Jake responded in kind. He noted that removing the barmaids would kill the most lucrative element of the Couer d'Alene's business. While he could succeed anywhere, Goetz doubted that Spokane could thrive without his resort, where the weekly payroll alone averaged $1,400—more than the payrolls of the streetcar and electric companies combined.[80]

May, June, July, and August came and went in succession and still the barmaids remained. In late September, when Henry "Fisky" Barnett tried to obtain a license for the Comique, Comstock gathered his strength and again demanded that the resorts comply with municipal demands.[81] But the mayor had not chosen the most politic moment for a renewed morality push, because Spokane was days away from the remunerative Industrial Exposition. If the divisiveness of the situation needed any emphasis, it came at the next council meeting, when the Stockholm and Coeur d'Alene tried to renew their licenses. On paper the 1899 city council looked like a group that could at least agree with itself (see table 4 in the appendix). Republicans all, the councilmen were generally middle-aged businessmen who had lived in Spokane for some time; as a local GOP leader said, their elections meant a "good, clean business administration." These demographically similar men represented well the difficulty of the variety theater question among middle- and upper-class Spokanites. In the Barnett case, the city legislature was torn, voting on the Comique license thrice, each time evenly split. As they had demonstrated for several years, respectable Spokanites could not decide what part variety theaters should have in their city.[82]

The matter of the Stockholm and Coeur d'Alene licenses made the city's social cleavage even more evident. The request for a vote occurred when one councilman was absent, allowing the decision to fall in favor of the varieties. Theater opponents immediately cried foul play. Fueled by righteous indignation, the reform camp gained the upper hand for a moment and the varieties remained unlicensed.[83] The rejoinder was equally swift and indignant: councilman James Omo suggested that if his colleagues wanted to be "so remarkably and exceedingly good," they could support their virtue with their votes and their constituents' business. Omo proposed a series of "shut tight" resolutions that would align Spokane to a strict standard: variety theaters closed; gambling laws enforced; businesses, especially saloons, closed on the Sabbath; prostitutes and gamblers no longer exacted the monthly fine tantamount to a license. Shut tight.[84]

The choice between profits and morality stood at the heart of Omo's bluff, though he claimed that the $30,000 Spokane gathered annually from vice district fines and licenses was immaterial to him. Even so, Omo crossed the hardening lines of the city council to vote with the anti-theater camp and pass his measures. But the reform councilmen did not adequately represent bourgeois Spokane. Howard Street proprietors predicted that the "holiness" resolutions would so upset merchants that the city would soon be forced to reopen the bars, brothels, and variety houses.[85] Indeed, one day after Omo's proposal, a host of wholesalers, retailers, property owners, and community giants—much the same demographic that lobbied on behalf of varieties in 1895—presented a petition to the city council requesting that decent "vaudeville or variety shows" receive licensing. The petitioners knew what they wanted from their city. Spokane had moved beyond the depression of the mid-1890s and the future finally looked bright. With all their hope for and investments in Spokane, the merchants could not "sympathize with any conduct on the part of city authorities to retard or hamper the growth of the natural prosperity of the community."[86]

The petition contained an important caveat that articulated a compromise Spokanites increasingly made with themselves and with nineteenth-century ideals: the variety theaters must be orderly and law-abiding. Perhaps the theaters did present romping, lowbrow shows, but if their worst features (namely, the "commingling of the sexes" and connection to gambling joints) were eliminated, what, precisely, was the problem? The city's businesses—from the I.X.L. Clothing Company to the German Savings and Loan Society—certainly had no objections to profiting from the laborers who frequented the variety theaters. Even councilmen who voted against licensing the theaters admitted that, if in compliance with the law, variety theaters were not entirely distasteful. With this stance, Spokanites deviated significantly from Victorian aesthetics, which required performances to be uplifting and eschewed mere amusements.[87] Spokane's shopkeepers, on the other hand, felt that as long as a theatrical establishment did not break the law (and earned them and the city money), it had value.

Furthermore, in contrast to those who tried to position Spokane favorably within a geography of morality, these petitioners cared more about the city's place within regional and urban hierarchies. In its defense of theaters, the petition played on Spokane's sensitivity to urban ranking by remarking that "all cities of any size and importance license and permit vaudeville theaters." Likewise, the petition reminded the council that "Spokane is the center of a large and continually growing mining center. It is visited annually by thousands of people who visit these [variety] shows simply as a place of entertainment."[88] The theaters, in other words, increased Spokane's role as a regional hub. Eliminating the varieties would decrease both the city's importance to its hinterland and the profits realized from that arrangement. It was this calculation that made the question of whether the varieties would remain open during the Industrial Exposition—which the Omo resolutions precluded—so hot.

While businessmen promoted one vision for Spokane, the editors and ministers had their own ideas. For its part, the *Spokesman-Review* answered pro-theater arguments with a renewed appeal to concerns about Spokane's place within the enlightened world. The experience of the West, the newspaper argued, proved that the combination under one roof of stage, music, alcohol, gambling, "and the presence of reckless women" led to demoralizing shame. "Resorts of that kind smack too strongly of the dare-devil days of San Francisco and the wild abandon of Dawson City." Spokanites might gratefully accept the profits of mining, but they must not let their city fall off the map of civilization by throwing away the moral code that could give it a place within Victorian America. The clergy, meanwhile, tried to shame the local bourgeoisie into accepting reform. An Episcopal bishop chastised businessmen who considered themselves upstanding and yet supported the variety theaters on the grounds that such places increased spending. Was money "their God"?[89] A group of Protestant ministers tried to change the direction of the debate toward morality and away from the fear of lost revenue, and they questioned the character of a man or a city that stooped to depending on "bawdy house inmates and gamblers."[90] There it was: would Spokane be a place that capitalized on the miners and their alleged sins, or would it be a place that flourished, somehow, without the spending money of laborers?

Omo's "shut tight" resolutions had received hasty support from the council, which rethought its actions with equal haste after the businessmen expressed their displeasure with the strict new standards. Their quick return to the drawing board had another, related, cause: the imminence of the industrial exposition. The councilmen knew that if the variety theaters were closed during the fair, the city could expect a sharp drop in receipts.[91] The petition had convinced them that, if nothing else, the city and its variety theaters must remain "open" during the exposition. As members of the council's pro-theater faction put it, the "shut tight" resolutions—ordinances that would give Spokane the blue laws of a New England village—would "work great and permanent injury to the business interests of the city; would seriously mar the success of the coming exposition" and were, on the whole, "impractical."[92]

Thus, with the fair's promised revenue nipping at their heels, the councilmen rescinded the Omo resolutions, dithered a bit more, and finally arrived at a milquetoast solution: the varieties would receive licenses but only if they closed their doors from midnight until early morning. By October 5, 1899, the three contested theaters were licensed, just in time for the exposition.[93] With this Spokanites had again decided that, while some among them worried deeply about how the variety theaters affected the city's character and image (could a "Wild West" mining center really exist within respectable America?), the great majority cared more about the immediate realities of urban hierarchies and bottom lines. They had, again, chosen to make a pragmatic rejection of the Victorian ethos.

James J. Hill may have called Spokane the "'worst old hole' in the West" in 1898, but much of what made the city so unattractive to people concerned with respectability—a downtown filled with bars, brothels, and variety theaters, as well as employment agencies, flophouses, and outfitters—made it an ideal gathering place for the thousands of migratory wageworkers who kept the region's extractive industries running.[94] Those features in turn made money. Throughout the 1890s (and beyond), Spokanites were torn between their desires to comply with images of middle-class propriety and their desires for profit. Indeed, the debates over the future of the Howard Street theaters revealed much about how Spokane's residents envisioned the future of their city and how they dealt with the troubles of its present.

The variety theater fights conveyed Spokanites' vacillating perceptions of their home and how it should fit within late-nineteenth-century America. The city's moral reformers talked a great deal about what might be called a geography of decency. They alternately attempted to place Spokane safely inside the boundaries of "civilization" (insisting, for example, that a mining center need not be a wild mining camp) or, more ambitiously, claiming a spot for Spokane at the center of the moral map by denigrating alleged centers of corruption and sin, such as Chicago and Paris. At a time of general and overwhelming urban change, these people were hesitant in their embrace of urbanization. On the other hand, boosters and burghers saw Spokane as the heart of another kind of geographic order: a commercial hierarchy that made Spokane the undisputed head of the Inland Northwest and allowed it to control the region's hinterland.[95] Through their support of the varieties, 1890s Spokanites chose this second geography.

Further, these debates showed how at least some Spokanites made the transition from the Victorian suppression of self and body to the twentieth-century celebration of those things: through the mundane. At other times, the people of the Inland Northwest walked away from Victorianism more dramatically (truly) when they viewed the work of Clyde Fitch or Florence Ziegfeld at showplaces like the Auditorium. But Spokanites also rejected the values of the nineteenth-century middle class by choosing to support, not reform, but the city's variety theaters. In these decisions—and hence in the region's culture development—Spokane's western setting mattered: Spokane's casual labor market was dominated by migratory young men largely because of the Inland Northwest's role as a supplier of resources for the East. These fellows wanted the fun and flirtation of variety theaters, local businessmen willingly answered the market demand, and the theaters became a defining force in Spokane's regard of personal propriety and public entertainment.

CHAPTER THREE

Variety Theater, Gender, and Urban Identity

Thomas McNally was a sucker. Like many patrons of Spokane's famous Coeur d'Alene in 1907, McNally paid dearly for the drinks sold to him by attractive barmaids working on commission. Of McNally's complaint, a jaded policeman remarked, "Conditions in the variety theaters are the same that they were . . . in the days of a boom mining camp. The work of the owners of the resort and of the women employés is just as coarse as it was in the pioneer days." Dr. C. O. Kimball held a different opinion of life in Spokane. That same year, when the proprietors of downtown resorts defended themselves by noting that Spokane was a "western city," he scoffed. "If they mean . . . that we are a town of the early frontier days I deny it. Spokane is an eastern city set down in the West. One thing is sure, and that is we have jumped the rowdy age." Kimball and the officer might have disagreed about whether Spokane was a Wild West town, but they agreed that such a place involved abandon, lawlessness, and not least, the visibility of a certain kind of woman.[1]

The relationship between gender ideals and urban identity preoccupied Spokanites during their many years of conflict over variety theaters for if the variety theater question was about anything it was about gender: womanhood, manhood, and the home. Those people who fought against the varieties generally subscribed to middle-class Victorian ideals, where a man who had forged his character through years of self-sacrifice presided over a homebound wife.[2] The varieties were anything but that: here bare-limbed, saucy, and largely single women were paid to entertain men said to have no proper home. The theaters' opponents worried about the influence of the women who worked at the venues, about the manhood of those fellows who allowed the varieties to exist, and about the young people who might learn gender-inappropriate behavior from the resorts. These concerns became a matter of urban identity because Spokanites were boosters, ever trying to attract investment, or "good" families, or both to the Inland Northwest. Some Spokanites, though surely not all, felt that creating a city conducive to family life was key to attracting the right kind of people; they feared that if Spokane appeared too wild and woolly, those people would not emigrate. And with variety theaters came drinking, thieving, gambling, gun-fights, and sex—a caricature of the unfettered West. Gender relations and variety theaters, therefore, mattered a great deal in the boosting of Spokane.

There were several political episodes and legal developments in the 1890s and 1900s that help with understanding gender in Spokane's variety theater fights. Although anti-vice advocates held up both male and female ideals, they portrayed manliness as the stronger force against evil. According to their rhetoric, pure womanhood was unstable and deviant womanhood was toxic. It was men—usually reform politicians or Protestant ministers—who led the local drives to clean up the variety theaters, and women filled the auxiliary roles. Further, while these same people railed against bankrupt manhood, they repeatedly argued that upright men were key to the protection of personal and civic virtue. For this was also a contest about urban identity. What, Spokanites asked again and again, would their city be? Often this boiled down to a question of whether Spokane would be a "western" city—a place without law, civility, or decent women—or whether it would be family-friendly. In other words, the per-ceived wantonness of the theaters, especially their women, made Spokane feel too western. Home and gender ideals played a central role in the variety theater debates and were a major weapon used by the anti-vice camp, which connected these ideals to the identity of Spokane itself.

"Exit, Pretty Barmaid"

Female desirability was the linchpin of the variety-theater business plan. As the venues developed in the mid-nineteenth century, they did so specifically to entertain men with the bodies, antics, and companionship of young women. On and off the stage, variety actresses and barmaids (often the same person) wore a costume—tights, knee-length skirts, and sleeveless bodices—designed to titillate. Between shows, the "waiter girls" or "box rustlers" tantalized male patrons with hugs, winks, and the like and pressured them to buy overpriced drinks. Some varieties contained back rooms with couches, the purpose of which was obvious; nearly all had private boxes that appeared shockingly sexual.[3]

Flaunting their limbs and flirting for pay, variety theater women were the reverse image of the "true" woman—she who remained at home, respected male authority, shielded her body from public view, and reserved intimacy for marriage. And in a society where pundits advised that wives should but endure marital relations, variety theaters provided men with the free-and-easy companionship of young women who seemed to be sexually available. On one hand, like prostitutes, variety actresses and barmaids acted as a kind of sexual safety valve; their work allowed middle-class wives and maidens to remain ostensibly passionless while men across the social spectrum enjoyed physical flirtations. On the other hand, the mixture of men, women, alcohol, and sex—in a commercial setting, no less—seemed to many observers a recipe for social chaos and misery.[4]

In the still developing state of Washington, the need to contain the moral disorder of variety theaters received specific, official public comment throughout the 1890s. Activists in Seattle, Tacoma, and Spokane conducted citywide campaigns against the venues—with mixed success. In the spring of 1895 they joined forces and descended on the state legislature to secure the so-called barmaid law, which rendered variety theaters unquestionably illegal. The act's text focused on the combination of women and alcohol, briefly stating that no woman could be employed in any capacity in any saloon, theater, or place of amusement where liquor was sold.[5] The law's legislative history was equally brief: the Committee on Public Morals examined it, both Republicans and Populists supported it, and the state legislature summarily passed it, on March 14, 1895.[6] Like other states and eventually the U.S. Supreme Court, Washington decided that the protection of public morals necessitated a separation between women and liquor.[7]

Uncontroversial on its surface, the barmaid law gave legal teeth to
a fight against lucrative interests. Spokane's law-and-order advocates
moved quickly to use it against the city's most notorious impresario, John W. Considine. In August 1895 a rival reported Considine's newly criminal activities and county authorities arrested him.[8]
He fought the charge of both employing women and selling liquor
in a series of cases. As Considine's suit graduated through the
court system, the arguments against him confirmed the gendered
logic of the barmaid law: that errant womanhood, especially joined
with drink, threatened public virtue and that, as the fathers of society,
lawmakers and judges had a responsibility to police that danger.[9]

The meanings of womanhood in an ordered society so dominated
the case that even Considine's side offered a defense grounded in
that discussion. His legal team skirted the perceived immorality of
variety theaters by considering, instead, the rights of women as
citizens. Citing the equal protection clause of the Fourteenth Amend-
ment, they argued that the barmaid law denied women the privileges
allowed others by restricting their right to choose employment.[10]
Yet Considine's team also tried to sanctify his cause by connecting
it to middle-class gender mores. At one point the subject of prostitution arose. The lawyers placed their client firmly on the side of
conventional morality by denouncing prostitution and praising,
instead, the "true mission of women, which it is one of our highest
duties to protect in social and domestic life."[11] The man derided
as a "variety pimp," in other words, paid homage to the ethos that
idealized women and charged men with guarding them.[12]

While Considine's counsel tried to shift the conversation away
from sexuality, prosecuting attorney John W. Feighan insisted that
the real subject of the "barmaid case" was the danger presented by
the volatile brew of men, women, and liquor. Guided by state law
Feighan argued that variety theaters offended because they used
the physical attractions of women to enhance the attractions of
drink. Following this logic no woman should work at the venues;
after all, managers employed singers and actresses to draw in customers. Feighan then emphasized the 1895 law's basis in traditional
morality. The strongest motivation for outlawing the "barmaid system,"
he argued, was surely the responsibility of lawmakers to guard against

the degradation of womanhood.[13] With that, Feighan expressed well the paternalism of reformers as they tried to contain and correct the behavior of variety theater women.

Feighan's interpretation of the situation—that the barmaid law was key to the protection of public morals—ultimately became the opinion of every judge involved in the case. When Considine petitioned the U.S. circuit court for habeas corpus, the verdict was no different. The court responded that the barmaid law existed in order to check sexual impulses in resorts where "the worst passions are aroused," not to work arbitrary injustice. Petition denied.[14] Where Considine claimed to see in variety theaters an opportunity for female employment, Feighan and the judges saw nothing less than the corruption of womanhood and the unleashing of sexuality from the bonds of marriage. As social guardians and father figures, lawmakers could not allow that to happen.

After his conclusive legal defeat, John Considine left Spokane in late 1897 for Seattle, then in the dizzying midst of outfitting Klondike gold rushers. There, the impresario laid the foundations of a vaudeville empire that Spokane theatergoers soon welcomed.[15] But that was in the future. In those fitful years when Spokane could not rid itself of the variety theater specter, residents of the inland city still had to deal with the problems they felt were presented by variety actresses and pretty waitresses, the problems suggested by the barmaid case: that young women who flirted for pay were morally derelict; that some, if not all, actresses stood on the edge of the abyss that was prostitution; that the combination of these creatures—weak, tempting, and uncontrolled—with alcohol could destroy a man's life and a city's reputation.

When Considine's attorneys claimed to uphold the "true mission of women," they tapped into a deeply important element of nineteenth-century life, the role of women and the meaning of so-called true womanhood. Middle-class mainstream norms presented as ideal the woman who existed for private family pursuits and who had not a scrap of sexual deviance about her.[16] Variety theater women—who generally lived outside the nuclear family and, worse, seemed to disrupt it—hardly fit this image. They were, according to many contemporaries, its opposite: home wreckers who transgressed the boundaries between the public and private worlds and tempted others to do the same. Cultural commentators portrayed these small-time actresses and barmaids as sirens, harlots, monstrosities, at best, foolish girls.

Spokane's newspapers were instrumental in creating and disseminating perceptions of variety theater women.[17] The journals taught their readers that these women endangered society because they were sexually available or appeared to be. Newspaper accounts, in Spokane and elsewhere, noted how free the barmaids were with their arms and smiles, how they might even sit on a man's lap.[18] In the context of Victorian gender prescriptions, this was perversion indeed. A *Spokesman-Review* editorial in 1897 demonstrated the destructive capabilities of the varieties, describing them as "places where fallen women fell still lower, where young men were estranged from the pure and wholesome influences of the home, and weak and foolish men were plucked of their hard earnings." The theaters themselves were not the only trouble. In the words of the newspaper, the women who worked the private boxes—"half-dressed women, immodest to lewdness, [who] wheedled and cajoled" men—represented a terrible threat to the home. The problem with these actresses and barmaids was their alleged ability to lure men into dissipation through the use of their physical charms. It was this sale of physicality that connected variety theaters in the public mind to dance halls (where men paid to dance with a female employee) and prostitution. Reformers did not hesitate to call variety theaters places of assignation and a mere stop on the career path of harlots. Whether the actresses and barmaids actually sold sex was beside the point. In contemporary opinion, they had removed themselves so far from the meanings of propriety that they might as well be prostitutes.[19]

The unsympathetic reactions of middle-class commentators to the sexual advances endured by these women made clear the perceived connection with prostitution.[20] Consider an exchange that took place in a Spokane courtroom between Patrick Murane and May Wrenly, a redheaded actress with a black eye. Murane testified that in a private box at the Comique, Wrenly held out "various promises." When Murane suggested sex, Wrenly allegedly beat her customer. The young woman told a different story. After drinking together Murane propositioned Wrenly, "grabbed her, and took other liberties." She managed to ring for a waiter but could not escape as Murane pushed her into a corner, seized her throat, and attempted to rape her. Murane's attorney dismissed the assault by asking Wrenly whether it was true that Comique women embraced male patrons and sat on their laps. A blushing Wrenly insisted that she did not do these things, but the counsel quickly dispensed with her protest. The judge agreed and told Wrenly that by associating herself with the Comique, she invited men to treat her as a sexual object.[21]

At times newspapermen and others contained the danger presented by variety theater women by portraying them from an angle that not only moved them outside the realm of true womanhood but also made them seem altogether unattractive. Many a reporter described box rustlers and variety actresses as cheaply dressed, overly made-up, raspy voiced, fat, and ungrammatical wenches: more freak show than temptresses.[22] Likewise, depictions of the women connected them firmly to Spokane's red-light district and its hardships, only rarely expressing sympathy for "tragedy in low life."[23] On the whole, observers believed that actresses and barmaids reaped what they sowed, as the death of Ollie Dolan demonstrated. Despondent over news from her jailed lover, the Comique box rustler killed herself late one night with a handful of morphine. This bitter end, the *Spokesman-Review* concluded, was the penalty of her dissipation. Dolan's drug use further connected her to racial minorities, specifically, the Chinese.[24] The stain of white women (for they were generally white) consorting with non-white men became evident with an 1891 article about Lottie Forbes. The small-time actress left her common-law husband for a Japanese wrestler and thus became newsworthy for her double transgression against race and gender prescriptions.[25] In the public discourse, box rustlers and variety actresses occupied a place among the most marginal of people.

Editors, ministers, judges, and legislators perceived variety actresses as dangerous, aberrant, and in need of containment. But what, in reality, did they experience? This is not an easily answered question. Flitting across newspaper advertisements and only resting in the columns when involved in the bad or the tragic, the names of small-time actresses are often all we have of them. These women are difficult to trace individually, but they can be understood as a group from the information left in public documents. From these records, we see women who—like the men they entertained—lived lives of meager itinerancy, whose domestic situations were as topsy-turvy as the reformers and boosters feared, and who did indeed have their brushes with the law. On the other hand, we see women who enjoyed a measure of personal independence by living outside of strict households.

Contemporary Americans had a name for women who worked for wages but did not live with a family. Such "women adrift" were stigmatized for being unmarried and working-class and were believed to be sexually active.[26] Variety actresses belonged squarely to this demographic. At the turn of the century, Spokane's average actress was a single white woman in her mid-twenties, who lived in a rented downtown room and floated from job to job and town to town.[27] While reporters exaggerated the lawlessness of variety actresses, they did get in trouble for such activities as disorderly conduct, drunkenness, larceny, and vagrancy. Bertha Miller, for instance, was arrested for drunkenness on a morning late in November 1898, with a mere fifteen cents in her pockets. Less than a week later Miller landed in jail once again—this time for vagrancy, during a midnight in winter. These were hardly the heights of glamour. Yet despite the images generated by the reform drives (namely, that downtown was awash in rowdy, thieving stage women), Spokane actresses were neither more plentiful nor more rascally than "theatrical men." Rather, actors and actresses formed just a part of Spokane's underclass: waiters, loggers, teamsters, prostitutes, gamblers, domestics, and tramps, guilty of petty crimes and unstable domesticity.[28]

Consider the thirty women listed as actresses in an 1895 city directory. All of them rented rooms—generally by themselves, apart from coworkers or family members—near variety theaters, railroad tracks, saloons, or brothels. And then they moved, either out of town or to another seedy downtown block. Public documents show ten actresses living in Spokane during both 1895 and 1896; five had identifiable addresses for both years, each changing locations from one year to the next.[29] Narrative records tell a similar story: of Eva Lester, a twenty-seven-year-old song-and-dance artist who in 1895 traveled from Kalso, British Columbia, to Spokane, where she performed at Considine's theater and stayed for seven weeks at the Metropolitan hotel; of actresses lately arrived from Chicago and San Francisco to play at the Comique in 1907; of Haydie Clarke, a Spokane girl who appeared onstage from "San Francisco to Victoria, and from Portland to Pocatello."[30] Well might an attorney in the Considine case argue that actresses and barmaids were as migratory as "the bird of passage."[31] Still, within their fluid world, these women created relationships—with a fellow chorus girl, a driver at the neighboring hotel, the aging proprietor, or a bar-tending lover—that provided a measure of safety and sociability.

More damning than the itinerancy of a variety woman's work life was the irregularity of her home life. In 1900 the next-door neighbors of Spokane's downtown actresses included miners, clerks, cooks, day laborers, merchants, saloon keepers, and "French prostitutes."[32] Marital status only compounded the disgrace of promiscuous living environments, as the case of Haydie Clarke demonstrated. Clarke made headlines in 1904 simply because by the time she was twenty two men had already married, abandoned, and divorced her, prompting her to turn to the stage. She had appeared as a witness in her elder sister's divorce trial some years earlier. For this the young woman endured not a little sarcasm from the *Spokesman-Review*.[33] In an era when women's prospects for respectability (let alone economic survival) were only just opening up to means other than marriage, the singleness of most actresses marked them as deviant. And although an occasional "Mrs." performed for Spokane audiences, turn-of-the-century actresses in that town were overwhelmingly single or divorced and childless.[34]

Why did these women choose to work in Spokane's variety theaters? The evidence strongly suggests that box rustlers and actresses saw their work as just that, as a way to support themselves and their loved ones. Variety theater women used the language of employment—skills, shifts, salaries, and commissions—to describe their experiences and arrived at that employment from a number of circumstances. They included girls who came to the city from regional hamlets; a Sunday-school innocent duped into variety work; an educated singer, fallen on hard times after her husband's death; a beautiful opium addict and thief; a young mother, twice divorced but still helped along by her own parents; and a song-and-dance woman, on stage since age fifteen and married to another local favorite. Such women worked at variety theaters out of both desperation and excitement. That variety employment required short skirts and coquetry does not mean that box rustlers and actresses considered themselves whores; on the contrary, some of them took pains to distinguish themselves from prostitutes and, in so doing, faced the violent responses of spurned male customers (not to mention dubious glances from the better element). Although variety theaters were less than respectable, perhaps some of these women were already accustomed to rough environments because of their origins, perhaps they cared more for personal independence than for social approval, or perhaps they had nowhere else to turn.[35]

Often living away from their families, peripatetic as the men they entertained, and tied through geography and perceptions to a seamy urban world—these were the circumstances of variety actresses and barmaids.[36] Such circumstances played out into a broad societal judgment of these women as foolish, fallen, and low, for purportedly abandoning the responsibilities and protection of families, for associating themselves with dissipation, and for stepping entirely outside the realm of true womanhood. As Brooks McNamara describes concert saloon waitresses—"there is no doubt that waiter girls were non-persons and any contact with them was never to be mentioned in conversation with respectable people"—so it was for Spokane's variety theater women.[37] Economic and social conditions created the category of variety actress and barmaid, but that same society did not allow the women who filled the role to be regarded as respectable.

Manhood and the Variety Theater, 1895–1899

While the opponents of variety theaters used idealized femininity to legislate, prosecute, and inform against the institutions, they also used model manhood as a major rhetorical tool in the anti–variety theater crusades. Morality advocates questioned the honor of men involved with the theaters and tried to disgrace them into reversing

their position; their critiques often had deep race and class connotations, which added to the intended ignominy. Despite the prevalence and intensity of these arguments throughout the 1890s, they
failed to convince Spokanites that the theaters should close. Spokane was a city with only a veneer of propriety to cover divorces in
its best society, middle-class men profiting from (and sometimes
attending) brothels and variety theaters, and of course reluctance
to rid the city of vice.[38] But though Spokane's middle-class men were
more complex than their newspapers and pulpits suggested, Victorianism yet dominated the public discourse.

In the spring of 1895 Spokane's Ministerial Association mounted
a campaign to close the Howard Street variety theaters, but it must
have soon recognized that its efforts were failing. After the ministers
and their allies circulated an anti-variety petition, a rival document
made its way through the city and garnered significantly more signatures, including those of powerful businessmen and community
figures. Likewise, though the city council passed an ordinance prohibiting alcohol at variety theaters, Mayor Horatio N. Belt promptly
vetoed it.[39] The churchmen, however, did have the language and
force of traditional morality on their side, which they deployed through
their own bully pulpits and the *Spokesman-Review*. As businessmen,
certain councilmen, and Mayor Belt sided with the theaters, the
preachers denounced their actions as unworthy of true men. Manhood for the ministers meant unswerving convictions and the development of character through years of "high-minded self-restraint."[40]
According to these ideals a Christian gentleman would never abdi-
cate his personal honor or his responsibility to protect weaker beings
by choosing expediencies over principles. Therefore, just as the
variety actresses allegedly did not deserve the title of true women,
so Belt and others lost their claim to true manhood when they supported the variety theaters.

These Protestant ministers attempted to shift the public discourse
in their favor through the use of shame and gender ideals. They chastised Spokane's merchants for abandoning their consciences in favor
of continued profit and called for men with backbone enough
to withstand the power of Howard Street. With these barbs the

churchmen hoped to prod the city's influential men into a change of position.[41] They reserved their strongest language for Belt, the person they felt had most thoroughly abandoned Victorian manhood. The Sunday after Belt vetoed the variety theater ordinance, half a dozen ministers detailed the ways in which he strayed from the code of middle-class conduct. In their estimation Belt's main sin was hypocrisy. The mayor, a longtime churchgoer, had been among the first signers of the anti–variety theater petition. Now, the reverends claimed, he had acted a double part, disgraced the church, aided corrupt institutions, and become a coward and poseur. One pastor went so far as to strike at the heart of Belt's manhood—his fatherhood—by reporting that the mayor's son frequented variety theaters. "It hurts me," the minister sighed, "to think men care so little for their boys."[42]

This gendered appraisal of variety theaters often veered into slander of the race and class credentials of the venues' supporters. Using an argument prominent in the late nineteenth century, the ministers and newspapermen attacked the patrons, employees, and managers of the varieties as less than male and almost less than Anglo-Saxon. During this era the American and British bourgeoisie worried that the combination of foreign immigration and unhealthful urban conditions doomed their supposedly pure racial stock to denigration.[43] At the same time, public discussion about manhood also took on a fevered tone. In the logic of cultural commentators, since the nuclear family and its head served as the locus of legitimate society, the future health of America depended on the virility and respectability of white husbands and fathers.[44] When white men abdicated their home responsibilities, they elicited fear and faced censure. According to local pundits, the itinerant laborers who "floated" through Spokane were such men, and the businessmen and politicians who allowed Howard Street to flourish were not far off.

A well-attended sermon delivered by A. G. Wilson addressed these concerns and specifically connected the evils of the variety stage with the bloodlines of the working class. Wilson argued that, while the Inland Northwest must have workingmen for its mines and fields, those laborers had a biological propensity for low, wicked behavior.

Even if the varieties were abolished and the city could rid itself of every prostitute and every saloon, Wilson concluded, dangerous men would still roam the streets "carrying around in head and heart and blood the causes of long growth which have developed these evils."[45] A letter to the *Spokesman-Review*, written by "Smilax," echoed the tone of Wilson's sermon. Smilax described the variety theaters as filthy places "where idiots congregate and gape. . . . Any man who is satisfied to sit in such a place night after night hadn't ought to be saved, and no effort should be made to save him. He has a soul of mud that couldn't possibly soar above a dog fight."[46] This picture of degenerate manhood smacked heavily of the pseudoscientific talk about the dwindling racial purity of poor whites that abounded in this era. Indeed, both Smilax and Wilson appropriated some of the most loaded ideas of their time to convince their fellow citizens that the varieties must close.[47] The social and ethnic tension of the 1895 debate could only have been increased by the fact that many of the theaters' supporters—men with names like August Vital or Sol Mayer—did not belong to the old Protestant stock, and that the kingpin of the vice district, Jacob Goetz, was a German immigrant (see table 1 in appendix).

The opponents of variety theaters also used the tool of racialized gender against the mayor himself. The *Spokesman-Review* especially tried to increase Belt's humiliation by insisting that, through his veto, he had crossed into the realm of degenerating manhood. Describing the abuse Belt experienced at ministerial hands, the newspaper assured readers that the mayor had escaped alive and run "to the wigwams of the dealers in firewater and the abodes of the dancing maidens." Safe in the arms of his protectors, Belt filed his "second naturalization papers"—in the vice district.[48] By using the language of cowardice, race, and immigration this editorial attempted to strip Belt, rhetorically, of his manhood, his whiteness, and even his citizenship. The newspaper continued the conceit as the 1895 mayoral campaign progressed. Although Belt had tied himself to Howard Street, at least something about him was commendable: he had found courage enough to come out and "fight like a Caucasian. A year ago he was everywhere and nowhere at the same time—skulking like an

Indian and smiling like the adroit politician he is."[49] In the opinion
of conservative Spokane, supporting the variety theaters meant abandoning a manhood that was both honorable and white.

Despite the intensity of the attacks on the variety theaters and
the politicians who allegedly succored them, Belt won reelection in
May 1895. Despite the state and local laws passed against them, the
resorts grew in strength throughout the remainder of the decade.
This did not stop the anti-vice crowd from employing Victorian
gender ideals to advance their cause. As Howard Street gained
political capital in the late 1890s, members of the local establishment on either side of the question flatly used the discourse of
middle-class manhood to discredit one another. A particularly notable
exchange occurred in September 1899, as the city council debated
the licensing of the Comique, Stockholm, and Coeur d'Alene. At
a September 19 meeting, a series of votes on the matter split the
council evenly and resulted in a draw. The body's next scheduled
meeting involved another vote on the theater licenses, but this time,
a member of the anti-theater camp, J. S. Phillips, was compelled to be
absent—a change that could swing the vote in favor of the varieties.[50]

That vote, however, did not take place. William Acuff, a councilman opposed to the licenses, seized the floor and accused the pro-
theater members of using Phillip's absence to push the licenses
through. Acuff denounced his colleagues as cowards in a speech
couched in the ideals of honor, reputation, and manhood. Every
member of the council was a white, middle- or upper-class businessman. Most were married and middle-aged. They were exactly the
demographic that could be hurt the most by charges of impeached
character leveled at them by Acuff. As Belt's enemies had done in
1895 Acuff manipulated the ideals of character and courage to
humiliate his opponents and change their positions. Not content
with this Acuff deepened his accusations against the pro-theater
men by insinuating that they were enslaved to Howard Street. In so
doing he targeted another key aspect of nineteenth-century manliness: independence. Men of the era measured their manhood in
part by their political, economic, and social independence and,
conversely, in the dependence upon them of women, children, and
employees. Acuff's suggestion that the pro-theater members had

abandoned their self-respect and become the toadies of the vice lords was the lowest of blows.[51]

Acuff's offended colleagues shot back responses equally caught up with Victorian gender ideals. At the next meeting one councilman proposed that the city investigate Acuff's suggestion of bribery, because "we are men of families; we are men of reputation; we owe this investigation to ourselves, to our families, to our good names." Another implicated politician refused to vote for the measure on account of his pride, instead accusing Acuff of actions hardly befitting "the father of a household."[52] A third councilman dismissed Acuff's speech as "unwarranted and ungentlemanly."[53] Pummeling each other with ideas such as pride, morality, reputation, fatherhood, and family, these were fellows deeply invested (at least rhetorically) in middle-class manhood.

Middle-class men themselves led the attacks against Spokane's variety theaters during the 1890s. Protestant ministers and good-government politicians acted as the most visible, vocal leaders of the morality drives.[54] This is not to say that women did not participate in these efforts, but they did so in an auxiliary manner. For instance, the Ministerial Association spearheaded the 1895 anti-variety campaign during which women attended mass meetings, canvassed the city for signatures, and sat in on city council debates. No record exists, however, of women speaking before crowds or council or of signing the petition they asked others to consider; those tasks fell to the divines and to the voters.[55] Civic-minded women surely guided and helped other causes during the 1890s, but regulating the variety theaters was either a less important or a less achievable mission for them. Further, by the late 1890s, female activists generally had less influence with Spokane's city hall, even as Howard Street enjoyed increased pull with officials.[56] This points to a likely explanation as to why men so dominated the variety theater debates. Control of those resorts was deeply tied to local politics and powerful interests, and in 1890s Spokane politics remained a male domain. Women remained chiefly visible in these discussions only as types—as either a "true" woman, who required male protection, or as a temptress, who required male control.

Accordingly, idealized manhood and womanhood formed major weapons in the anti-vice arsenal. Moralists such as Wilson or Acuff, realizing perhaps that the weight of political and business opinion was against them, tried to win by leveraging the desire of office-holders and shopkeepers to be seen as Christian gentlemen. Such tactics hinged on a definition of manhood—or, rather, white man-hood—as courage in the face of difficulty, as behavior that accorded to belief, and as the protection of dependents. The reformers did not hesitate to denounce officeholders and shopkeepers, as well as the working-class patrons of variety theaters, as inadequate and unmanly for their connections to the resorts. Yet for all the calumny described by Wilson or Acuff, Spokane's variety theaters thrived as the nineteenth century gave way to the twentieth. Victorian gender ideals might have had purchase with Spokanites but not enough to close the varieties. As the first decade of the new century pro-gressed, concepts such as home, virtue, and character remained powerful tools in the variety theater debates and, indeed, were key to the 1908 shuttering of those institutions.

"It May Be Your Daughter," 1900–1905

In the heat of the 1903 election season, a political advertisement asked voters whether they would choose "decency or the dives, virtue or vice, the cradle or the crib."[57] The advertisement's insistence that this was a struggle between home or slum conveyed a major concern of anti-variety activists: the effect of the theaters and their sister venues on families. While reformers used both ideal masculinity and femininity to punish their opponents, they invoked the home—that meeting place of gender roles—with equal frequency and force. Before the 1907–1908 morality drive that closed the varieties, certain Spokanites made several efforts to tame the vice district. Almost invariably, the home (or the nuclear family of husband, wife, and children) became a focal point of these efforts. Middle-class Spo-kanites worried that variety theaters lured men (as patrons) and women (as employees) away from wholesome influences; those con-nected with the theaters might, in turn, track depravity back into the home. The moralists especially feared the influence of Howard Street on young people. These anxieties fueled much of the debate over variety theaters in the early twentieth century, when politicians could frame the matter so starkly as a choice between an infant's cradle and a prostitute's crib.

The forces of virtue (as they would have it) did not prevail during those first years of the new century. Municipal elections in 1901, 1903, and 1905 each yielded administrations friendly to the vice district, which allowed the continued non-enforcement of rules like the 1895 barmaid law (see table 5 in the appendix). Reform faltered for many reasons. Spokane was once again booming, and during the 1900s the city increased from 36,848 to 104,402 residents.[58] This growth only heightened the variety theater dilemma for with economic progress came an increasing number of transient workers and an expansion of the city's sporting element.

The lumber industry exemplified the situation. Frederick J. Weyerhauser brought his empire to the Pacific Northwest in 1900 with the purchase of 900,000 acres of timberland. Spokane's involvement in the lumber industry had been small-time up to this point, but Weyerhauser's move set off a buying frenzy and an influx of eastern capital. From 1900 to 1903 one-third of the area's forested acreage changed ownership, and by 1909 the Inland Northwest had three hundred mills. Although the inland timber business never prospered on the scale of its coastal cousin, wood processing had joined mining and agriculture as powerful resource-extractive industries that required an army of laborers—young men who rolled into Spokane by the thousands when their contracts were up, looking for work, drink, and girls.[59]

This meant real influence for Howard Street. A 1902 accounting of Spokane businesses found that amusement resorts constituted a significant portion of local payrolls. The Coeur d'Alene and Comique employed a total of 211 people; the Coeur d'Alene alone boasted an annual payroll of $231,930, far more than Spokane's first-class legitimate theaters.[60] Critics had reason enough to suspect that the proprietors of the Coeur d'Alene resort, Jacob "Dutch Jake" Goetz and Harry Baer, reigned over city hall.[61] Meanwhile, the mayoral campaigns of those years were split among three or four candidates, which siphoned votes away from "clean" candidates. Finally, the political will to control vice seems to have been in short supply in

Howard Street in 1909, as it crosses Riverside Avenue. The Coeur d'Alene
building is two blocks north of this intersection, but this image captures
the vitality and commercial importance of Howard Street in the first decade
of the century. Courtesy Northwest Room, Spokane Public Library.

the early 1900s. Yet it was growing. So too was the conviction that
Spokane should be not just a commercial city (the refrain of those
who defended the variety theaters) but, rather, a city focused on
homes.[62] As the desire to improve Spokane's image mounted throughout the early twentieth century, the talk of home and family became
ever more connected to the debate over urban identity.

Spokane had gained a wild reputation, and the city's relationship
to respectable gender norms played a central role in turn-of-the-
century politics. That notoriety had developed in part because of a
lax city hall. In the first days of the new century, for example, the city
council refused to pass measures that would have made saloons less
sexual. Combined with the continued strength of brothels, variety
theaters, and gambling joints, this created a rollicking downtown.

As speakers at a ministerial convention put it in late 1900, the unwillingness of local officials to enforce morality laws made Spokane "rotten as hell."[63] The stage was set for another reform effort, which came with the mayoral race of 1901. That spring, a non-partisan Citizens' League ran John Anderson at the head of a ticket intended to restore the city's name. The men of the Citizens' League portrayed themselves as the fatherly rescuers of a wayward Spokane, striving to "protect the city from the peril of shame and debauchery that belong to a wide open town." With the identity and reputation of their city on the line, these men applied the ideals of upright manhood to municipal activism.[64]

Like a loose woman Spokane had been disgraced of late, and not by the clergy alone. *Finance*, a St. Louis journal, had lately warned its readers that Spokane's wide-open policies allowed downtown resorts to swindle visitors. The city's people and institutions recognized what was happening but refused to intervene. Spokanites, the journal continued, were less moral than the residents of the East and Midwest: though they could not deny their city's wickedness, the money motive kept them from improving it. The Spokane chamber of commerce replied with a worldly letter that pondered the nature of civic sin and, more conventionally, expounded on the quality of churches, schools, and homes in the inland metropolis. Spokanites, in other words, straddled the fence between settled respectability and the profits that came from abandon.[65]

Upright citizens responded to such embarrassments with the 1901 campaign, which sought to brighten the city's image and centered on the hope of clean home life. The Citizens' League and Anderson—supported by ministers, businessmen, the *Chronicle*, and the Women's Christian Temperance Union (WCTU)—ran on the premise that the "Howard Street element" was no longer good for business and that a family-friendly image would do more to attract money and settlers.[66] But Anderson's main rival, Dr. Patrick Byrne, also used the idea of urban identity. When asked if he would curb vice, Byrne gave a statement that both equivocated and hit at the heart of the issue: "The question asked here . . . enters deeply into the life of the western cities." In Byrne's estimation, being a western city meant accepting the fluidity that came with recent settlement and resource-extractive industries. Miners and lumberjacks would be entertained.

The *Chronicle* disagreed, countering with a catalog of the social problems caused by permissiveness and imploring men to think of their families as they voted. It was to no effect. Byrne won the election. Likewise, though postmortem editorials used the language of enervated manhood and unprotected homes to reproach the voters, the sporting district flourished under Byrne's city hall.[67]

One election did not define Spokane. Anti-vice advocates continued to assert that, despite its location, Spokane could be a city that enshrined family life and traditional gender norms. With the 1903 election they regrouped as the Spokane Municipal Party and ran a ticket headed by William Acuff. The party's message was clear: an unregulated Spokane threatened the family itself, but Acuff had backbone, honor, and Christian manhood enough to stand up to the slum bosses. Indeed, the Municipal Party staked its efforts almost entirely on the concept of impeccable manhood (as embodied by Acuff) and suggested that the choice was a simple one, between home or Howard Street, cradle or crib. Meanwhile, editorialists friendly to Acuff dismissed his opponents as timid, hesitant, and caught in dubious alliances. As the *Chronicle* put it, of the four mayoral candidates, only Acuff could say that he would categorically stand between evil and the home.[68]

Municipal Party allies made clear the evils Spokane faced with exposés of the lower Howard businesses; they framed their stories in terms of appropriate gender behavior and portrayed the resorts as cancers that threatened home and city.[69] Reports of the variety theaters especially played on gender ideals by depicting the box rustlers as femmes fatales; like the women targeted by the 1895 barmaid law, these women were considered doubly dangerous because of their connection to alcohol.[70] Newspapermen presented female theater employees as the opposite of true women: aggressive, physical, pleasure-loving, and public. Yet in these exposés and especially in Municipal Party advertisements, true womanhood was not stable. Reform materials recounted how local women and girls fell prey to Howard Street's temptations, suggesting that the red-light district could turn decent women into harlots.[71] In this calculation, the volatility of female virtue required an extra measure of masculine protection. The Municipal Party appealed to the manhood of Spokane's electorate by telling voters that "we need a genuine man"

(Acuff) and that they must vote to protect their own wives and children. After all, as a narrative advertisement cautioned: "IT MAY BE YOUR DAUGHTER."[72]

Although the 1903 exposés were built on the bad behavior of women, they contained another element designed to shock respectable readers: tales of men and women "mingling indiscriminately" and enjoying physical relations in a promiscuous public setting.[73] Both the *Chronicle* and the *Spokesman-Review* detailed the "orgies" that took place within the curtained variety theater boxes, where the sexes drank together and women sat on the laps of random men. The writers were particularly offended by the familiarity of these situations and used the term "familiar" often, as if to reinforce the impropriety of allowing intimacy to flourish on the public market. The reformers insisted that upstanding people would not countenance this kind of behavior, especially since it occurred in "the very heart of the city."[74] What did it mean, they seemed to ask, that this alleged debauchery existed within the "very heart" of Spokane? That it was a city whose core was corrupt? That it peddled perversion? That it was, somehow, morally inside-out?[75]

Accordingly, the Acuff partisans emphasized that Spokane did not have to be a place where Dutch Jake ruled city hall. They were plainly concerned with how elements of the city's nature, such as its reputation and economy, related to family and gender norms.[76] For instance, immediately before the elections, one of the many sermons devoted to local politics made a plea for the combined ideal of home and city. The sermon borrowed the language of local boosterism and argued that a clean reputation could become one of Spokane's best assets.[77] A *Chronicle* editorial questioned Spokane's character more directly. The newspaper outlined the barefaced operation of vice—cribs, saloons, dance halls, and variety theaters—along the city's central avenues and hard by its government offices and asked, "Are we to believe these are the supports on which rests Spokane's prosperity? . . . Are we to calmly accept the theory that this city's hope of greatness depends upon the shame of women and the folly of men?" Certain Spokanites, in other words, rejected the idea that the city must serve as a wide-open entertainment center in order to prosper; to these people, an adherence to respectability would profit Spokane much more.[78]

Acuff did not win the four-way race of 1903. Instead, L. Frank Boyd, the purported favorite of the Coeur d'Alene and other resorts, took the mayor's seat. Another four-way campaign in 1905 generated little excitement and resulted in the election of Floyd Daggett, a Democrat who, like his predecessors, was denounced as a puppet of "the dives."[79] Spokanites were not, however, entirely weary of reform. During the early 1900s, the feeling that Spokane must be attractive to itinerant workingmen decreased somewhat. Further, the economic diversification that accompanied growth might have lessened Spokane's dependence on variety theaters. Consequently, the venues enjoyed by workingmen gradually came to be seen as burdens, not magnets for trade. Acuff and other reform candidates did not win office in these years, but their campaigns reinforced the connection between gender norms and Spokane's identity. The concept of a home city was gaining ground. Combined with the Progressive-era activism building in the city, these ideas led to the closure of Spokane's notorious variety theaters.

The City and the Home, 1905–1908

A. H. Wright came to Spokane in 1904, a friendless job-seeker, twenty-one years old, and one of many young men flocking to the city in search of opportunity. In this tenuous situation Wright reached out to the Young Men's Christian Association (YMCA), which led him to employment and companionship. One year later, he donated fifty dollars to the YMCA, hoping it would place other youths on the path to respectable manhood.[80] Like Wright, many people moved to Spokane in the early years of the twentieth century, but the kind of city those newcomers would find or create was far from certain.[81] Would Spokane be a place of sensual Wild West entertainments or a city of orderly homes and happy families? This was the question moral crusaders presented to Spokanites in the final, successful battle against the variety theaters.

The anti–variety theater efforts of the 1890s failed because the revenue those resorts brought to local businesses led merchants to fight moralists. They failed in the early 1900s because of contentious politics and the continued might of lower Howard businesses. These influences continued in the mid-1900s but were eclipsed by other aspects of Spokane's public life, specifically, the combination of Progressive-style reform with boosterism. Spokanites became involved in causes that tied municipal progress to personal and civic cleanliness; this made the variety theaters feel like relics of a Wild West past that impeded the advertising efforts of a twentieth-century Spokane. In other words, when increasingly powerful organizations connected promotional efforts to municipal reform and middle-class morality, variety theaters then became civic liabilities.[82]

Reform-as-boosterism came to Spokane in the mid-1900s with a cluster of causes that contributed to the idea of a clean, beautiful city based on correct homes and gender; these included the 150,000 Club, the City Beautiful movement, and the YMCA. The boosterism that characterized Spokane's past became focused in late 1905 on the 150,000 Club, so named because of its desire to have that number of people living in Spokane by 1910.[83] The club's leaders were frank about their motivations: more residents meant higher business returns and real estate values. People would come, the boosters claimed, as Spokanites supported a publicity effort trumpeting the region's many advantages. These included water power, railroads, mining, agriculture, timber, and also a less tangible resource: the quality of its homes.[84]

The promotional focus on the home and other signs of social refinement became more pronounced after a Spokane luminary, Aubrey L. White, suggested that the 150,000 Club should ally itself with the City Beautiful movement.[85] Throughout the United States, the white middle-class men behind City Beautiful believed that cities could be brought to order through attention to cleanliness, careful planning, and elevated design. They believed that attractive urban environments would lead not only to cultural parity with Europe but also to a heightened civic loyalty that would in turn alleviate the moral chaos of cities.[86] The City Beautiful goals struck a chord with community-minded Spokanites—ever trying to burnish the city's image and declare their equality with the eastern United States—and White's advice to make Spokane more pleasant inspired them.[87]

The City Beautiful anthem opened a door for Spokane's anti-vice crusaders to tie boosterism once again to morality. A sinful city, they argued, could not attract the right kind of families. Accordingly, as the 150,000 Club and City Beautiful campaigns continued, a related discussion of the nature of the city's homes and the threats faced by those homes unfolded in public forums.[88] Like past reformers City Beautiful and 150,000 Club leaders recognized the challenge that the Inland Empire's migratory workforce, with its throngs of single men, posed to their venture. They attempted to solve this perceived problem by throwing their weight behind the local YMCA.[89] Americans imported the YMCA from Britain to answer the very anxieties suffered by the Spokanites: how could young men who came to the city—beset by temptations, cut off from the moral support of home—maintain their virtue? Spokane's reformers felt the YMCA gave them a fighting chance against the vice district, maintaining that the YMCA could produce men with wisdom, brains, and backbone.[90]

That Spokane had an abundance of men, women, and households that were the assumed opposite of the middle-class ideal was undeniable. Even as Spokane's bungalows and mansions multiplied, so too did its less conventional homes and people: resorts and lodging houses filled with casual male laborers and the women who entertained them. In a city that disdained the so-called floating population, the crush of new establishments catering to that group did not go unnoticed.[91] A 1909 *Chronicle* article noted that, whereas the 1898 city directory listed thirty-nine lodging houses, the 1909 directory listed eighty-eight. Such lodging houses—where small and crudely partitioned cubicles counted as rooms—epitomized the city un-beautiful. Together with businesses such as cheap cafeterias, these dwellings facilitated what contemporaries called a "civilization without homes": a menacing alternative to or even rejection of mainstream domesticity. Among those businesses was, of course, the variety theater.[92]

Middle-class Spokanites feared the men and women of this urban underworld precisely because they viewed them as the antithesis of the ideal family. Transient men—hobos—had long frightened other Americans, who attributed their itinerancy not to the vagaries of capitalism but to a conscious rejection of middle-class values. That is to say, Americans believed men tramped because they preferred the pleasures of "hobohemia" to the responsibilities of wives, children, and property ownership, and this was often the case.[93] Like male hobos, actresses and barmaids concerned middle-class Spokanites because they lived and worked in situations outside the pale of gender respectability. Variety theater women created anxiety for another reason as well: their alleged ability to seduce men into an acceptance of manhood based on bravado and prowess rather than on middle-class virtues.[94] Because reformers worried that such gender deviancy existed aplenty in their city, they promoted the YMCA as an environment far more wholesome than the downtown entertainments.[95]

According to respectable Spokane, the choice between appropriate manhood and its opposite was clear, and as another morality drive began in 1907 the crusaders repeatedly described it as a fight between men who stood for families and progress and those who supported vice and corruption.[96] Of course, home and gender ideals had been deployed throughout the many years of anti-vice campaigns in Spokane, but their growing strength, buttressed by the influence of Progressive movements, became evident in the 1907 municipal election when, at last, a reform candidate won. Throughout the mayoralty of Floyd Daggett (1905–1907), groups like the Law and Order League had accused him of running a machine and favoring dealers in liquor and vice, thereby sullying the city's opportunities for advancement. When election time came, the Republican Party championed C. Herbert Moore, a man who represented issues dear to conservative Spokane. Moore received the endorsement of the *Spokesman-Review*, the Civic League, the Federated Men's Clubs (FMC), and that amorphous group, "the businessmen." Not coincidentally, he also served in 1907 as the chairman of the City Beautiful committee of the 150,000 Club.[97]

The Republicans quickly reduced the 1907 campaign to a decision between home, growth, decency, and civic betterment, on one hand, and liquor, machine politics, fraud, transient men, and licentiousness, on the other. Daggett's enemies made him the symbol of everything respectable people eschewed. The *Spokesman-Review*, for instance, argued that Daggett could marshal hundreds of votes from unsavory characters who liked a wide-open town.[98] In contrast, the newspaper held that businessmen, wage earners, and property holders supported Moore. These groups reportedly knew that the forces behind Daggett would make of Spokane a "Klondyke town," driving away investors, residents, and immigrants.[99] The fear of a "Klondyke town" was telling. For years, middle-class Spokanites had shied away from the Wild West image of lawlessness and errant sexuality that the lower Howard area gave their city. To such people, the self-indulgence of Howard Street (as they would have it) spelled frontier barbarism and social malaise; modernity, on the other hand, would come with the ability to regulate vice effectively.[100] Thus, in the midst of the glorification of modernity that was the Progressive Era, these Spokanites especially wanted to rid their city of that "Klondyke" taint. Moore became mayor.

Moore's victory did not mean the automatic enforcement of morality laws or closure of the variety theaters. That required one last anti-vice drive, which—as if in symbolic denouement to the years of struggle—was spearheaded by middle-class men (and a few women) who saw themselves as the protectors of a city's virtue. It did not start as a crusade against the varieties. Rather, the variety theaters became caught up in a battle royal that began when the "best citizenship" grew tired of the Moore administration's failure to fulfill its promise of reform. Those best citizens—namely, Protestant ministers and leaders from the YMCA, the Law Enforcement League, the WCTU, and business organizations—started their campaign in late 1907 by rallying against the non-enforcement of a Sunday saloon closing law.[101] This, in turn, inspired the *Spokesman-Review* to investigate the police's false claim that box rustlers had ceased working at the variety theaters months ago.[102]

As before, establishing middle-class male authority meant diminishing the gender credentials of men who supported the varieties. In this last effort the *Spokesman-Review* consistently portrayed male theatergoers as being either too simple or too weak to withstand the barmaids.[103] If reformers pitied the laborers and youths "whose sense of manhood" vanished at the theaters, they tried to humiliate Howard Street's businessmen and impresarios.[104] In early January 1908, the Law and Order League increased its pressure on city hall and had 175 saloon keepers (including Dutch Jake and Harry Baer) jailed for their refusal to close on Sunday. Another group, perhaps the FMC, suggested that showmen should be part of the mass jailing. The *Spokesman-Review* depicted this event as the use of manly force over indecency; for example, on January 8, 1908, it described the city council meeting that upheld the jailing as a "spanking."[105] Likewise, newspaper accounts during this anti-vice drive applied a rhetorical device (the rendering of quotations in a ridiculous dialect) that they never had applied before to Dutch Jake, implying that the king of Howard Street was at last losing his place in the city's power structure.[106]

With the enforcement of the Sunday closing law came the enforcement of the 1895 barmaid law. For many years Spokane's police shared with city hall at least some culpability for the environment downtown; by 1908 civic groups had begun to humble the police force, if not transform it into a model organization.[107] On January 10, 1908, the chief of police, newly attentive to community demands, notified all resorts that featured both women and alcohol that one or the other must go.[108] Spokane's public, meanwhile, did not lobby on behalf of the variety theaters, as it had so many times before. Affordable alternative entertainments—such as "polite" vaudeville— had at last taken hold in Spokane, and this likely played a role in the public silence. Whatever the case, honest application of the barmaid law spelled the end of Spokane's variety theaters, which gave their final performances on January 11, 1908. After all, as Dutch Jake remarked, there was no money in it without the women.[109]

The variety theaters did not go down without a flourish. Although the O.K. Concert Saloon hosted a closing night as mediocre as its name, at the Coeur d'Alene, Dutch Jake made certain that his institution would be remembered. Speaking through "Kid" Emer Reel, Dutch Jake presented an interpretation of Spokane's past and present at odds with the reform vision. He was quick to remind the city that Goetz and Baer had a long relationship with Spokane, beginning with their grubstaking of the Bunker Hill and Sullivan mine. Once the partners sold their stake, they invested in the building that led to the fledgling settlement's first real boom. Dutch Jake claimed that with the 1885 erection of the Frankfurt block, Spokane's real estate values advanced 100 percent and men like J. J. Browne became millionaires. "This town was made, if I do say it myself, by

Goetz and Baer." And the town was about to be unmade by moralizing, carpet-bagging New Englanders. Why, he lamented, could businesspeople not see that the reform measures amounted to a "great curse" upon Spokane?[110] From Dutch Jake's perspective, prohibiting the rowdy, sensual variety theaters denied the reality (not to mention the history) of Spokane's western location and could only diminish the city's economic importance.

Four years later, Nelson Durham offered a very different interpretation of how closing the variety theaters affected Spokane's standing and identity. In his history of the town, the longtime *Spokesman-Review* editor hailed the 1908 event as the beginning of Spokane's taking its place among respectable cities. With the final performance "of a frontier type of amusement" on January 11, 1908, "Spokane passed forever from a stage that was highly picturesque, but unsuited to an aspiring city of the modern mold, eager to rank as a social, educational, and amusement center of a better kind." Here were the two views of Spokane that its middle- and upper-class residents had argued about for so long: would Spokane be a "western" or a "modern" city? Would it capitalize on the fluid lives of resource-extractive laborers, using the charms of supposedly immoral women to attract them, or would it regulate away such "frontier type amusements" so that families could feel safe?

Spokanites took a long road to answer these questions. From the mid-1890s to the late 1900s, local activists tried to control the variety theaters by creating city ordinances, influencing state law, and denying business licenses. Their hope, with these attempts, was to separate women and alcohol and thus harness physical passions. Ministers, politicians, and newspapermen constantly manipulated gender-based ideals to shame, cajole, or frighten Spokanites into accepting regulation of the theaters. These ideas must have carried some weight with Inland Northwesterners for them to have been so used and so often. Such tactics did not work, however, until 1908, when the advocates of reform finally convinced their neighbors that it was more valuable (and possibly more remunerative) to build a "home city" rather than a place of frontier revelry. The market in sin did not, of course, entirely disappear, but the 1908 closure of the variety theaters did mark a change in Spokane's western identity. With their city's "Klondyke" element somewhat tamed, middle-class Spokanites began to regard dime-novel westernness with more equanimity.

The breakthrough of 1908 hardly meant the end of the entertainment business in Spokane. Instead, during the first decade of the twentieth century, Spokane became a regional hub for more polite theatergoing. This occurred through the activities of home-grown businessmen and, perhaps more important, the growth of connections to outside organizations. Even Goetz and Baer tried their hands at respectability. Soon after the Coeur d'Alene resort shut its doors, the partners announced their plans make a first-class theater of the Coeur d'Alene and build a family-friendly vaudeville circuit on the ashes of their variety fame. It was to no avail.[111] That those giants of Spokane business could not succeed in the wider theater industry indicated the difficulty of the enterprise.

By 1912, when Nelson Durham described Spokane as an "amusement center of a better kind," Spokane boasted several legitimate, vaudeville, and movie houses. Because of the vagaries of the entertainment industry, these heights could not last. And just as variety theater became an issue of civic identity, so too did Spokane's place within national theatrical hierarchies correlate with its place among American cities. The city's relationship to national theater networks demonstrated how a different aspect of Spokane's westernness—namely, its dependence on outside financing and systems—affected its cultural development.

CHAPTER FOUR

The Geography and Hierarchy
of Show Business

In late January 1917 a Mrs. P. F. Chadwick traveled north from
Colfax, Washington, stayed at Spokane's Davenport Hotel, and
watched no one less than the Ballets Russes. Here was contrast. A
hardware dealer's wife, together with several other small-town gentry,
witnessed the absolute cutting-edge of European performing arts.
That Vaslav Nijinsky and Mrs. P. F. Chadwick could connect, however slightly, required coordination indeed. That coordination came
in the form of modern technologies and business practices that
linked American cities into "theatrical circuits" and disseminated
culture through them.[1] On this occasion, New York City's Metropolitan Opera cooperated with a powerful national circuit to manage
the Ballets Russes tour. For the Northwest, the appearance of Sergei
Diaghilev's famous company represented a particular opportunity.[2]

The opportunity was this: if first-class houses in Portland, Seattle,
Spokane, and Tacoma could draw audiences appreciative and remunerative enough to justify outlays of this level (the troupe required
fourteen train cars to transport its dancers, musicians, costumes, and
scenery), then the Metropolitan Opera would include the region in
an annual "grand opera" tour. Theater managers in the four cities
were working together to ensure that they passed this "test for the
West."[3] But the local managers did not rely solely on in-town audiences. For events of this caliber, Spokane's showmen specifically
advertised the availability of mail-order tickets for theatergoers in
outlying hamlets. So it was that Charles York, house manager of the
Auditorium, had a desk drawer overflowing with requests from throughout the Inland Northwest to see the Ballets Russes, and that Chadwick
joined a party of "Whitman County people" for the rare evening.[4]

The Inland Northwest's brush with the Ballets Russes illustrates well a central idea: how urban hierarchy, economic geography, and cultural hierarchy combined to affect business and the arts in one corner of the United States. Historians of the American West have demonstrated how western cities structured and stimulated that enormous region and linked it to a system of national and international power centers such as New York, London, and Amsterdam. Those linkages came in many forms (such as capital loaned from a faraway bank) and created a geography of capitalism. Among the most important and tangible links in this chain was the railroad: a capital-made network that facilitated the flow of goods, information, and people and allowed westerners to tap into "metropolitan corridors."[5] By the early twentieth century professional theater was as much a part of this economic web as any endeavor. Consider the technological and economic linkages required for "Whitman County people" to acquire mail-order tickets and arrive in Spokane by rail or automobile—and more dramatically, for Diaghilev's company to travel from Europe to New York to the Northwest.

Spokane did not exist within a system of cities without reference to other locales. Rather, regional and national cities fell into a kind of pecking order, a concept that historians call urban hierarchy and that contemporaries understood and encouraged. Where a city stood within that hierarchy depended on the resources—such as transportation, government, finance, or industry—that it could control.[6] Those cities that controlled more resources had a strategic advantage and could demand "tribute" of the lesser cities and hinterlands surrounding them. Spokane dominated the Inland Northwest and was at the head of the region's urban hierarchy; though it sat atop a regional pyramid, Spokane was also bound (as was the entire Pacific Slope) to San Francisco by a host of commercial ties.[7] Spokane further belonged to a wider national network revolving around New York City, one of the few places with great reach and power.

Among the resources New Yorkers controlled was theater.[8] The city possessed such a concentration of artists, troupes, producers, critics, and booking agencies that it became the nerve center of American (and perhaps even Canadian) show business, despite prominent theater scenes in San Francisco, Chicago, and elsewhere.

Because New York City was the headquarters of American theater, its firms could often dictate business strategies and artistic styles to the rest of the nation and especially to cities like Spokane, which had people enough to support touring shows but not enough of an artistic community to compete with major cultural centers. Thus when the Metropolitan Opera—significantly named—offered a "test for the West," western music lovers had to comply with the terms of that trial if they wanted the best opera to come to their hometowns.

One final hierarchical designation complicated professional theater in the early twentieth century—that of culture. As several scholars have established, the latter half of the nineteenth century saw the division of literary, performing, and visual arts into firm categories of "high" and "low."[9] By the early twentieth century the popularity of "low" styles like vaudeville had begun to erode the dominance of more celebrated genres, but the idea that not all arts were equal remained entrenched in American taste. In the theater world, "grand opera" and "legitimate" reigned artistically, if not financially. The frothiness of musical comedy put it a step below these styles while the mixed format and motley origins of vaudeville placed it lower still; throughout the 1900s and much of the 1910s, film was at the bottom of the theatrical heap, thanks to its mechanical nature and working-class edge.

The level of performance could also determine a show's place within the broader cultural hierarchy. Despite the quality of some companies, stock theater—wherein resident actors performed standard, often tired, plays on a rotating basis—was looked down upon as déclassé legitimate. Finally, in American show business, cultural hierarchies correlated with urban and geographical hierarchies: good acts usually came from the East and Europe. Such "metropolitan successes" were perceived as superior but small-town and western audiences had far fewer opportunities to see them.[10] Spokane's theaters hosted song-and-dance troupes on a regular basis; the Auditorium presented Nijinsky only once.

The interplay of geographies and hierarchies affected the progress of the professional stage in Spokane during the first two decades of the twentieth century. Spokane's relationships to such circuits hinged on geographic and capitalist calculations and played a tremendous role in how its commercial amusements evolved. The city's own physical location and qualities—which made Spokane both an inland link to more profitable coastal markets and the hub of a territory far from theatrical capitals—at times advanced its importance to theater chains but, more often, left it too isolated to be practical. On the other hand, regional cities like Spokane, as well as the towns and villages beneath them in the urban hierarchy, were not entirely without power in the entertainment industry. To pay for their wide-reaching schemes, New York moguls needed the Mrs. Chadwicks.

Yet altogether, urban hierarchy determined cultural hierarchy. The greater a city's resources and its connections to other cities, the more likely it would have a vibrant and praiseworthy stage. As Spokane's value to metropolitan forces waxed and waned, its theater scene rose and fell in quality.

Spokane in the New Century

Spokane's theatrical scene flowered at the turn of the century, finally allowing the city's residents and visitors to patronize venues beyond the expensive Auditorium or the naughty variety houses; this growth occurred against a backdrop of wider economic expansion in Spokane and the Inland Northwest (see table 6 in the appendix). That prosperity had its own roots in the final years of the 1890s when Spokanites engaged successfully in regional developments and made their city an inland hub for mining, fruit distribution, grain milling, and timber processing. These industries, as well as a service sector catering to the hinterland, laid the foundation for Spokane's second period of spectacular expansion, which lasted from the late 1890s to around 1911.[11]

As with the boom of the 1880s economic growth led to population and construction booms, and Spokane enjoyed almost visible momentum during the century's first decade. In 1900 the city had 36,848 people, 48 percent of whom were foreign-born or the children of immigrants; 747 people of color lived in Spokane. Appropriate to its economy turn-of-the-century Spokane had about 5,000 more men than women. One decade later, Spokane had increased by 183 percent, to 104,402 souls. Many of the newcomers moved from within the United States, but the city also attracted a large number of Canadians and Scandinavians. From 1900 to 1909 the city issued 17,521 building permits; the value of construction in these years totaled $38,220,905. Much of the new environment consisted of lovely parks, homes, office blocks, hotels, and club houses. Spokane had even paved its streets.[12]

The city's growth came with complications. In addition to their seemingly intractable class disputes, Spokanites were hampered by an economic structure that enabled initial prosperity but left local grandees without real power in the national and international marketplaces. For instance, by the 1900s Spokane firms sold Inland Northwest wheat through the world. But Palouse grain landed on tables in the Far East, not the East Coast, due to one of Spokane's essential weaknesses: its modest position in urban and capitalist hierarchies. Spokanites had to market their soft wheat abroad because easterners did not want it and smaller Washington towns did not need it. Worse yet, the complexities of international business proved too much for Spokanites, and outside concerns purchased their mills. A similar situation occurred with the remunerative mines that opened in the late 1890s. Although the mines contributed to the city's prosperity, insufficient local capital necessitated their sale to Canadian interests in 1899.[13] The hopes of Spokanites, in other words, were checked by the realities of geography and capitalism.

Geography and capitalism—those things that facilitated Spokane's development could also restrain it, as the city's relationship to transcontinental railroads exemplified. The financial troubles of the early 1890s resulted, by 1896, in almost complete control of the Great Northern and Northern Pacific railroads by James J. Hill, Spokane's erstwhile hero. Hill could set freight rates without the threat of competition. Because the city had no direct outlet to the Pacific Ocean, it was subject to higher shipping rates. Spokane's businessmen and boosters made a protracted fight against Hill's rate structure but never enjoyed a true victory. The mundane dealings of Spokanites in wheat and minerals—not to mention their rages against Hill— demonstrated how this mid-sized western city fared in the world of high-stakes finance and industry with all the vagaries and opportunities such an environment entailed.[14] Likewise, Spokane's involvement with the entertainment industry demonstrated how capitalist gamesmanship and continent-spanning enterprise could both give and take away.

The Structure of Show Business

The years of Spokane's greatest involvement with the business of touring theater, the 1880s to the 1910s, were also years of tremendous expansion and structural change in the American entertainment industry. In the late nineteenth century the industry comprised several elements, including physical properties, resident managers, production companies, and booking agencies. At one end were the theaters themselves, which were sometimes constructed or financed by local capital. In Spokane, for instance, J. J. Browne and A. M. Cannon built the Auditorium with their own (albeit mortgaged) fortunes. With the Panic of 1893, the Auditorium became the property of the Hypotheek Bank; from the mid-1890s to at least the late 1910s, no matter what productions played there, the theater remained in Dutch hands. When Harry Hayward, the Auditorium's longtime manager, received his salary, he did so from the Netherlands-based firm.[15] As the century turned, other wealthy Spokanites built or bought stock in local theaters, sometimes at the behest of national theater magnates.[16] Such property owners generally did not arrange the actual show business of a theater. This fell to a resident (or house) manager, a person with experience in the industry. House managers, working on contract with property owners or leasing the theater from them, had one overriding responsibility: to purchase performances.

This required someone to sell performances, a market opportunity filled by "combination" companies or "road shows." These units usually focused on one show and were organized by a producing manager or producer. New York City provided their base of operations, and through rail systems they traveled the nation. As the twentieth century approached combination companies became legion: 138 such troupes toured America in 1881, 234 in 1894, and 420 in 1904.[17]

Clearly, Americans outside the great metropolis wanted shows, and during the last decades of the nineteenth century they received those shows through a byzantine method. Circa 1870 "the out-of-town manager would come to New York in the summer, and hie himself to the 'Rialto' . . . where he would find every phase of the business itself conducted on the pavements." As troupes and theaters proliferated, this situation became unworkable.[18] Consequently, small theatrical circuits—or strings of theaters connected via railroad and financial arrangements—developed during the late nineteenth century. At the same time businessmen created booking agencies to act, remuneratively, as the coordinator between theaters and combination companies. Such agencies soon became concentrated in New York City, and in the hands of a very few men, which allowed the city to have almost dictatorial control over an industry. This too was unsatisfactory, and the monopoly inspired rebellion.[19]

Meanwhile, the structure of show business became increasingly stratified and professional. By the 1900s the trade included booking agencies, with their many departments and representatives; the producing firms, which created combination companies and included producers, stage managers, and publicity agents; circuits, with their owners, managers, representatives, and talent scouts; actors and their agents; local theaters, run by a resident manager and employing stagehands, carpenters, and ushers; and also the playwrights, critics, lawyers, bill posters, and ticket speculators. Allegiances overlapped throughout the industry. Producing firms, performers, playwrights, and circuits might work with a specific booking agency; producers might build their own show houses; theatrical lawyers might hold stock in production companies. In these endeavors capitalists—not impresarios or artists—realized the highest profits.[20] All told, early-twentieth-century show business was vast and systematized, creating a web of connections and hierarchies that spanned a continent and beyond.

When Julius Cahn listed Spokane contacts for traveling show people, he included not only house managers like Hayward but also agents for the Great Northern and Northern Pacific railroads. In guidebooks such as Cahn's, North American rail companies placed conspicuous advertisements that alerted readers to the major cities that their lines passed through. This attention to railroads was no mistake, for without trains the era's famous road shows could have hardly existed.[21] Modern technology underpinned turn-of-the-century show business. Moreover, through telegraph, printing, and rail once isolated spots like the Inland Northwest joined the networks emanating from America's entertainment centers.[22]

Becoming a part of these physical and financial networks signified much for westerners who wanted eastern culture. People in the region recognized that the greater their connection to the railroads the greater their chances to receive high-quality productions with some regularity. Spokane's growth as a regional transportation hub further demonstrated the tight relationship between railroads and show business. As the city's rail connections increased, so too did its ability to receive attractions from the East and to draw lucrative audiences from its own hinterland. Yet even as show business touched the most remote locales, modern devices allowed its administration to stay centered in New York City.[23]

Legitimate Theater Networks, 1896–1910

During the final decades of the nineteenth century American industry became increasingly consolidated as large businesses absorbed smaller concerns in an effort to curb competition, streamline methods, and increase profits. The creation of theatrical circuits was part of this move toward efficiency, concentration, and monopoly.[24] As the entertainment industry consolidated at the firm level and expanded geographically, Spokane and the Northwest became entangled in the efforts of magnates to control transcontinental networks of theaters. In this game, certain locations had greater strategic value; this was particularly true for those cities with rich hinterlands, a number of rail connections, or a location that helped break up the long distances inherent in North American travel. Provincial cities such as Spokane, therefore, were not without negotiating power, especially when they worked together or proved their market value. Yet as Spokane's theatergoers learned, the city's ability to attract first-class legitimate theater ultimately depended on the vagaries and decisions of outside firms and forces.

Circuit-building began humbly in the Inland Northwest but was founded on the same principle as in other regions: managers could acquire better acts by expanding the number of theaters or nights of work an act could expect. Because American theater was centered at the far end of the continent in New York City, taking a troupe to the West cost dearly. If a house manager could provide performers with even one more audience, he had an additional bargaining chip. Every theater buttressed a manager's ability to attract decent performers. Accordingly, throughout the 1890s Hayward reached into Spokane's hinterland and assumed management of opera houses in towns such as Wallace, Idaho—an arrangement that improved his leverage with theatrical companies. As the decade progressed, small networks like Hayward's covered the Northwest and much of the United States.[25]

The work of one regional showman, John Cort of Seattle, became significant for the entire West. Cort's activities exemplified the tactical, geographic nature of theatrical circuits and the ties between these financial networks and the railroads that facilitated them. Cort arrived in Seattle in the late 1880s and originally focused on variety theaters. By 1890 the young man had agreements with or control of theaters in Butte, Spokane, Seattle, Portland, San Francisco, and elsewhere, allowing him to attract good eastern variety acts and offer them sixteen weeks of work. Other Seattle impresarios such as J. P. Howe and John Hanna were likewise scrambling for mastery of the regional theater business. Their efforts were aided by Seattle's concentration of rail lines, which made it a hub for road shows: companies could travel north from San Francisco along the Union Pacific or overland through Spokane via the Northern Pacific, picking up audiences along the way.[26] Cort manipulated the situation best, however.

Cort's advantage came, in part, because of developments at the highest levels of show business. In 1896 the trend toward consolidation culminated in the creation of the so-called Theatrical Syndicate. The new booking concern comprised three firms and six men—Marc Klaw and Abraham Erlanger, Al Hayman and Charles Frohman, Samuel Nixon and J. F. Zimmerman. By coordinating booking through a pooling arrangement the Syndicate members gained control of more than five hundred American theaters. Though the Syndicate had western connections (notably Hayman, a San Franciscan), its clearinghouse was the Klaw and Erlanger firm and its center was

New York City. A number of production companies and artists as well as more theaters became allied with the Syndicate. Though others in the entertainment industry hated the group's monopolistic power, it was difficult to resist.[27] In the meantime, Cort turned his attention to legitimate theater and assembled a sizable regional circuit. When the Syndicate looked to the far western end of the Northern Pacific railroad, they found John Cort and found they could do little in the Northwest without him. For his part Cort saw in the Syndicate the hope of good productions; thus around 1900 he entered an agreement with Klaw and Erlanger and essentially became the Syndicate's western agent.[28]

For these barons of booking as well as for industry observers, theatrical circuits were conceived of as battlefields. Magnates concentrated on well-placed markets and spoke regularly and without irony of territories, invasion, Napoleons, and tsars. The *Coast* magazine, for instance, described Cort's dealings as an "efficient generalship" that allowed the Northwest to negotiate with the Syndicate from a position of power.[29] Yet Harry Hayward did not take the martial view. Rumors that Spokane (that is, Hayward's Auditorium) might join a larger legitimate circuit proliferated throughout the late 1890s but never came to fruition. The only circuit the Auditorium belonged to at this point was the one operated by Hayward between Spokane and Wallace, small potatoes indeed compared to developments elsewhere in the Northwest.[30] It was not Spokane itself—with its theater-loving public and many rail connections—that kept the Auditorium out of larger circuits. Whatever he may have felt about other circuits, Hayward despised the Syndicate as a trust. In early 1901 the opportunity came for Hayward and the Auditorium to join the Syndicate, apparently through Cort's newly formed Northwestern Theatrical Association (NWTA). Hayward rejected the offer.[31]

Hayward had the respect of show-business insiders, but his rejection of the Syndicate meant the humbling—if not the demise—of the Auditorium.[32] Because the city of Spokane possessed all the elements of a provincial cultural hub, it constituted a critical link in the northwestern circuit and provided a lucrative stop for attractions traveling on the Northern Pacific en route to Seattle. Cort and the Syndicate were not about to abandon a place of this value.

Accordingly, in mid-1901, they rushed the building of the Spokane Theater: a first-class legitimate house in competition with the Auditorium. Like the Auditorium a decade earlier, the new theater symbolized the desire of local people to have Spokane linked with and patterned after major metropolises. Advance reports, for instance, noted that the Spokane was styled on the Illinois Opera House of Chicago and would have the same amenities as theaters in more powerful cities. With the Spokane Theater, the city's entertainment scene became unquestionably tied to financial and theatrical forces outside the Inland Northwest. The NWTA installed a resident manager, Dan Weaver, but the Spokane was presided over by Pacific Coast showmen and connected to theaters in Oregon, Washington, and Montana.[33]

The link that mattered the most, however, was the one Cort provided to the East through the Syndicate. When Weaver announced the new theater to reporters, he was quick to mention that the Spokane was in Syndicate hands: "Klaw and Erlanger . . . control the bookings of every attraction except Mrs. [Minnie Maddern] Fiske. We have a contract for Spokane for all trust attractions for five years, beginning September 1."[34] At this point, Klaw and Erlanger did control almost every major star and attraction, which meant that Weaver and Cort's contract with them gave the Spokane Theater a tremendous advantage over the Auditorium. The NWTA, moreover, had five-year franchises for "trust attractions" throughout the Northwest. Hayward could not hope to compete and could no longer lure high-quality road shows to the Auditorium, as he had for a decade. With its opening in the fall of 1901, the Spokane Theater became the new darling of local society and the home for "highbrow" legitimate theater.[35]

With Syndicate-controlled productions sent exclusively to the Spokane, an important change occurred at the Auditorium: it dropped in the cultural and social hierarchies. Like J. P. Howe in Seattle (who also spurned the NWTA and suffered for it), Hayward struggled to find adequate substitutes for the best road shows, which he could no longer engage. His attempts to compete included renovations of the Auditorium and, more to the point, a renewed effort at circuit-building.[36] But the Northwest had become trust territory.

Through the Syndicate and other circuits, Spokane audiences watched many of the same productions as theatergoers elsewhere in the nation. *Ben Hur* played at the Spokane for a week in October 1905. While Spokanites welcomed shows from New York City, people also traveled from throughout the Inland Northwest to see those shows in Spokane. Essential for all of this were the newspapers, mail services, and rail lines that allowed people, information, and money to move across space. For *Ben Hur*, local railroads offered popular excursion rates. Strobridge and Company Lithograph, 1901. Courtesy Library of Congress, LC-USZ62-50782.

As the *Argus* put it, Cort and the Syndicate had the region "so bottled up" that performers "could not even play a water tank along the Northern Pacific" without the NWTA's blessing.[37] Hayward's solution was, eventually, a turn to stock theater. Stock companies had once dominated the American stage; however, by the new century they were considered middle-brow at best, legitimate that had "lost caste." Hayward had booked stock companies before but only to fill the empty summer months and at "popular" prices. With the Spokane Theater in town, the Auditorium became primarily a stock house— and a popular-priced one at that—for the rest of the 1900s.

To many Spokanites this was humiliating. Hayward and the Auditorium had long served as monuments of civic pride.[38] Now, more than ever before, the manager respected throughout show business and the house built to advertise Spokane were at the mercy of outside forces. In February 1903 Hayward relented and joined his theater to the NWTA and the Syndicate. Yet throughout the decade the Auditorium continued to play second fiddle to the Spokane, and with the Auditorium in the Syndicate, Hayward could not engage productions booked by other agencies. Howe, for instance, tried to assemble a circuit oriented along the Pacific Coast, but the Auditorium was not eligible for membership in it because of its new Syndicate affiliation.[39] Spokanites did appreciate the presence of another legitimate house, but the Spokane Theater never occupied the same place in local imaginations as the Auditorium. Built by local initiative during Spokane's first flush of growth, the Auditorium represented the energy and boosterism that Spokanites called the "Spokane spirit." It mortified them to have that spirit bested by a metropolitan trust: decades after both theaters had passed their prime, Spokanites still blamed the Syndicate for debasing their prized institution.[40]

Even though the Spokane became the home of "trust" shows after 1901, this did not ensure that its high-priced attractions were the best of contemporary show business. Like many Syndicate houses, particularly in the West, the Spokane often received "mediocrity and worse."[41] Throughout the 1900s the Syndicate did have booking rights for many major stars and productions, but it did not always send them out west. This was a function of economic geography and bottom-line decision making. New York City—not Chicago, not San Francisco—was America's theatrical hub, from which places like Spokane were far-flung, to say the least. The Syndicate and its allies made fortunes playing top productions in the East; why then, add the terrific cost of overland railroad fare to the expense of mounting a top-quality show? The combination of transportation costs, reluctance to leave the East, and eastern headquarters meant that western audiences often paid high prices for second-rate productions. Plainly put, provincial houses such as the Spokane Theater—however attractive and well-connected—occupied the lower levels of the theatrical order and prospered accordingly.[42]

Yet there was a reverse side to the economic geography of show business, namely, the gathered power of the provinces. As the 1900s progressed, patrons and managers outside the metropolis became increasingly dissatisfied with the Syndicate. This presented an opportunity for entrepreneurs throughout the United States and a number of "independent" managers (such as Howe) tried to create rival legitimate circuits.[43] The group that most famously capitalized on the wave of theatrical "trust-busting" was the Shubert Brothers, led by Sam, Lee, and J. J. Shubert. By seizing on the theatergoing public's desire for competition and by using a more efficient structure than the Syndicate's old-fashioned pool, the Shuberts "invaded" much Syndicate territory, including the Northwest.[44] While opportunities existed outside the Syndicate, they also existed within that organization, precisely because it monopolized so much of the American market on the basis of a gentleman's agreement. John Cort recognized this. By the mid-1900s observers called Cort the Napoleon, the "Klaw and Erlanger" of the West. But though "Cort controlled the West . . . the East controlled John Cort"—a conclusion he accepted less readily.[45]

During the spring of 1910 Cort led a successful protest against Klaw and Erlanger by leveraging the collective might of the hundreds of western and small-town theaters within the Syndicate: a revolt of the "one-night stands." In early May 1910 after several meetings regarding the mediocre Syndicate road shows, Cort and the representatives of twelve hundred American and Canadian theaters created the National Theatre Owners' Association (NTOA). The new association, a combination of several large regional circuits, was based on an "open door" policy. To join, member theaters must book independently. Making fair play its motto, the NTOA asserted that any good attraction could secure a continuous route throughout the United States and Canada. With circuits in the West, Midwest, South, and Northeast and houses in regional cities (including Spokane), this was no empty boast. Within the month, the number of houses in the NTOA had risen to sixteen hundred. At almost the stroke of a pen, the Syndicate was bereft of many of the geographical and financial links that had made North American tours profitable.[46]

Syndicate apologists responded by dismissing one-night-stand managers as "janitors" who profited from Klaw and Erlanger's prowess, but they could not dismiss the importance of provincial audiences to show-business success.[47] North America is an enormous continent. If a theatrical company performed only in the largest cities or best houses, it faced what show people called the long, awful, or uncertain "jumps": extended travel across space with much outlay and little income. Small towns and regional cities alleviated these jumps by providing the "connecting links" between more desirable gigs. Producing managers certainly recognized this and designed tours accordingly.[48]

Regional hubs formed an especially important element in this equation, as Spokane demonstrated. In cities such as Spokane with well-incorporated hinterlands, managers could pick up audiences composed of resident and out-of-town theatergoers (perhaps for multiple performances), as well as one-night stands in the outlying opera houses. For instance, the Spokane Theater encouraged out-of-town attendance at major shows by arranging excursion fares with rail lines, facilitating theatergoers as far as two hundred miles from the city.[49] Likewise, the Auditorium's resident stock company had fans even among Scandinavian farmers in a nearby hamlet.[50] City audiences represented only part of the revenue possible through an Inland Northwest tour: through the NWTA, Syndicate shows played at houses in Wallace, Wardner, Coeur d'Alene, Colfax, Oakesdale, Sprague, Ritzville, North Yakima, Ellensburg, and Walla Walla.[51] Performances in Sprague and Ritzville yielded little glory, but together, the Ritzvilles of North America meant more money and less "awful jumps."

The Syndicate and the northwestern managers (represented by Cort) finally reached an "armistice" in November 1910. Both sides had much to offer—the Syndicate, attractions; the northwestern independents, "so much rich territory." By utilizing the bargaining power of its "rich territory," Cort's group forced the Syndicate to relent. Both sides were now open to each other. Cort's 1910 revolt proved how otherwise impotent towns could benefit from the geography of show business; the physical geography of North America had much to do with this. Yet provincial theaters, even those in regional hubs such as Spokane, still remained beholden to the metropolis, as Cort's movement also proved: the NTOA was based in New York City.[52]

At the start of the 1910s, then, legitimate theater in Spokane looked much different than it had done a decade earlier. The Spokane Theater had humbled—and to an extent, replaced—the Auditorium as the city's finest house. Both theaters benefited from

Spokane's strategic location along several railroads and as the entrepôt for a large inland region. Because show-business magnates recognized the city's geographic value as well as its taste for the stage, Spokane claimed a thriving entertainment scene at this point. But those audiences were largely at the mercy of showmen outside Spokane and the Northwest, and the circuit wars had not concluded.

Vaudeville Networks, 1900–1910

Even as legitimate tycoons assembled their empires, vaudeville impresarios created organizations that fastened Spokane to national and international networks. As they built circuits these showmen also analyzed the North American map, planting theaters in cities that could yield revenue and break up the "jumps." Much more than legitimate businessmen, vaudeville organizers had to be careful in considering what role cultural respectability would take in their dealings, for both the content and the pedigree of this genre condemned it in the eyes of Victorian purists. Vaudeville shows consisted of a number of acts such as dance, acrobatics, animal tricks, broad comic sketches, and playlets, the kinds of performance that had been expunged from "highbrow" playbills when middle- and upper-class Americans began glorifying legitimate theater years earlier. After the Civil War, such smorgasbord entertainment was relegated to concert saloons and variety theaters.[53]

In the 1880s and 1890s vaudeville innovators (particularly Tony Pastor and B. F. Keith) had achieved success by moving mixed-format shows from the "smoky, boozy, licentious male atmosphere" of variety halls to a setting that was safer for middle-class women and children. Even the new genre's French name represented attempts at an air of European sophistication.[54] Accordingly, turn-of-the-century showmen devised business models based not only on the availability of hubs, hinterlands, and railroads but also on the propriety of acts, theaters, and neighborhoods. These were calculations involving both urban and cultural hierarchy. Stratification, moreover, became intrinsic to vaudeville as it bifurcated into the "big time" (which entailed two performances daily, and the best theaters, salaries, and stars) and the "small time" (several performances per day, at remote or dowdy theaters and lower prices).[55] A vaudeville organization advanced financially—and often geographically—when it ascended the cultural hierarchy by gentrifying or as it dominated one level of the genre's pyramid. This applied to circuits originating in the Pacific Northwest as much as it did to those from the East.

Late-nineteenth-century variety theater flourished in the Northwest, but with the new century "polite" or "advanced" vaudeville overtook its predecessor and became something of a boom industry in regional cities. As polite vaudeville developed, Spokane provided a logical outreach point for impresarios trying to expand a chain of regional theaters. In the 1900s circuits based in Portland (Northwest Vaudeville), Seattle (the Consolidated Star, Sullivan-Considine, and Pantages circuits), and elsewhere (Edison Display and Irving Vaudeville) attempted to make Spokane part of their systems; often they succeeded.[56] Yet, as Spokane businessmen learned, the inland city proved less ideal as the headquarters for vaudeville circuits, particularly when compared with Seattle. Though Spokanites loved vaudeville, the city was handicapped by unfavorable freight fares and had not capitalized on the 1897 Klondike gold rush—which incubated the careers of Seattle showmen—to the extent Seattle had.[57] Thus Spokane remained Seattle's inferior, almost its dependent, throughout the decades of vaudeville's popularity.

Spokane's old bête noire, John W. Considine, loomed large in the entertainment worlds of Seattle and Spokane, and his career demonstrated how cultural respectability, or at least the outside form of it, could drive success. During the 1890s Considine had scandalized middle-class northwesterners with his variety theaters and had waged failing legal battles to defend those barmaid-centered venues. Then around 1898 he apparently learned his lesson and moved "above the line" in every sense by relocating from Seattle's skid road to a better district and by separating liquor from the stage.[58] Having ostensibly left the underworld Considine began assembling a regional small-time vaudeville circuit. The showman started his polite vaudeville dealings in 1902 by purchasing a half-interest in an Edison ten-cent theater, which featured moving pictures and live acts. But securing that live talent meant facing the old problem of western theater managers: how many weeks of work could Considine offer the performers? Like other impresarios he solved this dilemma by establishing outpost theaters in nearby cities, Spokane among them. This required capital. Consequently, early in the 1900s, Considine approached a fraternal-order acquaintance and fellow Irish Catholic for financial help: Timothy "Big Tim" Sullivan, the celebrated Tammany Hall politician. The men entered a partnership. Sullivan provided money and clout, Considine expertly managed the show-business end, and they created the Sullivan-Considine (S&C) vaudeville circuit.[59]

Sullivan and Considine quickly gained control of a host of mid-level venues; they did so by purchasing other circuits and by opening their own theaters, mortgaging one house to pay for the next. In 1905, for instance, the partners bought the Consolidated Star Vaudeville circuit. This led to the acquisition of the new Washington Theater in Spokane, a house of middling quality that allowed Spokanites to see better vaudeville than they yet had. By 1907 the S&C circuit encompassed some forty theaters and was becoming a dominant force in western popular-priced vaudeville. Key to Considine's strategy was a shrewd use of cultural expectations. Although the circuit generally featured small-time acts, it did so in plush settings. As the impresario and author Robert Grau put it, Considine served up inexpensive vaudeville but he did so in theaters that are "as fit for grand opera as for popular priced vaudeville." Considine had determined that lovely theaters would fool audiences into feeling that his small-time performers were stars, a calculation that proved profitable.[60]

While the Sullivan-Considine circuit spread across western North America, Considine himself acquired regional franchise rights with big-time Orpheum vaudeville and became the general manager of the Pacific Northwest Orpheum circuit.[61] For Spokane audiences, this meant access to the best touring acts at the local Orpheum theater, built in 1906 by George Turner and leased to the Washington-Columbia theater company. The Spokane Orpheum (originally the Columbia) was a fine theater that played at higher prices and attracted local society.[62] It did not, however, compare to the gorgeous Orpheum that Considine opened in Seattle in 1911 at a cost of $500,000: Spokane was clearly a second-place city in theatrical hierarchies, even regional ones.[63] Perhaps, in Considine's case, the city deserved its lower status; Spokane's leading citizens had roundly denounced the showman a decade earlier, at which point he had returned to Seattle and begun his vaudeville empire. On the other hand, perhaps Considine would not have succeeded so well in the inland city, given its shortcomings of geography and finance.

Considine's success exemplified the fabulous growth of vaudeville in the early twentieth century. During those years the light-hearted and fast-paced genre overtook legitimate theater in popularity. This fostered the development of organizations that rivaled the might and reach of the Theatrical Syndicate. Around 1910 the most potent players included the Keith-Albee and Orpheum circuits, which respectively controlled the big time in the East and the West; the United Booking Offices of America (UBO), an eastern agency dominated by the Keith-Albee group and allied with similar western concerns; William Morris's independent booking agency; and Marcus Loew's eastern circuit, which, like S&C, made the small time seem big. This created an extensive economic geography, as well as relations of power and dependency between different points on the vaudeville map. Major organizers had agents scattered throughout America and Europe; financial arrangements in scores of North American towns; and headquarters in Seattle, San Francisco, Chicago, and New York. The nexus of it all—the "hub of American vaudeville"— was the Long Acre building near Times Square, which housed the systematized offices of the Orpheum and UBO and where artists and agents haggled and hawked, as surely as if they worked at a stock exchange.[64]

Through Seattle-based organizations, northwestern cities like Spokane joined this increasingly global network. Put differently, local audiences wanted to see cosmopolitan talent; impresarios answered that demand by establishing foreign offices and relationships. To secure European acts, for instance, Considine had booking offices in London and Europe until mid-1910. At this point the S&C and Orpheum circuits negotiated a deal with Variety Theaters Controlling Company of England that facilitated tours of American, British, and Continental acts in all directions. Considine could then claim to operate the sole international, popularly priced vaudeville chain.[65] But at this point, also, Considine had a serious small-time rival: Alexander Pantages, a Greek sailor and Klondike showman turned Seattle vaudeville magnate. Pantages had a knack for understanding what audiences wanted and used his knack to find, among other things, European talent. By 1910 his representatives included the "globe trotting" Berlin-based Richard Pitrot, who toured annually "in search of foreign novelties and specialties." By 1914 Pantages was advertising his houses (including the Spokane Pantages, opened in October 1907) in London's *Stage Year Book*.[66]

One week of vaudeville in August 1909 demonstrates how John Considine and Alexander Pantages had joined Spokane to both national and international markets and styles. At the Pantages, audiences watched a smattering of acts that included Irene Lee and Her Candy Boys, a dance ensemble "direct from England," and the Spiller Musical Bumpers, an African American group advertised as the "original ragtime musical act." Considine's Washington Theater, meanwhile, presented a female acrobat; an Australian "comedy of comedies"; Rinaldo, "the wandering violinist"; and the "Live Snake Dance," an "Oriental burlesque" wherein a female impersonator depicted Cleopatra's Egypt. Finally, the bill at the Orpheum centered on "At the Country Club," a musical comedy that portrayed the world of high-society New York and featured metropolitan fashions.[67] Local audiences, in other words, could watch interpretations of black American, Knickerbocker, and "Oriental" styles, and artists headed to or from England, Australia, and Europe. Because of Considine, Pantages, and others circa 1910 Spokane's theatergoers enjoyed a wide and growing spectrum of vaudeville talent. While the city's many vaudeville houses connected Spokanites to the world, however, Spokane itself was only a minor junction in America's complicated theatrical web.

Florescence and Decline, 1910–1917

The second decade of the twentieth century opened happily for the capital of the Inland Northwest. Spokane boasted two skyscrapers, numerous rail connections, mansions, theaters, and cathedrals, the largest concrete-arch bridge in the nation, a population of over a hundred thousand, a newspaperman whose home was open to Theodore Roosevelt, and representation in the U.S. Senate by Miles Poindexter.[68] Part of Spokane's vitality was its theatrical scene, which

attracted artists from Anna Held to Sergei Rachmaninoff. Professional
theaters had surely multiplied in the first decade of the century. For
legitimate theater, Spokanites could attend the Spokane (advertised
as the "leading" playhouse and featuring Syndicate road shows) and
the Auditorium (which continued its long engagement of the Jessie
Shirley stock company); for big-time vaudeville, the Orpheum; for
good small-time, the Washington and Pantages; and for mixed-format
shows of lesser quality, the Arcade, Novelty, and Empire.[69] Two years
later, in the fall of 1911, the Pantages, Washington (now the Empress),
and Orpheum still presented national touring vaudeville, and store-
front venues like the Amusement Parlor still provided cheap fun,
but much had changed. Because of NWTA decisions, the Auditorium
and the Spokane had traded status: the Auditorium now hosted
expensive road shows, while its rival was downgraded to vaudeville
and pictures. What the American, Spokane's newest first-class theater,
would present was anyone's guess.

At the start of the 1910s, then, Spokane had a theater scene at
once abundant and unstable. From roughly 1909 to 1914, the professional stage flourished and provided audiences with access to
much entertainment—often good, sometimes stellar—across a range
of prices. But the heights of the early 1910s were unsustainable
because they had been forced by short-sighted competition among
theater moguls. By the latter half of the decade, Spokane's value to
national circuits had declined, which local observers both recognized and regretted. This happened at a time when legitimate road
shows were becoming unprofitable in the face of the popularity of
vaudeville and moving pictures. In Spokane, even the plummiest
houses switched from genre to genre, based either on what the
public wanted or, more likely, on what the circuits offered. For highbrows, it must have felt as though the theatrical sky had fallen. All
told, Spokane's slippery theatrical fortunes in this era illustrate
well both the fruits and the vulnerabilities of participation in the
national marketplace.

Indeed, the progress and demise of Spokane's theaters during
the 1910s was indicative of the city's wider troubles. From its first
boom in the 1880s Spokane had belonged to the new West of "high
finance, nationwide markets, and rapid advances in communication

and transportation." Throughout the 1910s the dangers of that system became evident. To begin with, the Inland Northwest had long served as an "economic colony" that supplied natural resources to the East, rendering it vulnerable to market shifts. Then at the turn of the century a national trend of industrial consolidation and stratification became especially important in the Pacific Northwest. Local investors simply did not have the capital required to keep the region's extractive industries afloat, and so the area became increasingly reliant on external investors.[70] By around 1910, Spokane's foremost businessmen had generally divested themselves of their holdings and ceased to innovate.

Spokane lost its drive socially as well as economically. Around 1911 the rush of immigrants began to fizzle out. The city still had some cachet, as demonstrated by the 1914 opening of Louis Davenport's opulent hotel, but people across Spokane's social spectrum and outside its city limits noticed a shift from vibrant to insular. By 1920 the inland metropolis claimed only thirty-five more residents than it had in 1910—this from a town that once grew by 6,000 percent—and the sources of local fortunes were becoming part of nationwide monopolies.[71] Spokane had entered a funk that took decades to shake. A similar stagnation took place in the city's theatrical scene because local people could not control the power of outside trends, financing, and events.

But as Spokane's many theatergoers knew, before the fall comes the climax. During the first several years of the twentieth century, entrepreneurs great and small tried to capitalize on the growth of the entertainment industry.[72] The competition among the biggest players—such as the Shuberts versus the Syndicate or William Morris versus the vaudeville "Combine"—created a fast-paced environment. In their zeal to control the North American "road," these organizations not only entered leasing or booking arrangements with venues and managers they also built theaters by the score. When John Cort's 1910 coup d'etat deprived the Syndicate of over twelve hundred "one-night stands," for example, the Syndicate scrambled to acquire rival houses throughout the Midwest, building when necessary. For provincial cities this meant more theaters—often symbols of civic pride—and improved connections to mass national culture. Such

Playbills along Howard Street, December 1912. These advertisements provide insight into Spokane's theater scene of the 1910s—about to decline but still vital because of metropolitan connections. Through John Considine's franchise, the Orpheum showed big-time vaudeville. Meanwhile, Alexander Pantages's "big small-time" featured actual and imagined international performances. Finally, stock players at the troubled American theater presented a recent Broadway offering, *The Greyhound.* Northwest Museum of Arts and Culture/Eastern Washington State Historical Society, Spokane, Washington, L2003-24.804.

places may have appreciated multiple competing playhouses, but they could not always support them. Accordingly, the competition among circuits became ruinous and glutted the market with unprofitable theaters.[73] Precisely this situation occurred with Spokane and its American Theater.

The American had a dizzying, if not glorious, career. Yet it began life auspiciously. In 1909 the Shubert Brothers openly challenged the Syndicate with their announcements to build or acquire legitimate theaters throughout the West. They brought this campaign to

Spokane that autumn when work began on a 1,650-seat house planned to be among the finest in the West.[74] When it opened a year
later, the American was certainly modern and attractive but it was
no longer a Shubert theater. What happened in the months between
groundbreaking and debut demonstrated how the high stakes and
geographic realities of the North American entertainment industry
could play out. In the midst of constructing the American, the Shuberts redrew their proposed route to the Pacific Coast. Instead of
killing the space between Winnepeg and Vancouver with inland
American cities, the Shuberts decided to open "new territory" in
the Canadian heartland, thereby picking up more performances
along the way. This meant abandoning the American Theater. As
the *Spokesman-Review* put it, "the designs of the 'open door' on this
city [fell] victim to the 'long jump.'"[75] Such were the brass tacks of
show business.

   While the Shuberts reconsidered their western strategy, another
so-called insurgent became interested in the theater under construction in Spokane. William Morris, a New York talent agent, had received
underhanded treatment from the Shuberts, the Syndicate, and particularly the UBO. He responded in 1909 by assembling a competitive
and high-grade vaudeville circuit. Morris's theaters were often built
by local capital and were predominantly located in major western
cities.[76] In March 1910 Spokanites learned that the Shubert theater
on Front and Post Streets now belonged to the American Building
Company, a new corporation of local stockholders from whom
Morris would lease the property for twenty years. Spokanites were
flattered to read that Morris's general agent described this acquisition as the key move in Morris's "campaign to gain a foothold in
the West."[77] These announcements signified nothing. Morris had
overextended himself financially and his western "invasion," with
some fifteen houses planned, soon collapsed. The American Theater
—unused and unopened—went back on the market in late 1910, again
a casualty of the volatile continental schemes of theater magnates.

   The American Building Company, meanwhile, was left with an
expensive theater that had no scheduled attractions because it had
no clear connections to any major circuit. The bitterness of this
situation became obvious in November 1910 when a house manager,

Charles Muehlman, remarked that no Syndicate shows would come to the American and that "through the work of Marc Klaw, Abraham Erlanger, John Cort and Lee Shubert, Spokane people have been double crossed." These men, he complained, had never intended to book their attractions at the American because they had all the Spokane business they wanted at the Auditorium.[78] Muehlman immediately recanted, but Cort and the Syndicate (now reconciled) evidently concluded that the inland city could not support two first-class road-show theaters. In the early 1910s the NWTA chose to send its best acts to the Auditorium, and the American was demoted accordingly.[79]

With no Shuberts, no Morris, and no Syndicate, the American Building Company could not fill the American with the shows it was built for. Still, local investors put on a brave face. After an emergency meeting with the city's house managers, the American Building Company secured an engagement with the Del S. Lawrence stock theater company.[80] When the American finally opened on Christmas Day, the Spokane banker who dedicated it boasted that this venue, among the finest in the Northwest, would prove an asset "to the city as a commercial enterprise, being owned by Spokane men." Enormous crowds did turn out that first week, but Spokane's zest for the stage supplied only one of the requirements needed to support a theater of this caliber. Furthermore, although the Lawrence troupe ranked among the higher grade of stock companies, the American had taken undeniable steps down the cultural hierarchy—from legitimate road shows to first-class vaudeville to regional stock players—in its very infancy.[81]

The American Theater only continued its downward path. Rumors occasionally circulated of a place for it within various circuits, but favorable alliances never developed. In the meantime the American existed from hand to mouth, presenting moving pictures, ten-cent vaudeville, cheap stock, cheap musicals, or nothing at all. Within a few seasons it had become "taboo in the minds of better class of theatergoers."[82] By 1916 the state of Washington had struck the American Building Company from official records for its failure to pay licensing fees.[83] The American, initially advertised as the "Theater Beautiful," now exemplified the dangers of the boom-and-bust amusement industry. Local money could build a theater as elegant as anything in the West, but without strong national connections Spokanites could not keep it booked with attractions from the top or even the middle of the cultural hierarchy. Theater barons might consider Spokane a useful regional hub, but a change in routes or fortunes could quickly shift attention away from the inland city. Show-business rivalries could lead to a proliferation of theaters but they could also create a fatally saturated environment.

Even as the American's star was falling, wide-reaching developments in vaudeville circuits attested to the risks faced by provincial theaters. The western market caused several careers and circuits to prosper, but individually most western cities had a limited ability to influence the entertainment industry. And as with the American Theater, Spokane's vaudeville experiences of the mid-1910s demonstrate that a city with relatively little sway in the urban hierarchy could not expect the best in cultural hierarchy. Throughout the early 1910s vaudeville impresarios continued to deal with the North American stage as though it were a true theater of war, wrangling over "territory" and negotiating rights regarding each other's spheres of influence. In 1911, for instance, Marcus Loew and John Considine—who respectively dominated the "big small-time" in the East and the West—agreed that Considine would not open theaters east of Chicago, and Loew not west of Cincinnati.[84]

Indeed, it was the dealings of Considine and Loew that initially showed how beholden Spokane's vaudeville audiences were to outside forces. Considine had for years linked Spokane to good vaudeville through his S&C chain and Orpheum franchise rights, but this all began to disintegrate in 1913 when Big Tim Sullivan died. Without his "New York anchor," Considine lacked the necessary financial security to sustain the S&C circuit.[85] Within months Loew had spent millions and acquired over one hundred S&C houses. These included the Spokane Orpheum Theater, which was rechristened Loew's Theater in August 1914.[86] For Loew, who began his entertainment career with penny arcades, the S&C purchase led to a period when observers hailed him as the "king of vaudeville." Significantly, it was the western theaters that made

Loew king; operating from coast to coast he threatened Pantages, UBO, and Orpheum interests.[87] As John Cort had taught the Syndicate four years earlier, there was power in the West and in small towns.

The Loew-Considine deal set off a number of realignments within the vaudeville world during the spring of 1914. This shuffling of interests affected Spokane unfavorably and deprived the city of big-time vaudeville. The West could make a king, but most western markets were pawns in the show business wars. For Spokanites losing the big time meant more than decreased access to entertainers. Commercial amusements drew Inland Northwesterners to Spokane; without the big time, merchants lost revenue and Spokane lost something of its regional appeal. Consequently, when Spokane businessmen learned in May 1914 that Considine might bring Orpheum big time back on a subscription basis, they jumped at the opportunity.

Spokane's role as the area's entertainment capital was illuminated by those elements of the community that pushed for the Orpheum's return: the Ad Club, the hoteliers, the chamber of commerce, and the Elk's Club—groups invested in the promotion of Spokane and its success as an entrepôt. The city's hotel men were especially active for "They, more than many others, realize just what high-class vaudeville attractions in the city mean to them in attracting show lovers from the surrounding towns." Meanwhile, a local columnist argued that if theatergoers turned out in force, they could convince the impresarios of Spokane's profitability.[88] After working throughout the summer of 1914 to secure their place within national circuits, Spokanites did earn the right to Orpheum shows. Then came the outbreak of war in Europe and a solid end to that season's big-time hopes.[89]

At that point Spokane's theatrical hopes began to fall apart altogether. This occurred because of the industry's wild fluctuations, a market overburdened with theaters, the weight of international events, and particularly, the unequal relationship between metropolis and province. In the vaudeville arena Spokane's audiences and business people continued to beg for the big time, and they watched as another round of leasing deals and rumors surrounded the Loew's (née Orpheum) Theater. Because of Marcus Loew's changing plans, that venue remained dark for a good portion of 1915 until Eugene Levy—

a small-time Seattle showman—leased it and reopened it as the Hippodrome Theater that autumn. Critically, these and other decisions regarding the local vaudeville scene were made in New York City, San Francisco, and Seattle, not Spokane; Spokane interests were represented at distance, and most Spokanites learned the results through secondhand newspaper reports. Furthermore, metropolitan decisions often led to provincial decline: as the Orpheum-Loew's-Hippodrome passed from one circuit to another in 1914 and 1915, it clearly lost status in the vaudeville hierarchy.[90]

The Loew's uncertainty happened in mid-1915, concurrent with a second fruitless campaign to bring Orpheum productions back to Spokane. That summer, house managers both negotiated with "big-time powers" and asked local Orpheum fans for pledges. The effort's outcome demonstrated Spokane's middling position within the system of cities: community leaders—hoteliers prominent among them—again lobbied for the big time, knowing it would draw people from the hinterland, but the Orpheum chiefs no longer saw Spokane as a worthwhile link in the northwestern chain.[91] Though big-time (or even big small-time) vaudeville service mattered very much to Spokanites and their business interests, Spokane mattered less and less to the New York moguls.

The vaudeville stage in Spokane suffered in the mid-1910s, but (largely because of Alexander Pantages) the big small-time recovered and even flourished in the city into the 1920s. The same could not be said of the "legit." Despite its cachet, legitimate theater had been in trouble since the late 1900s, partially because of the public preference for vaudeville and partly (increasingly) because of the movies.[92] The race to build theaters throughout North America left the Syndicate, the Shuberts, and others financially incapable of sending the best productions on tour, which augmented the frustrations of already skeptical audiences. Added to the hardships of World War I, these conditions made unsound business out of legitimate road shows and left places like Spokane starved for the cream of New York. For highbrows (of whom Spokane had its share), access to good legitimate theater signified the cultural advancement of themselves and their city, and the loss of legitimate made the Inland Northwest feel like a backwater.

Still, in August 1914, the *Spokesman-Review* predicted Spokane's "fattest" season ever.[93] The Great War, however, rendered the season exceedingly slim—even on Broadway—as productions were postponed and production companies fell apart. Broadway soon revived; the stage in Spokane did not.[94] By the spring of 1915 Spokanites had to admit their dependency on metropolitan forces for high-quality theater. After a series of mishaps, "garbled" information in "eastern trade papers" portrayed the Spokane market as unprofitable, despite evidence of the city's regular and profitable theatergoing. Communication networks and geography had again combined to Spokane's disadvantage. Five theaters sat dark that summer, and although the theater columnists divined a fine fall season, notable attractions remained few and far between. This dismal situation was only to continue into the latter half of the decade, by which point most Spokanites had lost whatever taste they had for straight drama.[95]

As legitimate road shows dwindled, well-heeled theatergoers welcomed performers and genres that had been shunned by their social class only a few years earlier. This occurred in part because of changing preferences but also because of the kinds of shows Spokane's houses could offer. For instance, highbrows had long regarded stock theater as legitimate's poor relation—a format troubled by overworked actors, out-dated plays, cheap prices, and vulgar crowds. By the mid-1910s, however, stock was the best straight theater Spokanites enjoyed with any regularity. City newspapers noted the recent improvements in stock and hailed it as the hope of the legitimate stage. When stock companies began their residencies at Spokane theaters, local critics praised them; when the same troupes proved mediocre, the critics were somewhat quieter. This is not to say that respectable or affluent Spokanites had in the past avoided all performances from the middle and lower ends of the cultural spectrum; these groups had a record of theatrical slumming. What had changed was the frequency and broad acceptance of formerly déclassé genres such as stock. Because Spokane society could no longer turn out in force for famous Shakespeareans, it did so for the American Players.[96]

By 1917 Spokanites understood that they were living in the theatrical hinterland. Critics for the *Spokesman-Review* particularly noted the city's diminished status in relation to New York. The newspaper's theater page referred repeatedly to Spokane as an outpost in "the provinces" and remarked that plays with the full New York cast and production intact could arrive in Inland Northwest only rarely, happy though such an event would be.[97] Twice that year the dream was realized; critically, this happened through the New York chiefs Klaw and Erlanger and not because of any native clout or persuasion. Just so, the prospect of stellar shows did not diminish the sense of civic envy, which Hannah Hinsdale made clear by writing that, with *Very Good Eddie*, "Spokane can fool itself into being New York for three nights at least."[98] Similarly, Wilbur Hindley described his cynicism with the advertising ploy of "New York production," and how Klaw and Erlanger answered that doubt with a tour of *Miss Springtime* that (with seven railroad cars) would preserve every detail of the metropolitan production and bring to smaller cities the best theatrical spectacle they could hope for that fall. When the publicity proved accurate, the *Spokesman-Review* commented that "Klaw and Erlanger waved their fairy wand and a bit of old Broadway appeared at the Auditorium."[99]

The lesson was obvious. New York controlled the American stage, and Spokane was New York's far-flung subject. If Inland Northwesterners wanted blue-ribbon entertainment, they depended on the decisions of big-city businessmen as well as the transportation networks that delivered such amusement. At other points, notably the 1890 opening of the Auditorium, Spokanites had insisted that their artistic achievements and choices situated the city within the so-called borders of civilization. During the late 1910s Spokanites could surely claim a spot in this geographic imagining of the American cultural order, but as in earlier years, not without qualification— the geography of capitalism determined Spokane's place within the geography of urbanity. The final proof of this came with a development that became the Auditorium's coup de grâce. As the *Spokesman-Review* critic Margaret Bean put it, sometime after World War I, the construction of a road south from Seattle made Spokane an unprofitable outlier for touring shows, which "would come up the line into Seattle [from Los Angeles], and we were left over here in the boondocks. Then nothing but stock companies played in that theater."[100]

To argue that Spokane's professional stage deteriorated after the mid-1910s suggests that the city welcomed uniformly superior shows until that point. This was not the case. From the 1890s to the 1910s local managers often struggled to secure leading attractions. Even at the climax of their careers Spokane's premier houses—the rival Auditorium and Spokane—presented shoddy, middling productions that gave no glory to their names. During their best years, moreover, these theaters made ends meet by serving as a venue for rallies, benefits, or ceremonies, or they simply sat dark.[101] Conversely, Spokanites received a few outstanding acts such as the Ballets Russes even as professional shows increasingly passed by the city. What made the difference, by World War I, was that Spokane was no longer a growth market that metropolitan decision-makers wanted to capture and capitalize on. Consequently, the inland city no longer possessed the quality of connections it needed to maintain a vital theatrical scene.

CHAPTER FIVE

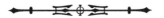

The Respectable Stage and the Sources of Indecency

Helen Campbell lived a glamorous life. Born to Amasa and Grace Campbell in 1892, she enjoyed both the luxury that her father's mining wealth could buy and the growing personal freedom available to the twentieth-century new woman. In her diary, which she kept from 1913 to 1917, Campbell recorded a life of golf, tennis, and voting, metropolitan shopping trips, and débutante balls. Theatergoing—whether to opera, legitimate, vaudeville, or movies—counted among Campbell's most frequent activities. From April 1913 to April 1916, she watched at least 195 shows in Spokane, New York City, and elsewhere, either with a party or with a male companion.[1] Moreover, activities and styles adapted from the stage became part of her social life. Around 1914 she began attending the tea dances that society called *thés dansants*. Dansants had gained popularity in New York about two years earlier when cabaret impresarios built dance floors that allowed their affluent patrons to try the new steps performed by exhibition dancers. After a pair of fashionable sisters imported dansants to Spokane, elite young women like Campbell spent many an afternoon dancing the tango at the Davenport Hotel.[2]

Only a decade earlier, upright Spokanites had been protesting—or, rather, continuing to protest—the presence of variety theaters and dance halls in their city, institutions that, while much seamier than the venues attended by Campbell, offered similar entertainment. The differing standards of acceptance were not solely a matter of change over time, for concurrent with efforts to close the varieties was a flowering of legitimate and vaudeville theaters that often presented off-color or challenging acts. How did Spokanites respond to provocative shows at what might problematically be called respectable

The Davenport Restaurant in downtown Spokane, 1908. Louis Davenport added a large hotel to his restaurant in 1914. Here, Spokane's elite enjoyed

theaters—places where women and girls could appear without ruining their reputations? In Spokane, such theaters ranged from posh venues dedicated primarily to legitimate performances (especially the Auditorium and the Spokane) to the city's many vaudeville houses (especially the Orpheum and Pantages). The difference between variety and respectable theaters did not necessarily come from the content performed on their stages; both types of theaters presented plenty of the light farcical material and mixed-format shows that highbrows disdained. Rather, Spokane's legitimate and vaudeville theaters remained above the variety theater taint because of the national or regional reputations of the artists they presented, their disassociation from local politics and working-class male culture, and particularly, the absence of alcohol and gambling from their premises. Thus, a young woman of irreproachable standing such as Helen Campbell could safely watch vaudeville lineups and dance in a public setting.

a lavish setting for their social life, which included the tango. Haines Photograph Company. Courtesy Library of Congress, 2007662982.

This is not to say that clerics and columnists did not wring their hands over the material billed at allegedly respectable theaters. Certain shows frequently offended certain Spokanites, overwhelmingly because of how those acts treated womanhood and sexuality. In this regard, the houses that exhibited such shows had much in common with the variety theaters. A number of genres and styles were denounced as obscene—namely, problem plays, bedroom farces, girl shows, and staged ragtime dances.[3] Meanwhile, three themes emerge: the changing ideal of womanhood, the transition from Victorian to modern values, and the perceived sources of impropriety, tied to places, racial groups, and social classes.

Performances across a spectrum of genres in Spokane manifested the trend toward a more public, pleasure-seeking, and loosened atmosphere as well as a less controlled femininity. Spokanites cast this shift in mores in a geographic light by blaming immorality on outside places, particularly New York City and Paris. The local apologists had a point: most of the acts they watched at legitimate and vaudeville houses came via the "road." That enormous network of financial agreements and transportation technologies was centered on New York and annually shipped thousands of performers to the far reaches of the continent, thereby repackaging and distributing cultural elements from a host of sources.[4] Filtered through New York producers, many of the offending acts originated in the slums of Paris, Buenos Aires, or San Francisco. Occasionally, however, Spokanites could not ignore that the perceived smut was grown (and obviously enjoyed) in their own backyard. On such occasions the city's residents shunned those entertainments and artists that made them look vulgar and welcomed others that made them appear cosmopolitan.

The Staging of Womanhood and the Geography of Indecency

Throughout the nineteenth century, women and femininity served as key markers of the respectability of a theater or a performance. At midcentury, when showmen began expanding the appeal of their theaters, they did so by courting the patronage of middle-class women. While the presence of "decent" women in an audience could certify a theater's propriety, the women behind the footlights were just as important. From the foundations of their nation, Americans had looked askance at theater and particularly the women who performed on its stages. Doubts about actresses lingered on through the nineteenth century, though many of these women had clean reputations. Things visual, after all, played a major role in things theatrical: when women appeared onstage, they offered themselves up to public—and perhaps sexual—view.[5] The respectability of an actress and the decency of a show were never quite iron-clad.

By the first years of the twentieth century, however, the substance and appearance of touring productions made it clear that perceptions of women, the place of women in the public sphere, and the relations between the genders were undergoing enormous change. For instance, the growth of theatergoing had allowed some actresses to build successful careers, which in turn inspired female audience members on to their own achievements. On the other hand, American tastes had moved away from the Jacksonian-era preference for the spoken word toward a celebration of the visual; for women, this meant a glorification of youthful beauty and an objectification of actresses.[6] Meanwhile, both the legitimate and vaudeville industries joined the debate over modern femininity by presenting plays and sketches on issues such as female suffrage, working women, and shifting marital expectations. Spokane audiences watched such plays and witnessed these trends.

Patrons of the city's best theaters strongly supported three genres—problem plays, farces, and girl shows—that reflected and influenced the evolution of womanhood. Local conservatives, meanwhile, denounced the shows precisely because they dealt so directly with sexuality and unconventional femininity. Conservative Spokanites blamed outsiders for these shows and imagined a geography of indecency, where perversion from Europe and the East traveled through show-business networks to corrupt Spokane. Yet these detractors never developed adequate methods for censoring the popular shows. When clergymen castigated one of the city's favorite daughters for portraying lewd women and wearing clinging gowns, Spokanites rallied behind the actress, not the ministers: the dynamics of stage, morality, and local identity were complicated indeed.

Problem plays, as contemporaries called them, were works from the late nineteenth and early twentieth centuries that used realism to probe social dilemmas such as the double standard in social conventions or the introduction of demimondaines into the haut monde. The genre included Arthur Wing Pinero's *The Second Mrs. Tanqueray*, George Bernard Shaw's *Mrs. Warren's Profession*, and Clyde Fitch's *Sapho*; the genre was especially associated with the work of Henrik Ibsen. Problem plays often focused on strong, sensual, or tainted women, and several actresses spent their careers portraying these characters. Despite the literary quality of many problem plays, their frank exploration of taboos and the vigorous "emotional" style of the leading women rendered them shocking, even filthy, in the eyes of some viewers. The problem of the play was often the unorthodox behavior or sexuality of a woman, whether this woman was character or actress.[7]

Scandalous though the problem plays may have been for the more conventional, Spokane's theatergoers loved them. Throughout the

1900s newspapers reported that large audiences attended high-priced productions of *Zaza, Sapho, Magda, Camille, Ann LaMont, Hedda Gabler, Ghosts, Mrs. Dane's Defense, The Second Mrs. Tanqueray,* and *The Notorious Mrs. Ebbsmith.*[8] Likewise, the Women's Club of Spokane noted that its members had benefited much from their study of *A Doll's House,* Ibsen's treatise on female independence.[9] Spokanites had a particular affinity for a play and an actress, *Sapho* and Olga Nethersole, described as animal, vulgar, passionate, and salacious—the very opposite of controlled Victorian womanhood.

Fitch and Nethersole's version of *Sapho,* taken from a French novel, told the story of a worldly artist's model and her involvement with a young man from the country. It concerned the consequences of illicit passion and contained moments of unmistakable intent. By the time of *Sapho*'s premiere in February 1900, New Yorkers and many of their countrymen had watched the agonies of more than one fallen woman. Conservatives, however, saw something different in *Sapho* and moved immediately to have it suppressed. The difference was Nethersole. Onstage the British actress threw off the rules of female propriety with her presence and behavior, which included actions appropriate to the character (baring her feet, blowing her nose, crawling, wailing, smoking) but not at all appropriate to Victorian womanhood. Offstage, Nethersole—single, self-made, and successful—personified the new woman. The petitions and sermons of disgusted anti-vice crusaders landed Nethersole in court, but after highly publicized proceedings, both play and player enjoyed great popularity in New York and across the nation.[10]

Throughout the 1900s Spokanites turned out in force for repeat engagements by Nethersole and of *Sapho.* Whether given by Nethersole or less famous emotional actresses such as Florence Roberts, these engagements always included performances of other problem plays, for which local audiences had an obvious taste. Yet these were still shows about courtesans, music-hall girls, illegitimate children, and ruined innocents, facts that did not prove affluent Spokanites to have the cleanest of taste. Local theater critics dealt with this civic embarrassment by admitting the brilliance of a production and then figuratively shaking the dust from Spokane's feet by assigning the moral blame of problem plays to decadent European mores. *Sapho* provided a perfect opportunity for this, with its British star, French origins, and "thoroughly French" setting.[11]

For instance, immediately before an appearance of Nethersole in *Sapho* and similar vehicles in 1907, the *Spokesman-Review* reprinted commentary on George Ade's *County Chairman* that readers could not help but take as a critique of the problem plays and their sources. *County Chairman* portrayed midwestern life in the 1880s. Of his subject, Ade asked, "Why bother about foreign problem plays, which are foreign in every sense to the American understanding? I know the country people of the middle west, loved them, was brought up among them and still spend my happiest hours in their society."[12] Coming, as it did, just prior to a week of Nethersole shows, this statement provided a pointed contrast between perceptions of American purity and French depravity. Spokanites, in other words, might have enjoyed—and financially supported—stories about seduction at Parisian masquerades, but the debauchery did not originate with them.[13]

Problem plays such as *Sapho* dealt with taboos, promoted female autonomy (to a degree), and criticized the inequality inherent in the Victorian marriage. For all of these reasons they offended conservatives.[14] In contrast to the dread seriousness of problem plays, bedroom farces and girl shows treated sex flippantly: they winked at marital indiscretions and presented women as objects of desire. These genres were also enormously popular in Spokane and, at the same time, easy to blame on the purported wickedness of outsiders. Like problem plays, local reception of farces and girl shows followed something of a formula: through national circuits, a traveling show would play at the Spokane or the Auditorium to large audiences. After Spokanites realized the show's nature, a critic would express his disgust using the same forum—city newspapers—that had recently advertised the play. If the critic sought an explanation, he chose to find it in the metropolitan or foreign producers and degenerating modern tastes. At this point, however, audiences had supplied theater managers and circuit officials with evidence enough that such shows would thrive in Spokane. Both daring acts and lucrative crowds kept returning to Spokane's theaters, and by the 1910s plays that were free of innuendo or immodesty were a surprise to the critics.[15]

Farces—light comedies with fantastical plots—had filled Spokane's theaters since the 1890s, far more than the serious legitimate plays championed by the highbrows.[16] But Spokanites also enjoyed a variant of the farce that might be called the bedroom farce; playwrights introduced these shows to English-speaking audiences in the late 1800s when they began adapting the "well-made-plays" of French authors. In the "deodorized" English versions, these comedies used humorous situations and double entendre to dance around sexual issues in a manner titillating to genteel audiences.[17] A decade after the "Frenchified" plays of the 1890s had run their course, another batch of bedroom farces, often adapted from continental sources, crowded the American stage. As with the earlier shows, the farces popular around 1910 had plots built on divorce, remarriage, and at least the suggestion of infidelity; furthermore, they were set among people and places reputed for fast living.[18] In plays such as Fitch's *The Blue Mouse* and Paul M. Potter's *The Girl from Rector's* and *The Queen of the Moulin Rouge,* middle Americans became acquainted with the showgirls and rakes rumored to haunt the nightspots of Paris and Broadway; accordingly, audiences in Spokane and around the nation found these farces both exciting and prurient.[19]

Turn-of-the-century Spokanites flocked to a final type of charged performance: the girl show. Visual display, and hence female display, supplied the raison d'être for productions within this broad category, which included burlesques, musical comedies, and chorus girl revues. Spectacles and burlesques gained popularity in America after the Civil War, when impresarios discovered that the overt use of female beauty almost guaranteed monetary success. By the twentieth century American producers were staging musical comedies that replaced the beefcake appeal of burlesque queens with the youthful suggestiveness of chorus girls. Finally, with the rise of Florence Ziegfeld in the mid-1900s, objectified, interchangeable, and gorgeously costumed young women became the focus of revues. The local theatergoers who consumed the many touring girl shows could not fail to grasp that these were exhibitions of physical, bodily appeal, and consequently, female sexuality.[20]

As with problem plays, Spokanites were predictable in their reactions to girl shows and bedroom farces: critics and ministers might have been scandalized but the audiences were enthusiastic. Those who disapproved of the shows gave the facile explanation that these things originated outside Spokane. They could do so in part because of the transmission of plays across the theatrical circuits but also because of the persistence and growth of negative stereotypes. This was especially the case with representations of French culture. Since at least the early republican period, Americans had characterized the French as decadent, a perception Americans likely acquired from the English. For Spokanites and others, the mere connection of a play with France was almost enough to condemn (or recommend) it as wanton. The *Spokesman-Review*'s appraisal of *The Red Rose* exemplifies this association of France with lasciviousness. Of the girl-filled extravaganza, the newspaper remarked, "If the old Paris settings and plot, hovering near the brink of true Paris licentiousness, have not lost their appeal in the years of burlesque and musical comedy, the one charm of *The Red Rose* is assured."[21]

With the twentieth century New York City acquired a similar reputation. Americans for decades had considered cities to be sites of moral danger, but with the development of a famous public nightlife New York came to rival Paris in provincial imaginations.[22] Beginning in the late 1890s, for example, restaurateurs established "lobster palaces" along Broadway that, despite lavish interiors and menus, welcomed the fast after-show crowd. Rector's especially became known for its late-night "bird and bottle suppers," where wealthy roués treated the chorus girls. To many Americans, these restaurants were dressed-up places of assignation. Broadway's nightlife pushed against the edges of Victorian morality by creating spaces for men and women to socialize publicly, indiscriminately.[23] The city's reputation was assured.

Lobster palaces and cabarets were not the sole reason Americans raised their eyebrows at Broadway. As the entertainment industry centralized in the late nineteenth century, New York became the national hub for all aspects of the business. Middle-class Americans had long suspected show people of loose living, and now great numbers of show people congregated in the metropolis. More important, because New York was the point of distribution (and often production) for new styles and shows, provincial Americans considered New Yorkers to be guilty of sending the country smut. For example, in 1913, Howard Hindley of the *Spokesman-Review* laughed at the metropolis's reaction to a "white slavery" play, comparing it to shows like *The Girl from Rector's*, a bedroom farce about a demimondaine. Hindley remarked that "to one at all familiar" with *The Girl from Rector's* and other ribald plays, "New York's little spasm of virtue over *The Lure* and *The Fight* seems amusing. Just why the metropolis should grin satyr-like over the gilded vice in the first-mentioned and recoil from its darker phases in the latter productions is something of a mystery."[24] Hindley went on to mention the presence of out-of-town theatergoers—including himself—at questionable Broadway shows, but he ultimately blamed the cynicism of New Yorkers for both the production and the acceptance of "gilded vice." Hindley and other Spokane critics would have agreed with the *American Magazine* writers who attributed the prevalence of salacious road shows to the New York chieftains who controlled the American theatrical circuits.[25]

Between Rector's and Ritzville

Ostensibly, then, Spokane's response to provocative shows at respectable theaters could be summarized by the *Spokesman-Review*'s appraisal of a Gaby Deslys revue. In January 1914 the Parisian dancer packed the Auditorium and took with her one of the largest profits in the history of that house. According to the newspaper, Deslys's display of "flesh and fringe" left the audience with a "disillusionment too deep for words." The reviewer noted that many a spectator had whispered, "If that is Paris, then give me Spokane, Washington!"[26] Here was the alleged substance of Spokane's moral geography: middle- and upper-class Spokanites may have contributed to the commercial success of daring plays and performers, but in the end they recognized these things as foreign to their way of life, as imports that sullied Spokane and must be rejected. The reality of Spokane's experience with the staging of modern womanhood and the reputed sources of prurient theater was, of course, more complicated than the refrain of "If that is Paris . . . give me Spokane."

To begin with, affluent Spokanites could engage in a reciprocal relationship with the metropolises caricatured on stage and in print. Consider the education of Helen Campbell. At sixteen the mining heiress moved to Paris for a year of finishing school. Campbell's peers, the Murphey sisters, similarly spent a year in Europe in anticipation of their joint 1911 debut. For that event and "in order to live up to Spokane's expectations," the young women purchased their entire wardrobes in the French capital.[27] Campbell had a direct relationship with theater and nightlife in New York, as well, as did other wealthy Spokanites. Campbell and her mother spent several weeks each winter in the East, the bulk of it in New York City, to shop and visit friends. While in New York Campbell seemed hungry to enjoy as much theater as possible, attending Broadway productions almost every evening and sometimes more than once a day. This was not all. During her 1915 visit Campbell apprehensively "went to 'Rectors'"—sports and chorus girls notwithstanding—and made the telling remark, "Didn't want to go there but couldn't help myself."[28] Spokane moralists might denounce Paris and Broadway, but the city's first families allowed their daughters to travel to the belly of the beast.

Second, Spokane's place within a geography of indecent theater had far more points of contact and exchange than is suggested by the concept that put the inland city simply on the receiving end of questionable shows. Spokane theaters belonged to several national circuits that connected the city to American and European cultural centers and allowed it to host productions from around the world. But while Spokane had a middling, receiving position within these broader urban hierarchies and economic geographies, it sat squarely atop the hierarchy of regional towns and hamlets: New York was surely the cultural center of American, but Spokane was the cultural center of the Inland Northwest, the local seat of obscenity. In 1912, for instance, the Auditorium presented Anna Held in *Miss Innocence*, a Ziegfeld extravaganza thick with girls and innuendo. What purpose, then, did Spokane serve to the bankers who traveled from throughout the Inland Northwest to do some business but especially to attend the opening night of *Miss Innocence*?[29] While the promise

Helen Campbell and her cousin Hazel Lease, dressed in Turkish costume, c. 1910. Campbell watched productions with Orientalist themes, such as *Omar the Tentmaker*, throughout the 1910s. Northwest Museum of Arts and Culture/ Eastern Washington State Historical Society, Spokane, Washington, L90-272.

of Held's "transplanted-from-Paris" brand of entertainment could draw regional theatergoers to Spokane, the inland hub also had its share of actors and actresses who tried for national success in legitimate, vaudeville, and film.[30] These Spokane natives might have included the young women who graduated from Pauline Dunstan's acting school, but they certainly also included a man who had passed as a chorus girl in several New York productions.[31] Spokanites, in other words, both bought and sold on the marketplace of theater and sexual choices.

Perhaps early twentieth-century Spokanites gave such mixed reactions because they lived at a time of tremendous social and cultural change. By the late 1900s and early 1910s Victorian ideals were becoming increasingly outmoded. Theater reflected this shift in ideals—especially the evolving nature of womanhood—and it was certain to prompt discussion among those who felt the order of their world threatened by the spectacle on stage. At times the sense of anxiety and transition seemed palpable. In 1909, for instance, the *Chronicle* noted that the most "vicious, subtle, immoral, and brutal" aspect of the modern stage was its mockery of marriage and fidelity.[32] Yet the *Chronicle* itself advertised and reviewed many a show with just these tendencies. Spokanites vacillated in their opinions regarding the social change that theater brought and reflected; this became especially apparent in two instances involving stock actresses, Frances Slosson and Jessie Shirley. Because Slosson and Shirley led resident stock companies and were accepted in local society, they could not be dismissed as contagions introduced via the road. Their treatment revealed much about how Spokanites dealt with proof of shifting values among themselves.

The Slosson incident began in February 1911, in the dressing rooms of the Spokane. As Slosson, lead actress of the Baker Stock Company, read her lines for an upcoming production of *If I Were King*, she realized she was cast in a role that required her to wear scarlet tights.[33] She immediately protested, but her superiors let her know that she could choose the tights or her job. Her response was significant: "I won't! I won't! I have never worn [tights] and I never will. What would my friends think if I started to wear tights now?"[34] Slosson had good cause to object to the tights. For decades women's

Anna Held at the turn of the century. This image of the Polish-born French actress portrays her charm as well as some of the polite naughtiness associated with her brand. Held played in Spokane to appreciative audiences. Aimé Dupont, 1900. Courtesy Library of Congress, LC-USZ62-55901.

clothing had kept the lower half of the body concealed, hiding a woman's form beneath a barrier of cloth. The sight of a full female silhouette, therefore, had erotic appeal. Further, tights were associated with genres such as burlesque that cultivated "sporting" male audiences and pushed social boundaries.[35] By 1911 theatergoers had become somewhat inured to risqué costumes, but the sight of a woman's legs could still be electrifying. Not long after Slosson's protest, for example, a preacher asked Spokanites if they would like to see their own daughters and sisters "strut out on stage in tights" for the pleasure of "men with lustful eyes."[36]

There was more to Slosson's stance than the tights, however. She also worried that if she wore the tights, polite people would reject her. As the *Spokesman-Review* put it, Slosson had been "ushered into Spokane society . . . and has always had her ideals of stage life. On this she bases her refusal to wear the tights."[37] At this point American social leaders had finally accepted some performers into their company as equals—but only just.[38] An actress could still carry the stain of a public woman who offered her life and her charms up for indiscriminate enjoyment. It was telling that Slosson insisted she had "ideals" that safely guided her through "stage life" and that she must maintain the respect of her friends outside the theatrical world. After Slosson's protests became widely known, she grew even more sensitive about how the *If I Were King* role might affect her reputation. She was slated to play Huguette, a fifteenth-century French woman dressed in men's clothing. During the play a male character asks Huguette the purpose of her garb, to which she responds, "to please myself, and to show my fine shape to please others."[39] Slosson feared that this line might leave the impression that she went onstage to gratify male desires and insisted that it be changed. Altogether, her grievances hinted at the minefield of inferences and expectations that an actress faced in society.

Slosson won the day in the end. She received more than a score of notes and telephone calls congratulating her resolve and urging her to continue steadfast. Meanwhile, Baker Stock officials resolved the conflict by devising a less revealing costume.[40] The "tights fight" of February 1911 suggested that Spokanites wanted to protect the

purity of women and of their own polite society—that is, if one
ignored the Baker program for March 1911. The troupe opened
March with Fitch's *The Blue Mouse*, a farce with a checklist of racy
elements: partial undress, hints of adultery, broad flirtation, and the
attentions of a lecher. Its most culturally laden character was the
"blue mouse" called Paulette Devine, a showgirl who was kept by her
lovers and famed for her "Salome" dance—an Orientalist, sometimes erotic style descended from Richard Strauss's opera. In this
comedy, which was far more suggestive than *If I Were King*, Slosson
played Devine, with no reported objections and no public commentary. Rather, the newspapers only noted that Slosson made a "decided
hit" and that full audiences packed the Spokane Theater for an entire
week of shows.[41] Why did Slosson and Spokanites accept *The Blue
Mouse* and reject the red tights? Perhaps Slosson had worn out
whatever power she had with the tights affair and was loathe to risk
her career. As for middle-class Spokanites, they had every reason not
to vilify a woman whose virtue they had already certified and a play
they had so plainly supported.[42]

While Spokanites welcomed Frances Slosson, they made an institution of Jessie Shirley.[43] Beginning in 1902 the Jessie Shirley Stock
Company played a string of summer gigs at the Auditorium, and in
1905 the company took up residence there. This engagement lasted
for an astounding four years and six weeks. Throughout their time
at the Auditorium, Shirley and her troupe kept the 1,500-seat house
filled with carefully staged productions of stock repertoire.[44] Shirley
herself became particularly beloved of Spokanites, who flocked to
her performances, received her socially, and adopted her as one
of their own.[45] The intensity of Shirley's identification with middle-
class Spokane—and how that identification related to feminine
ideals—became clear in 1909 when the actress engaged in a public
conversation about the place of theater in decent society. That January a group of ministers brought the evangelist Billy Sunday to
Spokane, hoping that his plainspoken, slang-filled style would appeal
to the masses of workingmen who passed through the city.[46] During
his visit Spokane became saturated with the preacher's ideas, which
the local newspapers covered at length. Sunday's sermons lingered
on the evil effects of certain amusements and especially condemned

theater, portraying it as a wasteland hated by God and kept afloat by leg shows.[47]

This was too much for Jessie Shirley, who responded with a long and confident exoneration of the stage. Shirley defended her profession with arguments couched in the Victorian values of religiosity, high thinking, pure womanhood, and self-control. For instance, she opened by stating her credentials as "the daughter of a minister, and a student of the Bible" and then discredited Sunday by noting his popularity among "low brows" for his use of "smut and slang." Likewise, though Shirley admitted that not all plays were clean, she connected the theater to accepted forces of morality. Finally, she answered the one accusation that touched her personally—that actresses were almost harlots—by stating that, in all her years on stage, she could only recall one or two women "of whose morality there was the slightest question." Yet Shirley made a complex case. To Sunday's assertion that theater must go, she replied that the dark ages of witch hunts and bigotry had happily given way to "twentieth-century progress" and an appreciation of the stage's power to uplift. Even as she sought the sanction of nineteenth-century ideals, Shirley claimed twentieth-century modernity.[48]

Shirley's ruffled answer hinted at the opprobrium an actress might endure. Many Spokanites, however, soon demonstrated their preference for the ideas of the actress over those of the evangelist. After the *Chronicle* published her letter, Shirley received numerous notes and telephone calls, most of them approving her position. Her supporters included at least one clergyman and, perhaps more important, many women. Like Shirley they claimed the Victorian high ground in their defense of the stage and Shirley's public persona. They could do so because of Sunday's sensational, street-smart style. Sunday studded his sermons with patois ("low down," "tommyrot," "lobster") that felt vulgar in every sense to bourgeois listeners, since much slang originated in peripheral subcultures.[49] Several correspondents remarked that Shirley's article expressed the opinions of "thinking," "civilized," "educated" people repulsed by Sunday. These writers did not connect themselves to the "higher thinking class" in a vacuum.[50] Sunday's revival, though sponsored by ministers, became thoroughly associated with the hundreds of transient workers who crowded into his tabernacle that icy winter. Further, in a few months Spokane would erupt with class-based anger as the Industrial Workers of the World (IWW) and the city government scrimmaged over the rights of laborers.[51] The tensions that led to the IWW free speech fight of late 1909 certainly existed earlier in the year, making the statements of Shirley's supporters pregnant indeed.

These people upheld one element of the Victorian code—the manifestation of intellectual refinement through clean speech—but they walked away from the insistence that women should remain cloistered and submissive and that performances must be uplifting, not merely entertaining. First, the letters commending Shirley expressed a belief that a woman could display spunk, live at least part of her life publicly, and still remain a true woman. The Reverend W. L. Bull congratulated Shirley for her moxie but took pains to address her as a lady.[52] Mrs. W. R. Brown praised (and employed) a combination of gameness and propriety when she commended both Shirley's response to the evangelist and her stage productions, none of which Brown considered "the least bit objectionable." She wrote, "I read your attack on the famous Billy Sunday and I am so glad that one lone little woman has nerve and spirit enough to 'sass him back.'" That a woman could appear on stage, openly "sass" a man, and still merit ladylike treatment signified much. Likewise, Anna Deems associated Shirley with ideal femininity even as she noted the actress's public role as an entertainer. "I honor you," Deems wrote, "for your noble defense of your faith, your work, and your matchless womanhood." To Deems and others, dignity, education, and an avoidance of sensationalism mattered more than homebound femininity or strict religiosity. Second, Shirley's supporters rejected the Victorian disdain for amusements as they noted—in twentieth-century fashion—that one could and should seek enjoyment. And yet they could not abide Sunday's twentieth-century casualness. T. W. Butler portrayed this ambivalence when he commented, "I indulge the pleasure of seeing and hearing you frequently on the stage, but have seldom had a greater pleasure than in reading your reply to Sunday. . . . Billy is surely disgusting."[53]

As with the problem plays and other risqué shows, the response to Shirley's letter proved that the move to modern values was halting and mixed. The actress's detractors, like her supporters, placed certain aspects of Victorianism above others: Sunday's profanity could be tolerated, but Shirley's worldliness could not. One Adolph Cameron called the actress a hypocrite for espousing Christianity and yet keeping youth away from church with her Sabbath-day performances. Even worse, he argued, were the hints of sensual or unorthodox femininity in Shirley's productions. Cameron knew all of this because he had attended Shirley company shows "time and again." Cameron's opinions were reprinted in *War on the Theater,* a pamphlet in which the Reverend Henry Brown compiled several open and private letters about the Shirley article, indicating the level of comment the article had generated among opinion leaders. Like Cameron, Brown's polemic especially attacked Shirley for displaying her body and for introducing to Spokane a form-fitting French gown, the directoire. He castigated Shirley as a public woman, almost as a pariah, despite her acceptance in polite company as Mrs. Harry Smith.[54] But though Brown wanted to turn back the clock on social approval of the stage and its personnel, he represented a decided minority.[55]

The minister's efforts to connect Shirley's alleged corruption to outside standards fell flat in the face of evidence that bourgeois Spokane adored the stock actress. Brown's harangue about a "nasty French play" meant little compared to the many northwesterners who wished Shirley well and the many more whose theatergoing made the Shirley Company an unqualified success.[56] Altogether, Spokanites gave a complicated response—but one that leaned toward permissiveness—to legitimate stage productions that challenged nineteenth-century ideals of womanhood and propriety. Ministers and columnists surely denounced the shows and attempted to blame them on external influences, but activities in and of Spokane belied such claims. Wealthy Spokanites like Helen Campbell frequented New York and Paris; Spokane's people made *resident* troupes welcome and profitable; and the inland city itself served as an exchange point between metropolitan trends and the provincial Northwest. Whatever they professed in their personal lives, middle-class Spokanites enjoyed watching depictions of physically attractive or socially daring women enough that they purchased thousands of tickets to see the Saphos, Miss Innocents, and Girls from Rector's offered up to them.

Ragtime: Vaudeville, Sexuality, and Civic Control

Between the heights of the legitimate stage (such as they were) and the depths of variety theater existed a vastly popular middle ground—vaudeville. In the late 1800s impresarios recognized the potential of a structure with the accessibility of variety and the respectability of legitimate and moved mixed-format shows into settings that were palatable to middle-class families. With animals, actors, acrobats, musicians, dancers, and comics, vaudeville had something for everyone, at the mid-range cost of between ten and twenty-five cents. How vaudevillians dealt with propriety provided much of the genre's appeal. On one hand, the managers of national circuits and individual theaters assured upstanding customers that they had scrubbed every act clean. On the other hand, artists slipped plenty of slang, slapstick, and innuendo into their routines, often because audiences demanded it. As Andrew Erdman notes, this made sense, for vaudeville thrived in an era of "contest and change" regarding human sexuality. Finally, the urbanism of vaudeville—with its fast pace, neat packaging, big-city themes, and ethnic performers—added to its danger and fascination. This genre, in other words, often hovered near the edge of disrepute.[57]

The outrageousness of vaudeville troubled reformers, educators, and politicians as much as it delighted audience members in search of snappy, modern diversions. In 1912, for instance, speakers at a Spokane parent-teacher conference warned that vaudeville was damaging the development of "sensation mad" youths. Students at that school did patronize the stage—160 students attended a theater once a month, 135 went once a week, 30 went two or three times a week, and 7 watched a show almost nightly.[58] With these rates of attendance, theatergoers could not help but be influenced by the trends presented onstage; this process created anxiety and carried significance because such styles often originated among the poor and the nonwhite, making vaudeville a conduit that transmitted culture from the margins to the middle of society. Intimate couple dances (including the *danse des apaches*, the animal dances, and the tango) figured prominently among the cultural forms dispersed throughout the United States by vaudevillians and others. In the years just prior to World War I, mainstream Americans became crazed with

the steps they saw presented by exhibition dancers. They participated in a tremendous restructuring of how men and women interacted in public. Spokanites, too, were swept up in the "freak dances"
and the changes to which they contributed.

The new dances had "savage," subversive genealogies and an air
of abandon. These aspects repelled traditionalists and attracted
individuals, particularly women and youths, who were yearning for
that very abandon. The apache dance, for instance, was inspired
by the underclass Parisian gangsters nicknamed "apaches" for their
violent behavior, supposedly redolent of Native Americans in the
Wild West.[59] The dance itself was built on interchanges between a
brutally masculine apache and his girlfriend; its dips, swings, and
throws depicted a stormy, sexual, and abusive romance, hardly the
middle-class ideal.[60] Who first discovered or choreographed the
"apache waltz" remained disputed but how it traveled from the Parisian slums to Britain and the United States was clear—the stage.[61]
Via vaudeville, revues, and cabarets, astonished Americans watched
the dance described by the *Chronicle* as "the limit for toughness."
For their part, Spokanites welcomed the gangsters' dance throughout the early 1910s with enthusiasm and with little controversy. It was
obvious, however, that local audiences could only enjoy the alleged
savagery because of modern infrastructure: the city's first encounter
with an apache routine, scheduled for the Orpheum in 1910, was
delayed for days as the performers waited for the railroad car with
their scenery and costumes.[62]

Despite the sensation it caused, the apache dance did not transfer
easily from the stage to the ballroom; it was too physically demand-
ing. Amateurs could, however, replicate another set of dances filled
with "barbaric" pleasures. The animal or rag dances included the
Texas tommy, the turkey trot, the bunny hop, the grizzly bear, and
a host of other steps set to ragtime music. These exuberant couple
dances involved rocking, lifting, shaking, and hugging—a young man's
dream and a minister's nightmare. Their zoological names came
from joyful animal-like movements, such as jutting out the elbows to
resemble a turkey's wings. As Erenberg has argued, this alone disquali-
fied ragging from Victorian propriety, which demanded a suppression
of the animal and bodily in favor of the spiritual and mental.[63]

The source of the animal dances made them even more suspect in white middle-class eyes for, like ragtime music, they originated among African Americans.[64] The history of the Texas tommy and the turkey trot illustrates how rag dances spread from black vernacular to mainstream white culture. Around 1910 black artists performed the dances at cabarets such as Purcell's in the Barbary Coast, San Francisco's entertainment and red-light district. Among the "slummers" who watched the turkey and the tommy were Broadway figures who immediately recognized the commercial potential of the dances and hired black dancers to teach them the steps. Once the animal dances appeared on Broadway, they passed into numerous revues and routines and spread throughout the United States and Europe.[65] Here was a pedigree—at once black, underworld, working-class, Wild West, and theatrical—entirely outside the pale of so-called civilization.

Yet how Americans loved the rag. It was a style brimming with vitality, the excitement and release that affluent whites felt starved for, and after 1910 people of all sorts were trying the ragtime steps. From 1912 to 1914 about one hundred new dances were introduced to the stage and the ballroom. In the words of the *Spokesman-Review*, the craze burned across America like "prairie fire." Contemporary newspapers detailed the trend's progress in New York and Chicago, of course, but also in Wichita, Texas, in Anaconda, Montana, and Dayton, Washington.[66] Exhibition dancers, vaudeville theaters, and railroads were key to this transmission. Largely because of the stage, Spokanites had already heard ragtime music. When the animal dances arrived in town, they proved to be eager students. By January 1912 enough Spokanites had ragged that local clergymen specifically condemned the bunny hug, turkey trot, and grizzly bear as too sensual. In their lodges, hotels, dance halls, high schools, and homes, Spokanites danced on.[67] By January 1913 Mayor W. J. Hindley warned that things had reached a "serious pass." The city's youth particularly resisted the efforts of authority figures to subdue their enjoyment. How, one resident complained, could moralists stop freak dancing when couples watched "all sorts of 'rag' and fancy dances on the vaudeville stage every day, and nothing is said about

Spokane's experience with the movies during these years, especially with moviemaking, demonstrates that, though much had changed, much remained the same. Spokane was still a city trying to work out its identity and still an outpost in the entertainment industry—even as twentieth-century boosters called on J. J. Browne's old playbook by using theater to promote the Inland Northwest. Yet the city's people and critics accepted styles, subjects, and a medium that would have been seen as loose and cheap thirty years earlier.

Certainly, not everything was the same, for Spokane's flirtation with moviemaking occurred in a new theatrical era and represented the new order of things. For approximately twenty-five years, from 1890 to the mid-1910s, traveling legitimate, musical comedy, and vaudeville productions had visited Spokane theaters with frequency and success; from about 1900 to the 1920s, stock theater companies also played an important part in the city's entertainment scene. During these years the professional stage influenced and reflected the shift in ideals so evident in the years between the close of the nineteenth century and the beginning of the "Jazz Age." That Spokanites had conflicting responses to these changes became evident with their reactions to such episodes as the animal dance craze or the "tights fight." Then, by the 1920s—and with the exception of moving pictures—the city's professional stage began to lose steam.

Highbrow road shows, the productions for which J. J. Browne and A. M. Cannon had built the Auditorium, declined precipitously in the 1910s both because of competition among the theater moguls and because of the evolution of tastes and technology that fostered the movies. The Auditorium itself went through a protracted demise—complete with rats, candy wrappers, and third-rate entertainment—that ended in its destruction in 1934. Yet for residents of the inland city, the glory days of the Auditorium long served as a symbol of Spokane's "age of elegance."[5] Meanwhile, Spokane remained a good vaudeville market for much of the 1920s; it received a particular boost in 1926 when Alexander Pantages gave his theater there a lavish renovation. Publicity for the Pantages reopening echoed the intense local satisfaction evident at the Auditorium's 1890 debut: full-page advertisements announced that the Pantages's foremost purpose was to inspire pride that Spokane had such a showplace. This opening night featured a musical duo and a comic "photoplay," not an opera company.[6] Times had changed and would continue to change, with even vaudeville eventually losing ground to the movies.

As moving pictures rose to prominence in the 1910s, gender and sexuality remained topics of popular fascination and official concern, and Spokanites alternately flocked to and fussed over films that took up such issues as birth control and infidelity.[7] While the subject of theatrical controversies remained quite constant, the social character of Spokane's audiences became increasingly democratic from the 1890s to 1920. This happened largely because of the venues and genres available to Spokanites: expensive road shows, presented at the Auditorium and the Spokane, predominated from 1890 to the mid-1900s, when vaudeville finally provided a regular and somewhat respectable option at a "popular price." With the proliferation of movie houses in the 1910s, theatergoing became ever more accessible to Spokane's working class.

The increasing openness of the twentieth century was reflected in another trend in the city's theatergoing: a growing enjoyment of the western. Throughout the first decade of the century Inland Northwesterners watched many a staged western; these shows came to town because of both national touring companies and resident stock companies. Critically, western plays presented the Wild West at a remove. Their white heroes and heroines were people with whom middle-class Spokanites could identify, while dangerous "others" were safely contained as villains or stock characters.[8] All the while, the city's people debated the propriety of institutions such as the variety theaters—where wildness was not at a remove.[9] After the varieties closed in 1908 Spokanites, even the city's boosters, gradually looked back on them with a bit of nostalgia. In 1912 and 1915 two high-profile conventions took place in Spokane and both concluded with staged mining camps that featured sanitized versions of the old frontier sins, including variety theaters.[10] With the rise of movie culture, the western increased in popularity. By the late 1910s the Wild West seemed so distant and alluring that Spokanites thronged by the thousands to watch western film stars such as William S. Hart.[11] It was in this setting that a goodly number of Spokanites began to set their hopes on moviemaking.

Rutgers University Press, 1991); Tera W. Hunter, *To 'Joy My Freedom: Southern Black Women's Lives and Labors after the Civil War* (Cambridge, Mass.: Harvard University Press, 1995); Katie N. Johnson, *Sisters in Sin: Brothel Drama in America, 1900–1920* (Cambridge: Cambridge University Press, 2006); Joanne J. Meyerowitz, *Women Adrift: Independent Wage Earners in Chicago, 1880–1920* (Chicago: University of Chicago Press, 1988); Gillian Rodger, *Champagne Charlie and Pretty Jemima: Variety Theater in the Nineteenth Century* (Urbana: University of Illinois Press, 2010).

30. Berelson and Grant, "Pioneer Theatre"; Michael R. Booth, "Theatrical Boom in the Kootenays," *The Beaver* 292 (Autumn 1961): 42–46; Dilgard, *Mill Town Footlights*; Eugene Clinton Elliott, *A History of Variety-Vaudeville in Seattle: From the Beginning to 1914* (Seattle: University of Washington Press, 1944); Richard H. Engeman, "The 'Seattle Spirit' Meets *The Alaskan*: A Story of Business, Boosterism, and the Arts," *Pacific Northwest Quarterly* 81, no. 2 (April 1990): 54–66; Ernst, *Oregon Country*; Lawrence James Hill, "A History of Variety-Vaudeville in Minneapolis, Minnesota, from Its Beginnings to 1900" (PhD diss., University of Minnesota, 1979); George L. Lufkin, "The Spokane Spectacle: A Study of Spokane, Washington, Theaters between 1883 and 1983," rev. ed. (Shelton, Wash.: Published privately, 1984); Murray Morgan, *Skid Road: An Informal Portrait of Seattle*, rev. ed. (New York: Ballantine Books, 1971), ch. 3; Danny Ival Reams, "Spokane Theatre, 1880–1892" (master's thesis, Washington State University, 1970); Bruce Martin Wasserman, "Early Theatre in Spokane, Washington, 1889–1902 (PhD diss., Washington State University, 1975). See also Felicia Hardison Londré, *The Enchanted Years of the Stage: Kansas City at the Crossroads of American Theater, 1870–1930* (Columbia: University of Missouri Press, 2007). Kansas City was, like Spokane, a railroad hub and regional capital; accordingly, the two cities had similar theatrical scenes.

31. Berglund, in *San Francisco*, provides the best example of a complex, book-length examination of commercial amusements in a western city. See also Bonnie Christensen, *Red Lodge and the Mythic West: Coal Miners to Cowboys* (Lawrence: University Press of Kansas, 2002), 1–63; Richard Etulain, *Re-imagining the Modern American West: A Century of Fiction, History, and Art* (Tucson: University of Arizona Press, 1996); Brenda K. Jackson, *Domesticating the West: The Re-creation of the Nineteenth-Century American Middle Class* (Lincoln: University of Nebraska Press, 2005); Polly Welts Kaufman, *Women Teachers on the Frontier* (New Haven: Yale University Press, 1984); Sandra L. Myres, *Westering Women and the Frontier Experience, 1800–1915* (Albuquerque: University of New Mexico Press, 1982), 181–208.

1. Theater and Boosterism in Late Victorian Spokane

1. Lucile F. Fargo, *Spokane Story* (Minneapolis: Northwestern Press, 1957), 188–89. Spokane residents called their town "Spokane Falls" (also spelled

"Spokan") until 1891, when they officially dropped the "Falls." For the sake of clarity, I refer to it uniformly as "Spokane."

2. "Next Week at the Theater," *Spokane Chronicle*, June 8, 1900.

3. William Hudson Kensel, "The Economic History of Spokane, Washington, 1881–1910" (PhD diss., Washington State University, 1962), 21, 37; Pomeroy, *Pacific Slope*, 150.

4. Cronon, *Nature's Metropolis*; Meinig, *Transcontinental America.*

5. Spokane and Cheney particularly competed over which town would become the Spokane County seat. Spokane gained that title permanently in 1886 and quickly surpassed Cheney in growth and importance.

6. Schwantes, *Pacific Northwest*, 159. See also John Fahey, *Inland Empire: D. C. Corbin and Spokane* (Seattle: University of Washington Press, 1965), 3, 30, 49, 61–63, 80; Kensel, "Economic History," 41, 48–50, 56, 65, 98, 101–5.

7. Kensel, "Economic History," 72–74, 92; Zhenyu Wang, "A Study of Streetscape Evolution on Riverside Avenue in Downtown Spokane, 1881–1999" (master's thesis, Washington State University, 2001), 18.

8. Nancy Engle, "Benefiting a City: Women, Respectability and Reform in Spokane, Washington, 1886–1910" (PhD diss., University of Florida, 2003), xv, 4; Fahey, *Inland Empire*, 62; Schwantes, *Radical Heritage*, 15; Morrissey, *Mental Territories*, ch. 4.

9. Richard S. Kirkendall, "The Manifest Destiny of Spokane," *Journal of the West* 42, no. 1 (winter 2000): 4. The pamphlet was Harry H. Hook and Francis J. McGuire, *Spokane Falls Illustrated: the Metropolis of Eastern Washington; a History of the Early Settlement and the Spokane Falls of Today; Embracing the Commercial and Manufacturing Advantages of the City and Its Marvelous Growth, with Illustrations of Prominent Buildings, Beautiful Homes, and Portraits and Sketches of Leading Citizens* (Minneapolis: F. L. Thresher, 1889). See also *Settlers' Guide to Homes in the Northwest, being a Handbook of Spokane Falls, W. T., the Queen City of the Pacific Its Matchless Water Power and Advantages as a Commercial Centre* (Spokane Falls, Wash.: Dallam, Ansell, and Edwards, 1885), 25–27; Wasserman, "Early Theatre in Spokane," 25.

10. Berglund, *San Francisco*; Schwantes, *Radical Heritage*, 18, 125.

11. Edward Kohlhauff Sr., "Fifty Years of Theaters in Spokane," 1934, William Kohlhauff papers, MsSc 29, EWSHS, also available in the Northwest Room of the Spokane Public Library; Reams, "Spokane Theatre," 80; Wasserman, "Early Theatre in Spokane," 47.

12. Jonathan Edwards, *An Illustrated History of Spokane County, State of Washington* (San Francisco?: W. H. Lever, 1900), 301.

13. For *Spokane Falls Review*, see Nelson W. Durham, *History of the City of Spokane and the Spokane Country: From Its Earliest Settlement to the Present Time* (Spokane: S. J. Clark Publishing, 1912), 1:410.

14. Reams, "Spokane Theatre," 80, 83.

15. Morrissey, *Mental Territories*, 26; Kensel, "Economic History," 26–28, 91–92. Kensel makes clear how fully Spokane eclipsed Walla Walla and Lewiston, Idaho, another inland rival, by comparing their population growth: in 1880 Spokane had 350 inhabitants, Walla Walla 3,588, and Lewiston 739. Ten years later, their populations were, respectively, 19,922; 4,709; and 849.

16. Spokane and Walla Walla were hardly alone in connecting cultural attainment to urban hierarchy and identity. For similar episodes see Ernst, *Oregon Country*, 85; Jan L. Jones, *Renegades, Showmen and Angels: A Theatrical History of Fort Worth, 1873–2001* (Forth Worth: Texas Christian University Press, 2006), 45–46, 55; Londré, *Enchanted Years*, 65–67.

17. Fargo, *Spokane Story*, 197; Reams, "Spokane Theatre," 86; Wasserman, "Early Theatre in Spokane," 47.

18. Durham, *History of the City of Spokane*, 1:412, 428; Kohlhauff, "Fifty Years of Theaters"; Reams, "Spokane Theatre," 95, 134; Ernst, *Oregon Country*, 150; *Spokesman-Review*, April 2, 1933. The Falls City Opera House had a main hall of 50 by 90 feet, with six private boxes, and 350 chairs in the gallery.

19. Hook and McGuire, *Spokane Falls Illustrated*, 30.

20. Durham, *History of the City of Spokane*, 1:415–17.

21. Edwards, *Illustrated History*, 65; John Fahey, "When the Dutch Owned Spokane," *Pacific Northwest Quarterly* 72, no. 1 (spring 1981): 3; Robert Allen Henderson, "The *Spokesman-Review*, 1883–1900: A Mirror to the History of Spokane" (PhD diss., Washington State University, 1967), 29–30; Morrissey, *Mental Territories*, 43, 53.

22. Engle, "Benefiting a City," 13, 18; Wang, "Streetscape Evolution," 19, 36.

23. Kensel, "Economic History," 92; Jef Rettmann, "Business, Government, and Prostitution in Spokane, Washington, 1889–1910," *Pacific Northwest Quarterly* 89, no. 2 (spring 1998): 78.

24. Durham, *History of the City of Spokane*, 1:430; Morrissey, *Mental Territories*, 44, 51–55; Henderson, "Mirror to the History," 190.

25. Several secondary sources imply that the Auditorium came into being *because* of the great 1889 fire. Primary sources, however, clarify that construction began in the spring of 1889, months before the August fire. See Hook and McGuire, *Spokane Falls Illustrated*, 30; *Spokane Falls Review*, September 16, 1890; "Loved by Erato," *Spokane Chronicle*, January 27, 1896; Ernst, *Oregon Country*, 150; Reams, "Spokane Theatre," 110.

26. Barbara F. Cochran, *Seven Frontier Women and the Founding of Spokane Falls* (Spokane, Wash.: Tornado Creek Publications, 2011), 61, 99; Durham, *History of the City of Spokane*, 2:756–62; Edwards, *Illustrated History*, 513–14; Hook and McGuire, *Spokane Falls Illustrated*, 34; *Spokane Chronicle*, April 8, 1895; Wasserman, "Early Theatre in Spokane," 57–59; Morrissey, *Mental Territories*, 34, 42.

27. Ernst, *Oregon Country*, 149–50; Fargo, *Spokane Story*, 118, 191; Durham, *History of the City of Spokane*, 1:336–40, 399, 405, 2:757; Edwards, *Illustrated History*, 60. By 1889 Cannon was worth 1–2 million dollars, all made in Spokane; the *Chronicle* reported in 1891 that Browne paid the largest taxes of anyone in the state of Washington. Hook and McGuire, *Spokane Falls Illustrated*, 30, 34; Wasserman, "Early Theatre in Spokane," 57.

28. *Spokane Falls Review*, September 16, 1890. See also *Spokane Falls Review*, November 8, 1889; Ernst, *Oregon Country*, 149–50; *Spokane Chronicle*, September 16, 1890.

29. Margaret Bean, interview, December 8, 1958, pioneer voices series (OH 460, EWSHS); George S. Clarke, interview, June 17, 1958, pioneer voices series (OH 459, EWSHS); Henderson, "Mirror to the History," 81; Michael Page, "Sarah Bernhardt's Visit to Spokane," *Pacific Northwest Forum*, 2nd ser., vol. 5, no. 1 (winter–spring 1992): 130; Krista Anette Undeberg, "The Diary of Helen Campbell: Life during Spokane's Age of Elegance, 1913–1917" (master's thesis, Washington State University, 1997), 71.

30. Flynn to J. J. Browne, February 3, 1890, J. J. Browne to Alta May Browne, February 6, 1890, box 1, folder 26, Anna Stratton Browne to Earle Browne, February 9, 1890, box 1, folder 22, in John J. Browne papers, Ms 21, EWSHS; *Spokane Chronicle*, March 17, April 19, 1890; *Spokane Falls Review*, September 16, 1890.

31. Wasserman, "Early Theatre in Spokane," 25 (quotations), 61; Undeberg, "The Diary of Helen Campbell," 6, 48, 83; *Spokane Chronicle*, April 19, 1890.

32. *Spokane Falls Review*, September 16, 1890 (quotation); Kohlhauff, "Fifty Years of Theaters."

33. *Spokane Falls Review*, September 17, 1890. See also ibid., September 6, 16, 1890; *Spokane Chronicle*, September 16, 17, 1890. Fort Worthians made similar estimations of their own social status when that city's grand opera house opened in 1883; a newspaper hailed the theater's opening as a "memorable fashion event" in north Texas, wherein society enjoyed the most brilliant gems in the "operatic diadem." Jones, *Renegades*, 50.

34. *Spokane Chronicle*, September 16 (quotations), 17, 1890.

35. Civic leaders elsewhere used highbrow culture to advertise their cities. See Jones, *Renegades*, 48–50; Kasson, *Amusing the Million*, 17; Londré, *Enchanted Years*, 33–34.

36. *Spokane Falls Review*, September 16, 1890.

37. "The Auditorium Is Opened," *Spokane Chronicle*, September 17, 1890.

38. "New Effects in Music," *Spokane Chronicle*, February 4, 1893. During the 1890s most professional performances at the Auditorium were given by touring troupes; however, the theater also employed Hoppe's local, resident orchestra. On a few occasions, local talent supplemented outside companies appearing at the Auditorium.

39. Kasson, *Rudeness and Civility*, 231–46; Levine, *Highbrow/Lowbrow*, ch. 2; Durham, *History of the City of Spokane*, 1:452.

40. *Spokane Falls Review*, September 17, 1890. See also Robert B. Hyslop, *Spokane's Building Blocks* (Spokane, Wash.: Standard Blue Prints, 1983).

41. "New Effects in Music," *Spokane Chronicle*, February 4, 1893. See also Wrobel, *Promised Lands*, 25–33.

42. During the mid-1890s, a "popular-priced" ticket in Spokane cost from ten to fifty cents; Auditorium tickets ranged from $0.25 to $1.50. For most of the 1890s, Spokanites of middling means felt keenly the want of a theater at once respectable and affordable; on a few occasions, businesspeople and impresarios tried to address this market. In late 1897, for example, the *Chronicle* detailed how "people now in town" were pressing the city council to allow the construction of a sheet iron theater to host such shows. The newspaper did not doubt that even such a simple structure would draw crowds, for plenty of Spokanites "are ready and willing to patronize almost any sort of theatrical performance and kicks about the lack of entertainment are frequent." *Spokane Chronicle*, September 10, 1897. Harry Hayward tried himself to fill the "family house" void by engaging stock companies at the Auditorium during the summer (trials that met with varied success) and by booking less expensive shows for special family-priced events. The most important popular-price venture of the decade was the Arcadia, a pavilion theater opened in 1896 and located downtown, on Riverside Avenue between Washington and Bernard. Managed by a Mr. Daniels, the Arcadia featured the Hattie Bernard Chase Company, which performed stock standards and advertised cheap tickets ranging from ten to fifty cents. This tent theater did well enough to undergo a renovation in November 1896. Unfortunately, it soon burned down. *Spokane Chronicle*, April 24, July 8, 11, 14, 27, August 4, 11, 18, 27, 31, September 9, 24, October 19, 27, November 2–3, 11–13, 16–17, 19, 25, 27, 1896; *Spokesman-Review*, May 26, 1897; Kohlhauff. "Fifty Years of Theaters"; Wasserman, "Early Theatre in Spokane," 212–13, 225.

43. Henderson, "Mirror to the History," 84–85.

44. J. J. Browne to Anna Stratton Browne, July 6, 1890, October 10, 1892, box 1, folder 7, Anna Stratton Browne to Guy Browne, November 15, 1889, January 28, 30 (quotation), 1890, box 1, folder 19, Anna Stratton Browne to Earle Browne, February 9, 1890, box 1, folder 22, Ms 21, EWSHS.

45. J. J. Browne to Anna Stratton Browne, February 9, 1900, box 1, folder 9, Ms 21, EWSHS.

46. Mrs. Flynn to Anna Stratton Browne, February 7, 1890, box 1, folder 55, Ms 21, EWSHS.

47. Dorothy Woodward, interview by Mary Mitiguy, April 30, 1984 (OH 364, EWSHS). See also Durham, *History of the City of Spokane*, 2:344–49; Edwards, *Illustrated History*, 195, 646.

48. Erenberg, *Steppin' Out*, 16–19; Levine, *Highbrow/Lowbrow*, 135–46, 172–230; Singal, "Towards a Definition," 8.

49. Wasserman, "Early Theatre in Spokane," 29. See also Henry Matthews, "Kirtland Cutter: Spokane's Architect," in *Spokane and the Inland Empire: An Interior Pacific Northwest Anthology*, ed. David H. Stratton (Pullman: Washington State University Press, 1991), 142–77; Undeberg, "The Diary of Helen Campbell," 6, 38, 56, 62, 83; Wasserman, "Early Theatre in Spokane," 224; *Spokane Chronicle*, May 21, 1892.

50. Durham, *History of the City of Spokane*, 3:174. See also Edwards, *Illustrated History*, 313–14; Hook and McGuire, *Spokane Falls Illustrated*, 32.

51. Margaret Bean, *Spokane's Age of Elegance* (Spokane: Eastern Washington State Historical Society, 1960), 5; Reams, "Spokane Theatre," 150; Wasserman, "Early Theatre in Spokane," 65.

52. *Spokane Falls Daily Chronicle*, October 4, 1890; *Spokane Chronicle*, January 27, 1896, April 20, 1897, April 12, November 20, 1898.

53. Wasserman, "Early Theatre in Spokane," 358; Durham, *History of the City of Spokane*, 1:374–76, 473, 2:757. Local newspapers and their publishers figured largely in town-boosting throughout the West, and Browne surely used his daily to advertise Spokane. See Flynn to J. J. Browne, February 25, 1890, box 1, folder 55, Ms 21, EWSHS.

54. *Spokane Chronicle*, February 23, 1895, March 18, 1896. See also ibid., January 14, 15, March 21, April 8, 11, May 30, 1896.

55. *Spokane Chronicle*, April 20, 1897. Davenport presented *La Tosca* and *Fedora*. The *Chronicle* reprinted another such incident in 1899: Ignacy Paderewski's manager had his doubts about bringing the Polish pianist to the Northwest but not after seeing Spokane and its theater. *Spokane Chronicle*, October 20, 1899.

56. Wasserman, "Early Theatre in Spokane," 102.

57. *Spokane Chronicle*, October 15, 1891.

58. *Spokane Chronicle*, October 15, 17, 1891; see also *Spokane Chronicle*, December 28, 1896.

59. *Spokane Chronicle*, October 3, 1899. See also Wasserman, "Early Theatre in Spokane," 308. Earlier in the decade, the *Chronicle* promoted education by building a lending library of classic books, available for ten cents and a coupon. *Spokane Chronicle*, June 12, August 30, 1893.

60. *Spokane Chronicle*, October 16, 1899. See also Levine, *Highbrow/Lowbrow*, ch. 1.

61. *Spokane Chronicle*, May 29, 1896.

62. *Spokane Chronicle*, May 10, 1898.

63. Page, "Sarah Bernhardt's Visit," 134–35; Reams, "Spokane Theatre," 157; *Spokane Chronicle*, September 3, 22, 1891; also Edwin L. Nelson, "The History of Road Shows in Seattle, from Their Beginnings to 1914" (master's thesis, University of Washington, 1947), 57.

64. Adelaide Sutton Gilbert, "The Letters of Adelaide Sutton Gilbert," *Pacific Northwest Forum* 2nd ser., vol. 5, no. 1 (winter–spring 1992): 5, 11.

65. *Spokane Chronicle*, September 22, 1891; Bean, *Age of Elegance*, 5. For *Spokane Review*, see Page, "Sarah Bernhardt's Visit," 136. *Spokane Chronicle*, September 25, 1891.

66. Page, "Sarah Bernhardt's Visit," 138. See also Reams, "Spokane Theatre," 157; Durham, *History of the City of Spokane*, 1:441; Gilbert, "Letters," 5.

67. *Spokane Chronicle*, September 22, 1891. Audiences in Fort Worth, Texas, had a similar reaction to Sarah Bernhardt. See Jones, *Renegades*, 70.

68. *Spokane Chronicle*, February 10, 1892.

69. Wasserman, "Early Theatre in Spokane," 82–85, 148, 150.

70. *Spokane Chronicle*, October 15, November 4, 5 (quotation), 1891, February 10, 1892.

71. *Spokane Chronicle*, March 29, 1892 (quotation), February 12, 15, 1895; *Spokesman-Review*, February 3, 13, 1895.

72. *Spokane Chronicle*, April 12, 13, 1898; Wasserman, "Early Theatre in Spokane," 150.

73. *Spokane Chronicle*, June 18, 1898 (quotation); "Theatre % June 96–June 97," box 6, folder 26, Northwestern and Pacific Hypotheek Bank Records, Ms 46 (EWSHS). *Spokane Chronicle*, May 8, 9, June 18, 1898.

74. *Spokane Chronicle*, April 13, June 18, April 12, June 18, 1898. Audiences in Seattle and Kansas City showed a similar preference for light, gimmicky shows over legitimate drama and grand opera. Londré, *Enchanted Years*, 45–46; Nelson, "Road Shows in Seattle," 91, 102.

75. Digby Bell starred in Augustus Thomas's *The Hoosier Doctor*. Other shows deemed "worthwhile" by the *Chronicle* included contemporary touring favorites like Timothy Murphy in *Old Innocence* and Marie Wainwright in *Shall We Forgive Her?* and the more literary *The Dead Heart*, a Dumas adaptation starring James O'Neill. Edward Chauncey Baldwin, ed., *The Lake English Classics: A Tale of Two Cities, by Charles Dickens* (New York: Scott, Foresman, 1919), 42–43; Johnson Briscoe, *The Actors' Birthday Book: An Authoritative Insight into the Lives of the Men and Women of the Stage Born between January First and December Thirty-First, Second Series* (New York: Moffat, Yard, 1908), 98, 116; Jeffrey Richards, *Sir Henry Irving: A Victorian Actor and His World* (New York: Palgrave Macmillan, 2005), 367–69; A. D. Storms, ed., *The Players Blue Book* (Worcester, Mass.: Sutherland and Storms, 1901), 214; "A Young Favorite in 'Old Innocence,'" *Munsey's Magazine* 17 (April–September 1897): 460; "Jottings on Player-Folk," *New York Times*, December 8, 1918.

76. *Spokane Chronicle*, June 18, 1898.

77. "Inventor Tells the Secret of Amazing Stage Effects," *New York Times*, November 9, 1913; George Pratt, "Early Stage and Screen: A Two-Way Street," *Cinema Journal* 14, no. 2 (winter 1974–1975): 16–17.

78. Levine, *Highbrow/Lowbrow*, 163, 166.

79. *Spokane Chronicle*, June 18, 1898.

80. Those plays were Charles H. Hoyt's *Stranger in New York* and *Night*, with Nellie McKnight; both concerned the city's annual "French ball." See "Charles H. Hoyt's New Farce," *New York Times*, February 16, 1897; Gabrielle H. Cody and Evert Sprinchorn, eds., *The Columbia Encyclopedia of Modern Drama* (New York: Columbia University Press, 2007), 1:635; John Gassner and Edward Quinn, eds., *The Reader's Encyclopedia of World Drama* (Toronto: Thomas Y. Cromwell, 1969), 435; Timothy J. Gilfoyle, *City of Eros: New York City, Prostitution, and the Commercialization of Sex, 1790–1920* (New York: W. W. Norton, 1994), 232.

81. Kwame Anthony Appiah and Henry Louis Gates Jr., eds., *Africana: Arts and Letters: An A-to-Z Reference of Writers, Musicians, and Artists of the African American Experience* (Philadelphia: Running Press, 2004), 121; Colin A. Palmer, *Encyclopedia of African-American Culture and History: The Black Experience in the Americas* (New York: Macmillan Reference, 2006), 5:2096; Sally Sommer, "Dance," in *The Reader's Companion to American History*, ed. Eric Foner and John Arthur Garraty (New York: Houghton Mifflin Harcourt, 1991), 264.

82. *Spokane Chronicle*, June 1, 1896.

83. *Spokane Chronicle*, February 12, 1895. See also *Spokesman-Review*, February 3, 1895.

84. *Spokane Chronicle*, February 15, 1895. See also *Spokesman-Review*, February 13, 1895. The *Chronicle* reported that the evening version of *The South in Slavery* was well attended and appreciated, with the cakewalk forming the "crowning feature of the entertainment." *Spokane Chronicle*, February 16, 1895.

85. Eric J. Sundquist, *To Wake the Nations: Race in the Making of American Literature* (Cambridge, Mass.: Harvard University Press, 1993), 281–83; *Spokane Chronicle*, April 4, 6, 8, 1899.

86. Ashby, *Amusement for All*, 6–7; McArthur, *Actors and American Culture*, 130–31, 135; Anna M. Stratton, diary, March 4, 1891, box 1, folder 3, Anna M. Stratton Papers, MsSC 174 (EWSHS); "Can Stop at Any Floor," *Spokane Chronicle*, January 22, 1895.

87. Lewis O. Saum, *The Popular Mood of American, 1860–1890* (Lincoln: University of Nebraska Press, 1990), 11–15.

88. Anna M. Stratton, diary, September 17, 20, October 18, 22, 23, 30, November 4, 10, 15, 21, 22, 1890, February 20, 21, March 3, 4, 9, 17, 21, 31, April 6, 7, 18, 1891, box 1, folder 3, MsSc 174 (EWSHS).

89. J. J. Browne to Alta May Browne, February 6, 1890, box 1, folder 26, J. J. Browne to Irma S. Browne, February 9, 1890, box 1, folder 30, Ms 21 (EWSHS). Specifically, Browne discussed Edwin Booth with Alta May, and Elsie Leslie in *The Prince and the Pauper* with Irma.

90. J. J. Browne to Hazel Browne, January 7, 1900, box 1, folder 34, Ms 21 (EWSHS).

91. In an 1892 letter, for instance, Adelaide Sutton Gilbert reported that the famous actor Frederick Warde would not let his own convent-educated daughter enter a theater, which choice a friend of Gilbert's described as "in itself a sermon." Gilbert, "Letters," 51.

92. McArthur, *Actors and American Culture*, 70–73, 124 (quotation); Gilbert, "Letters," 51; Wasserman, "Early Theatre in Spokane," 148.

93. McArthur, *Actors and American Culture*, 135, 141, 152, 159–65.

94. Barth, *Instant Cities*, 192.

95. Saum, *Popular Mood*, 50, 55, also 42, 55.

96. Barber, *Reno's Big Gamble*, 45; Hamer, *New Towns*, 85–89, 198.

97. Barth, *Instant Cities*, 185, also ch. 7; Barth, *City People*, 30, 35; Pomeroy, *Pacific Slope*, 149.

98. Kensel, "Economic History," 73; Schwantes, "Wageworkers' Frontier," 128.

99. Fahey, "When the Dutch Owned Spokane," 4; *The Philistine* 22, no. 4 (March 1906): 123.

100. Durham, *History of the City of Spokane*, 3:434, 437; Henderson, "Mirror to the History," 112; Schwantes, *Radical Heritage*, 51; Schwantes, "Wageworkers' Frontier," 128; Henderson, "Mirror to the History," 112.

101. Durham, *History of the City of Spokane*, 1:449.

102. *Spokane Chronicle*, June 5, 1893. See also Durham, *History of the City of Spokane*, 1:449–50.

103. *Spokane Chronicle*, June 6, 7, 8, 12, July 26, 27, September 12, 1893.

104. Fahey, "When the Dutch Owned Spokane," 4–5. According to John Fahey, the catalog of bankrupt and heavily indebted Spokanites included James N. Glover, Benjamin Norman, Dr. Benjamin Burch, Sarah F. Moore, Eugene B. Hyde, Horace L. Cutter, and of course J. J. Browne and Anthony M. Cannon. They were among the most important businessmen, real estate owners, speculators, and bankers in the city.

105. Durham, *History of the City of Spokane*, 1:472, 2:758; *Spokane Chronicle*, September 8, 1893, April 7, 1895; *New York Times*, April 7, 1895.

106. Annual report, "1896 Bijlagen tot het Rapport," Annual Reports, 1889–1898, box 2, folder 9, Ms 46 (EWSHS); Fahey, "When the Dutch Owned Spokane," 5.

107. Fahey, "When the Dutch Owned Spokane," 2–3.

108. Annual Reports, 1889–1898, box 2, folder 9, Auditorium Building, 1898–1903, box 6, folder 26, Ms 46 (EWSHS).

2. Variety Theater, Politics, and Pragmatism

1. William A. Brady, *Showman* (New York: E. P. Dutton, 1937), 53–56.

2. Engle, "Benefiting a City," 19n89.

3. Coben, *Rebellion against Victorianism*; Kasson, *Amusing the Million*, introduction; Lears, *No Place of Grace*; Singal, "Towards a Definition," 7.

4. Gilfoyle, *City of Eros*, 67, 109–12; Claudia D. Johnson, "That Guilty Third Tier: Prostitution in Nineteenth-Century American Theaters," *American Quarterly* 27, no. 5 (December 1975): 575–84.

5. Allen, *Horrible Prettiness*, 73; Wilmeth, *Variety Entertainment*, 130–31. See also Ashby, *Amusement for All*, 48; Nasaw, *Going Out*, 13–14; Rodger, *Champagne Charlie and Pretty Jemima*, 17.

6. Allen, *Horrible Prettiness*, 74. See also Berglund, *San Francisco*, 62–63, 69; Gilfoyle, *City of Eros*, 129–30, 191, 225; Dilgard, *Mill Town Footlights*, 4–5; Dudden, *Women in the American Theatre*, 155; Ralph E. Dyar, *News for an Empire: The Story of the* Spokesman-Review *of Spokane, Washington, and of the Field It Serves* (Caldwell, Idaho: Caxton Printers, 1952), 55; Glenn, *Female Spectacle*; Hill, "Variety-Vaudeville in Minneapolis"; Rodger, *Champagne Charlie and Pretty Jemima*, chs. 6, 14; Toll, *On with the Show*, 208, 238; Wilmeth, *Variety Entertainment*, 131.

7. *Spokesman-Review*, March 22, 1895, November 29, 1896, April 8, 1899, March 10, April 30, May 19, 1901, June 15, 1902; Cochran, *Seven Frontier Women*, 233; Kohlhauff, "Fifty Years of Theaters"; Reams, "Spokane Theatre," 18–25; Wasserman, "Early Theatre in Spokane," 374; Wilmeth, *Variety Entertainment*, 131.

8. Secondary scholarship on variety theaters vis-à-vis their urban settings is quite sparse, but it suggests that Spokane's difficult relationship with these venues bore much resemblance to the place of varieties in other cities with similar economies. In Fort Worth, Texas, for instance, raucous variety theaters opened in the late 1870s, after the arrival of the railroad; the houses were aimed at a male audience of traveling men, farmers, and especially cowboys. As in Spokane, these houses featured mixed-format shows, expensive alcohol, and women. Similarly, Fort Worth's leaders wrestled with their conflicting desires to regulate the theaters and their (apparently greater) desire to reap municipal or personal profits from them. City officials would pass and then quickly repeal toothless ordinances aimed at controlling the varieties and their sister establishments. Likewise, attempts at reform in the cow town were short-lived and unsupported by local merchants, who in 1884 killed a morality drive with a petition in support of the theaters. Indeed, the loyalty of merchants to the varieties was such that what was likely Fort Worth's first variety theater (opened in 1875) was bankrolled by businessmen hoping to capitalize on the trade of stockmen and cowboys. Finally, and as in Spokane, Fort Worth's variety theaters finally closed in the mid-1900s, when tougher regulation of theaters and alcohol combined with the rise of other popular-priced entertainments to make the variety theater business plan untenable. See Elliott, *Variety-Vaudeville in Seattle*; Hill, "Variety-Vaudeville in Minneapolis"; Jones, *Renegades*,

1–36; Londré, *Enchanted Years,* 137; Rodger, *Champagne Charlie and Pretty Jemima,* 69, 74, chs. 14–15.

9. *Spokane Falls Review,* December 17, 1889; Edwards, *Illustrated History,* 299–301; Elliott, *Variety-Vaudeville in Seattle,* 22; Henderson, "Mirror to the History," 75; Kohlhauff, "Fifty Years of Theaters"; Lufkin, "The Spokane Spectacle," 4, 7; Nelson, "Road Shows in Seattle," 25, 51; Reams, "Spokane Theatre," 18, 22–23; Wasserman, "Early Theatre in Spokane," 25–29, 368.

10. Schwantes, *Radical Heritage,* 41. See also Frick, *Theatre, Culture and Temperance Reform,* 43, 49; Dyar, *News for an Empire,* 125. In 1891 the Seattle city council passed a short-lived ordinance that tacked a thousand dollars onto the annual license fee paid by saloons with concert halls or theaters. Three years later, the council tried again by revoking the licenses of Seattle's variety theaters. Elliott, *Variety-Vaudeville in Seattle,* 24.

11. Wasserman, "Early Theatre in Spokane," 375.

12. Schwantes, "Wageworkers' Frontier," 125–26.

13. Charles Gallinger, interview, January 30, 1976, page 14 (OH 072, 073, 074, EWSHS).

14. Fargo, *Spokane Story,* 170; Jef Rettmann, "Prostitution in Spokane, 1880–1910" (master's thesis, Eastern Washington University, 1995), 43. For Spokane's notoriety, see "Gambling at Charity Ball," *New York Times,* December 18, 1901.

15. Schwantes, *Radical Heritage,* 51, 114. See also John Fahey, *The Ballyhoo Bonanza: Charles Sweeney and the Idaho Mines* (Seattle: University of Washington Press, 1971), 33; Thomas Riddle, "Whitman County Populism and Washington State Politics, 1889–1902" (master's thesis, Washington State University, 1971), 40. Many historians have chronicled how, in mid-1892, violence broke out between Idaho silver miners and the capitalists who exploited them. See J. Anthony Lukas, *Big Trouble: A Murder in a Small Western Town Sets Off a Struggle for the Soul of America* (New York: Simon and Schuster, 1997), 101–4; Morrissey, *Mental Territories,* ch. 3; Schwantes, *Radical Heritage,* 41.

16. Dyar, *News for an Empire,* 40, 93; Fahey, *Ballyhoo Bonanza,* 125; Henderson, "Mirror to the History," 32, 35, 44, 93; David Fridtjof Halaas, *Boom Town Newspapers: Journalism on the Rocky Mountain Mining Frontier, 1859–1881* (Albuquerque: University of New Mexico Press, 1981), 9–10; David Paul Nord, *Newspapers and New Politics: Midwestern Municipal Reform, 1890–1900* (Ann Arbor, Mich.: UMI Research Press, 1981), 9.

17. Morgan, *Skid Road,* 120–21. See also U.S. Federal Census, 1900; Berglund, *San Francisco,* 64; Elliott, *Variety-Vaudeville in Seattle,* 25; Ernst, *Oregon Country,* 142; Gilfoyle, *City of Eros,* ch. 5; T. J. Jackson Lears, *Something for Nothing: Luck in America* (New York: Viking Press, 2003), 154–56; Londré, *Enchanted Years,* 138.

18. Durham, *History of the City of Spokane*, 1:429–30; Fargo, *Spokane Story*, 170–72; Hyslop, *Spokane's Building Blocks*; Morrissey, *Mental Territories*, 54. In 1890, after the fire, Goetz and Baer built a second Frankfurt block, and it was here, to number 123, that John Considine moved his variety theater in December 1894.

19. *Spokesman-Review*, January 15, March 22, 1895. The other houses Harry Baer referred to were those run by Holland, Brown, and Pratt.

20. Goetz, Baer, and Considine defended the People's Theater at a series of Spokane city council meetings in early 1895. At these events, several people noted that reformers had singled out the People's Theater, perhaps for political reasons, while other varieties (not to mention saloons and brothels) remained open. Indeed, it was not just ministers who discriminated against the People's Theater: the council itself often approved saloon and resort licenses at meetings filled with contention over variety theater licensing. For instance, even as the council and community debated the Considine case, a petition from S. J. Holland regarding the consolidation of the Comique and the Louvre passed through the council without comment. Council minute record book E, September 5, 1893–December 27, 1895, Spokane Municipal Government, EA598-3-7 (Washington State Archives, Eastern Regional Branch, Cheney, Washington; hereafter WSAEB), 675, 688, 689, 696; *Spokane Chronicle*, January 25, 1895; *Spokesman-Review*, January 15, 1895.

21. *Spokesman-Review*, January 23, 1895. See also *Seattle Post-Times*, January 25, 1895; *Spokesman-Review*, February 6, 1895.

22. *Seattle Post-Times*, January 25, February 8, 1895; *Spokesman-Review*, January 26, 1895.

23. *Spokane Chronicle*, January 7, 1893. See also *Spokane Chronicle*, January 9, 1893, November 5, 1898. In the 1890s many of Spokane's variety theaters sold tickets at prices lower than premium Auditorium seats, but they were still outside a daily middle-class budget. These fees—from 10 to 50 cents—were at the higher end of the "popular price" spectrum and perhaps accessible to single migratory workers with fresh wages in hand. Other houses had no cover charge. In January 1893, for example, the Comique, the Palace, and the Casino charged from 10 to 50 cents, while the Louvre was free.

24. *Spokane Chronicle*, February 27, 1895; *Spokesman-Review*, March 13, 1895. The ministerial association drew up the petition; it was presented to the council on March 13 by representatives of that body and a councilman from the residential fourth ward, Orlando G. Cooper, with 1,393 signatures.

25. *Spokesman-Review*, March 19, 1895. See also Council minutes record book E (WSAEB), 740; "The Variety Theaters," *Spokesman-Review*, March 14, April 22, 1895; Rettmann, "Business, Government, and Prostitution," 82. The Louvre cost an annual $14,000 in rent and $43,000 in salaries.

26. *Spokesman-Review*, March 14, 1895; Wasserman, "Early Theatre in Spokane," 353.

27. Stuart M. Blumin, *The Emergence of the Middle Class: Social Experience in the American City, 1760–1900* (New York: Cambridge University Press, 1989); Higham, "The Reorientation of American Culture"; Paul E. Johnson, *A Shopkeeper's Millennium: Society and Revivals in Rochester, New York, 1815–1837* (New York: Hill and Wang, 1978); Kasson, *Amusing the Million*, introduction; Kasson, *Rudeness and Civility*; Lears, *No Place of Grace*, 12–18; Mary P. Ryan, *Cradle of the Middle Class: The Family in Oneida County, New York, 1790–1865* (New York: Cambridge University Press, 1981); Singal, "Towards a Definition"; Alan Trachtenberg, *The Incorporation of America: Culture and Society in the Gilded Age* (New York: Hill and Wang, 1982).

28. "Plea for the Variety Theater," *Spokesman-Review*, March 14, 1895 (Onderdonk); *Spokane Chronicle*, January 22, 1895 (Wilson). See also R. L. Polk and Co., *Spokane City Directory*, 1895; *Spokesman-Review*, March 19, 1895.

29. *Spokane Chronicle*, March 27, 1895; *Spokesman-Review*, May 15, 1894, January 23, February 6, 1895; Morrissey, *Mental Territories*, 55–57.

30. "The Variety Theaters," *Spokesman-Review*, March 14, 1895.

31. Berglund, *San Francisco*, 48, 71; Christensen, *Red Lodge and the Mythic West*, 10–27.

32. *Spokesman-Review*, March 27, 1895. See also *Spokane Chronicle*, March 27, 1895.

33. "The Variety Theaters," *Spokesman-Review*, March 20, 1895.

34. Dyar, *News for an Empire*, 123; also *Spokesman-Review*, April 1, 1895.

35. Council minutes record book E (WSAEB), 748.

36. Edwards, *Illustrated History*, 383; Riddle, "Whitman County Populism"; Thomas Riddle, "The Old Radicalism in America: John R. Rogers and the Populist Movement in Washington, 1891–1900" (PhD diss., Washington State University, 1976), 182; Robert E. Ficken and Charles P. LeWarne, *Washington: A Centennial History* (Seattle: University of Washington Press, 1989), 77.

37. *Spokesman-Review*, March 30, May 3, 1895; Durham, *History of the City of Spokane*, 1:435; Riddle, "Old Radicalism," 182.

38. Edwards, *Illustrated History*, 384.

39. *Spokesman-Review*, May 5, 7, 1894. See also Durham, *History of the City of Spokane*, 1:457; Edwards, *Illustrated History*, 384; Fahey, *Ballyhoo Bonanza*, 85; Henderson, "Mirror to the History," 38; Lukas, *Big Trouble*, 411; Schwantes, *Coxey's Army*; Schwantes, *Radical Heritage*, 121; Schwantes, "Wageworkers' Frontier," 131. Belt's seemingly contradictory political and social positions illustrate the almost schizophrenic nature of Spokane politics during the 1890s. When the "Northwestern Industrial Army" came through eastern Washington in 1894, for instance, Spokanites variously reviled and cheered its members.

40. *Spokesman-Review*, March 30, 1895; Schwantes, *Pacific Northwest*, 267.

41. Council minutes record book E (WSAEB), 750–51. See also *Spokane Chronicle*, March 28, 1895; *Spokesman-Review*, March 28, 1895.

42. *Spokesman-Review*, April 1, 1895. See also *Spokane Chronicle*, March 29, April 1, 1895; *Spokesman-Review*, March 28, 30, 1895; Durham, *History of the City of Spokane*, 1:472.

43. At this time, many otherwise conservative Inland Northwesterners backed left-leaning, pro-silver policies because of the importance of the Idaho silver mines to the region's economy. Meanwhile, the American Protective Association (APA) became increasingly favored in the Inland Northwest during the early 1890s, especially among mine owners. Not incidentally, great numbers of wage-working miners were Catholic and foreign-born. Early in 1895, union miners became convinced that the APA (which connected Catholics with Populists) had an ulterior motive, that is, the destruction of organized labor. The APA exercised political power in the region through the Republican party, but it was also associated with an organization called the Citizens Party. The issue of religious prejudice became heated during the 1895 municipal campaign, particularly because of the Citizens ticket, which was headed by Walter French, a councilman who favored shutting down the varieties and who secured the city's APA vote. Belt, local Populists, and (late in the campaign) the *Chronicle* specifically denounced religious tests and prejudice. Further, in a region with a significant Catholic presence, Protestant ministers took the lead in attacking Spokane's variety theaters. I have not found evidence of Catholic clergy doing the same thing in the mid-1890s. All told, these ethnic and religious arguments increased the ferment of the 1895 election. *Spokane Chronicle*, April 24, May 3, 4, 6, 1895; *Spokesman-Review*, April 19, May 7, 1895; Fahey, *Ballyhoo Bonanza*, 71, 85; Donald L. Kinzer, *An Episode in Anti-Catholicism: The American Protective Association* (Seattle: University of Washington Press, 1964), 161; Riddle, "Old Radicalism," 197.

44. Durham, *History of the City of Spokane*, 1:473; *Spokesman-Review*, May 7, 1895.

45. "Just a Week More," *Spokesman-Review*, April 30, 1895; "Belt Raked 'Em In," *Spokesman-Review*, April 18, 1895. Belt's Populist opponents were J. H. Boyd and John Hearn.

46. "Not a Day of Rest," *Spokesman-Review*, April 22, 1895. See also *Spokesman-Review*, April 20, 22, 25, 27, 29, 30, May 3, 5, 7, 1895; Schwantes, *Radical Heritage*, 92.

47. *Spokesman-Review*, May 7, 1895.

48. Registers of the city prison, July 1, 1898–December 31, 1899, ad January 1, 1900–June 30, 1901, Spokane Municipal Government, EA598-3-7 (WSAEB); Edwards, *Illustrated History*, 84; Engle, "Benefiting a City," xvi,

13–25; Fargo, *Spokane Story*, 182; Annika Herbes, "Rescuing the Destitute: The Salvation Army in Spokane, 1891–1920," *Columbia* (fall 2004): 13–14; Rettmann, "Prostitution in Spokane," 39–41; Carl H. Trunk, interview, May 28, 1964 (OH 475, EWSHS).

49. *Spokesman-Review*, April 18, 1895. See also *Spokane Chronicle*, April 20, 1898, October 3, 1899; *Spokesman-Review*, April 27, May 7, 1895, October 3, 1897; Kristine Stilwell, "'If You Don't Slip': The Hobo Life, 1911–1916" (PhD diss., University of Missouri–Columbia, 2004), 237, 254.

50. Schwantes, *Radical Heritage*, 65, 86; Riddle, "Whitman County Populism," 55, 62.

51. *Spokesman-Review*, March 30, 31, April 20, 22–23, 25–27, 29–30, May 3, 7, 1895; Barbara Cloud, *The Business of Newspapers on the Western Frontier* (Reno: University of Nevada Press, 1992), 130; Dyar, *News for an Empire*, 35–37.

52. *Spokesman-Review*, April 28, 1895; also April 21–24, 29, May 7, 1895.

53. "Votes were Cheap," *Spokesman-Review*, May 7, 1895.

54. "Slum Politics," *Spokesman-Review*, May 5, 1895.

55. *Spokane Chronicle*, May 3, 1895; also April 19, 26, 29, May 1, 1895.

56. *Spokane Chronicle*, April 1, 18–19, 24–26, 29–30, May 1–4, 6–7, 1895.

57. *Spokane Chronicle*, April 1, May 1, 1895.

58. "All Belt's" and "Where Were the Nine?" *Spokane Chronicle*, May 6, 1895.

59. Council minute record book E, 750–51 (WSAEB); *Spokane Chronicle*, May 6, 7, 8, 1895; *Spokesman-Review*, March 28, May 5, 7, 1895. For the victory, see "Belt Is the Man," *Spokesman-Review*, May 8, 1895. Belt had 1,518 votes; Charles Hopkins had 1,228; and Walter France had 1,131, which gave Belt a plurality of 290 over Hopkins, the Republican.

60. Edwards, *Illustrated History*, 384. See also *Spokane Chronicle*, March 29, May 5, 8, 1895; *Spokesman-Review*, February 6, May 8, 1895; Riddle, "Old Radicalism," 180; Riddle, "Whitman County Populism," 66.

61. *Spokane Chronicle*, January 7, July 1, 1899; *Spokesman-Review*, January 1, 1897; Kensel, "Economic History," 174.

62. Kensel, "Economic History," 113–18, 162–69; Kirkendall, " Manifest Destiny," 5.

63. "In Drunken Revels," *Spokane Chronicle*, November 11, 1896.

64. *Spokane Chronicle*, November 10, 27–28, 1896; *Spokesman-Review*, November 29, 1896, May 18, 1899; Wasserman, "Early Theatre in Spokane," 374.

65. Margaret Bean, interview by Mary Mitiguy, April 23, 1984 (OH 366, EWSHS); Bean, *Spokane's Age of Elegance*, 11–12; Durham, *History of the City of Spokane*, 1:484 (quotation); Dyar, *News for an Empire*, 123; Fargo, *Spokane Story*, 182; Kensel, "Economic History," 114–17, 124.

66. "To Close Saloons," *Spokesman-Review*, January 3, 1897; "Saloons May Close," *Spokane Chronicle*, January 5, 1897. The 1897 anti-vice drive targeted

several kinds of resorts, including saloons open on Sundays, gambling rooms, dance halls, and varieties. See *Spokesman-Review*, May 27–29, June 8, 10, 12–13, 15, 19, 1897.

67. Council minutes record book F (WSAEB), 440; *Spokane Chronicle*, April 7, 1899; *Spokesman-Review*, May 27, 1897; Washington State, *Session Laws of the State of Washington, Session of 1895* (Olympia, Wash.: O. C. White, State Printer, 1895), 177; Dorothy Sue Cobble, *Dishing It Out: Waitresses and Their Unions in the Twentieth Century* (Urbana: University of Illinois Press, 1991), 156.

68. Council minutes record book F (WSAEB), 452–55, 467–71; *Spokane Chronicle*, June 2–3, 12, 1897; *Spokesman-Review*, May 29, June 8, 1897. For the People's Theater, see "Gambling Not Stopped," *Spokane Chronicle*, June 16, 1897; "Council Is Defied," *Spokesman-Review*, June 9, 1897. For September, see Council minutes record book F (WSAEB), 581, 590; *Spokesman-Review*, September 4, 20, 22, 1897.

69. *Spokesman-Review*, January 3, 1897; also June 1, 12, 1897.

70. Berglund, *San Francisco; Spokesman-Review*, May 29 (quotation), June 1, 1897.

71. "Business Streets of Spokane," *Spokane Chronicle*, May 26, 1897.

72. "Life on the Farm," *Spokane Chronicle*, June 1, 1897.

73. *Spokane Chronicle*, June 14, 1897.

74. "To Close Saloons," *Spokesman-Review*, January 3, 1897 (Spalding); "Standing on Clean Ground," *Spokesman-Review*, June 9, 1897.

75. Council minutes record book F (WSAEB), 472–75, 578, 581, 590; *Spokane Chronicle*, September 20, 1897; *Spokesman-Review*, September 4, 22, 25, 1897; Gilfoyle, *City of Eros*, 141.

76. Fahey, *Ballyhoo Bonanza*, 87; Lukas, *Big Trouble*, 112–15; Morrissey, *Mental Territories*, 100–11; Kathryn G. Morse, *The Nature of Gold: An Environmental History of the Klondike Gold Rush* (Seattle: University of Washington Press, 2003), 18; Schwantes, *Radical Heritage*, 21, 65; Schwantes, *Pacific Northwest*, 243–45, 273.

77. *Spokesman-Review*, October 2, 1899; Durham, *History of the City of Spokane*, 1:484; Henderson, "Mirror to the History," 88–91; Kensel, "Economic History," 135, 161, 169; Morrissey, *Mental Territories*, 139; Rettmann, "Business, Government, and Prostitution," 82; J. William T. Youngs, "Spokane's Northwest Industrial Exposition of 1890," *Pacific Northwest Forum* 7, no. 1 (winter–spring 1994): 38.

78. "He Roasts the Theaters," *Spokane Chronicle*, April 7, 1899; *Spokesman-Review*, April 4, 8, May 16, 1899.

79. "That Theater License," *Spokesman-Review*, April 8, 1899. For the controversy over varieties in spring 1899, see *Spokane Chronicle*, April 7, May 30, June 16, 1899; *Spokesman-Review*, March 17, April 4, 7–8, May 16–18, June 1, 1899.

80. "Wave of Moral Reform Rolls In," *Spokesman-Review*, May 18, 1899. See also Council minutes record book G (WSAEB), 490.

81. Council minutes record book G (WSAEB), 667; "Acuff Whips the Theaters," *Spokane Chronicle*, September 22, 1899; "No Variety Shows," *Spokesman-Review*, September 22, 1899; Rettmann, "Business, Government, and Prostitution," 81; Wasserman, "Early Theatre in Spokane," 380.

82. *Spokesman-Review*, May 3, 1899; also Council minutes record book G (WSAEB), 667.

83. Council minutes record book G (WSAEB), 675, 676, 679; *Spokane Chronicle*, September 22, 25, 1899; "Fiery Speech in the Council," *Spokesman-Review*, September 23, 1899.

84. "Omo Is in a Rage," *Spokesman-Review*, September 24, 1899; Council minutes record book G (WSAEB), 682–85.

85. *Spokesman-Review*, September 24, 26–27, 1899.

86. *Spokane Chronicle*, September 29, 1899. See also Council minutes record book G (WSAEB), 692; *Spokesman-Review*, September 29, 1899; Rettmann, "Business, Government, and Prostitution," 81–82.

87. "May Revoke Them," *Spokesman-Review*, September 29, 1899; Singal, "Towards a Definition," 15.

88. *Spokane Chronicle*, September 29, 1899.

89. *Spokesman-Review*, September 29, 1899; Berglund, *San Francisco*, 62.

90. *Spokesman-Review*, October 3, 1899.

91. "Bitter Words Were Spoken," *Spokesman-Review*, September 27, 1899.

92. "Put It Off Again," *Spokesman-Review*, September 30, 1899.

93. Council minutes record book G (WSAEB), 696, 697, 702; *Spokane Chronicle*, October 2–5; *Spokesman-Review*, October 1–6, 1899.

94. Engle, "Benefiting a City," 19n89.

95. Morrissey, *Mental Territories*.

3. Variety Theater, Gender, and Urban Identity

1. "Man Dislikes 'Dutch Jake's' Prices," *Spokesman-Review*, May 2, 1907; "Denies Executive Right to Lift Lid," *Spokesman-Review*, December 23, 1907. See also Barber, *Reno's Big Gamble*, 260n65.

2. Bederman, *Manliness and Civilization*; Leonore Davidoff and Catherine Hall, *Family Fortunes: Men and Women of the English Middle Class, 1780–1850* (New York: Routledge, 2002); John Tosh, *A Man's Place: Masculinity and the Middle-Class Home in Victorian England* (London: Yale University Press, 1999).

3. *Spokesman-Review*, February 13, 1895. See also Allen, *Horrible Prettiness*, 146; Berglund, *San Francisco*, 62–63; Dilgard, *Mill Town Footlights*, 4–5; Dudden, *Women in the American Theatre*, 154, 176; Dyar, *News for an Empire*, 55; Erenberg, *Steppin' Out*, 18–19; Hill, "Variety-Vaudeville in Minneapolis," 259; Londré, *Enchanted Years*, 119–38; McNamara, *New York Concert*

Saloon, 1; Toll, *On with the Show*, 208, illustration; Wilmeth, *Variety Entertainment*, 131.

4. Abbott, *How Cities Won the West*, 136; Erenberg, *Steppin' Out*, 8, 21, 82; Gilfoyle, *City of Eros*, 141; Tosh, *A Man's Place*, 179.

5. Berglund, *San Francisco*, 69; Dyar, *News for an Empire*, 125; Elliott, *Variety-Vaudeville in Seattle*, 24–26; Hill, "Variety-Vaudeville in Minneapolis," 124; Wasserman, "Early Theatre in Spokane," 369–82; Washington State, *Session Laws, . . . of 1895*, 177.

6. Washington State, *House Journal of the Fourth Legislature of the State of Washington. Ellis Morrison, Speaker, January 14–March 15, 1895* (Olympia, Wash.: O. C. White, State Printer, 1895), 283, 378, 557; Thomas C. Hoemann and Richard Nafziger, *Members of the Washington State Legislature, 1889–2005* (Olympia, Wash.: Secretary of the Senate, 2005), 57; Washington State, *Senate Journal of the Fourth Legislature of the State of Washington. January 14–March 15, 1895* (Olympia, Wash.: O. C. White, State Printer, 1895), 426, 433, 739. R. B. Milroy, a Yakima Republican, proposed the bill, which moved on to a committee composed of two Populists (one from Spokane) and two Republicans. After receiving the committee's full endorsement, House Bill 405 proceeded through that body with 55 ayes, no negative votes, and 23 absentee votes; it passed the state senate with 20 ayes to 14 absentee votes. Neither the *Seattle Post-Intelligencer* nor the *Seattle Post Times* mentioned it in their coverage of the 1895 state legislature.

7. Cobble, *Dishing It Out*, 156; Barbara F. Reskin and Patricia A. Roos, *Job Queues, Gender Queues: Explaining Women's Inroads into Male Occupations* (Philadelphia: Temple University Press, 1990), 242. The U.S. Supreme Court considered the "barmaid" issue in *Cronin v. Adams* (1904) and *Goesaert et al. v. Cleary et al., Members of the Liquor Control Commission of Michigan* (1948).

8. "The Barmaid Law," *Spokesman-Review*, August 22, 1895; Wasserman, "Early Theatre in Spokane," 371.

9. *State of Washington, Plaintiff, v. John W. Considine, Defendant*, November 1895, case no. 552, reel no. 6, criminal 68.7, Spokane County Courthouse Archives (hereafter SCCA); *State of Washington, Respondent, v. John W. Considine, Appellant*, no. 2466, Supreme Court of Washington, 16 Wash. 358, 47 P. 755, 1897 Wash. Lexis 322; *In re Considine*, Circuit Court, D. Washington, N.D., 83 F. 157, 1897 U.S. App. Lexis 2834, October 20, 1897; *Spokesman-Review*, November 30, December 2, 12, 15, 1895, January 9, 12, 1896, October 21, December 18, 1897. The first installment of Considine's barmaid case occurred in September 1895; he was charged with employing women in a place where liquor was sold. He was judged guilty and fined $500; he then took his suit before the Spokane Superior Court, where Judge James Moore found him guilty. The case went before the Washington State Supreme Court in 1896, which affirmed the lower court's decision and refused to grant Considine a second hearing. Considine and

his team claimed they would take the case to the U.S. Supreme Court, but that did not happen. The closing moment in the barmaid case seems to have been Judge Hanford of the U.S. circuit court's decision to deny Considine's petition for habeas corpus, which would have both interfered with the lower court's ruling and secured Considine's release from the custody of Spokane's sheriff. Considine's attorneys included John Wiley; Jones, Voorhees, and Stevens; Nulton Nuzum; and especially Richard W. Nuzum, who made a career of defending the Spokane underworld. John W. Feighan acted as the prosecuting attorney at all levels of the case.

10. *Washington v. Considine*, no. 2466, pages 15, 16, 21, 29; see also, "The Law Was Loaded," *Spokesman-Review*, May 16, 1894.

11. *Washington v. Considine*, no. 2466, pages 20.

12. "Men Who Cannot Endure Belt," *Spokesman-Review*, May 7, 1895.

13. John W. Feighan, Respondent's Brief, *Washington v. Considine*, no. 2466, pages 6, 13; Timothy J. Gilfoyle, *A Pickpocket's Tale: The Underworld of Nineteenth-Century New York* (New York: W. W. Norton, 2006), 111.

14. *In re Considine*, Circuit Court, D. Washington, N.D. 83 F. 157, 1897 U.S. App., October 20, 1897; also *Spokesman-Review*, May 27, October 21, 1897.

15. "Settled the Case," *Spokesman-Review*, December 18, 1897; Joe Laurie, *Vaudeville: From the Honky-Tonks to the Palace* (New York: Holt, 1953), 411–12; Morgan, *Skid Road*, 120–28; Wasserman, "Early Theatre in Spokane," 372–73.

16. Erenberg, *Steppin' Out*, 7–8.

17. *Spokesman-Review*, September 17, 1892, March 24, 1894, January 15, September 25, 1897, May 27, 1907; Hill, "Variety-Vaudeville in Minneapolis," 150–52; Rettmann, "Business, Government, and Prostitution," 50.

18. Hill, "Variety-Vaudeville in Minneapolis," 259.

19. "City House-Cleaning," *Spokesman-Review*, June 11, 1897. See also Allen, *Horrible Prettiness*, 76; Dilgard, *Mill Town Footlights*, 5; Hill, "Variety-Vaudeville in Minneapolis," 150; Rettmann, "Business, Government, and Prostitution," 62; Wilmeth, *Variety Entertainment*, 131.

20. "A Tragedy in Low Life," *Spokane Chronicle*, March 27, 1891; *Spokesman-Review*, February 23–24, 1904, May 6, December 20, 1907, July 30, 1916; Brady, *Showman*, 55; Wasserman, "Early Theatre in Spokane," 371; Hill, "Variety-Vaudeville in Minneapolis," 150.

21. Dyar, *News for an Empire*, 56–57.

22. *Spokesman-Review*, March 23, 1895, March 2, 1899, December 29, 1907; Hill, "Variety-Vaudeville in Minneapolis," 292; Kohlhauff, "Fifty Years of Theaters"; McNamara, *New York Concert Saloon*, 84; Wasserman, "Early Theatre in Spokane," 371.

23. "A Tragedy in Low Life," *Spokane Chronicle*, March 27, 1891.

24. *Spokesman-Review*, May 19, 1894. See also "Women in Opium Joints," *Spokane Chronicle*, September 5, 1898; *Spokesman-Review*, May 27, 1897,

October 15, 1907; Berglund, *San Francisco*; Hill, "Variety-Vaudeville in Minneapolis," 150; Gilfoyle, *A Pickpocket's Tale*, 87–90.

25. "Her Latest Act," *Spokane Chronicle*, September 11, 1890.

26. Todd DePastino, *Citizen Hobo: How a Century of Homelessness Shaped America* (Chicago: University of Chicago Press, 2003), 83, 148; Paul Groth, *Living Downtown: The History of Residential Hotels in the United States* (Berkeley: University of California Press, 1994), 105–29; Jacquelyn Dowd Hall, "Private Eyes, Public Women: Images of Class and Sex in the Urban South, Atlanta, Georgia, 1913–1915," in *Work Engendered: Toward a New History of American Labor*, ed. Ava Baron (Ithaca. N.Y.: Cornell University Press, 1991), 261; Marybeth Hamilton, *When I'm Bad, I'm Better: Mae West, Sex, and American Entertainment* (Berkeley: University of California Press, 1997), 13; Meyerowitz, *Women Adrift*, xix, 41.

27. Women listed by the U.S. Federal Census in 1900 as living in downtown Spokane were an average of twenty-five years old and overwhelmingly native-born. Spokane County marriage license records from 1891 to 1903 paint a similar picture: the twenty-seven women listed as actresses (or married to actors) in those records had an average age of twenty-three years; with the exception of three English women and one Canadian, all were native-born Americans.

28. Registers of the city prison, July 1, 1898–December 31, 1899, and January 1, 1900–June 30, 1901, Spokane Municipal Government, EA598-3-7 (WSAEB); see also Rettmann, "Business, Government, and Prostitution," 74.

29. R. L. Polk and Co., *Spokane City Directory*, 1895, 1896; *State of Washington, Plaintiff, v. John W. Considine, Defendant*, November 1895, SCCA; Registers of the city prison, July 1898–December 1899 (WSAEB); *Spokesman-Review*, March 22, December 10, 24, 1895.

30. *Spokesman-Review*, October 23, 1904. See also *State of Washington, Plaintiff, v. John W. Considine, Defendant*, November 1895 (SCCA); *Spokesman-Review*, December 28, 1907.

31. *Washington v. Considine*, no. 2466, page 22.

32. U.S. Federal Census, 1900, Spokane County, Washington.

33. "Twice Divorced at Twentieth Birthday," *Spokesman-Review*, October 23, 1904.

34. U.S. Federal Census, 1900, Spokane County, Washington; Eastern Washington Genealogical Society, *Spokane County Washington Marriage Licenses, 1891–1903* (Spokane: Eastern Washington Genealogical Society, 1993). For instance, census takers counted sixteen actresses living in downtown Spokane in 1900; of these women, nine were single, three divorced, and four married. Only three of them had children. Similarly, eight of the twenty-seven actresses (or wives of actors) who received marriage licenses in Spokane County from 1891 to 1903 were signing up for at least their second marriage, some at a tender age.

35. For descriptive information—however flawed—about theater women, turn to the *Spokane Chronicle*, September 11, 1890; February 11, March 4, 27, 1891; April 20, 1899. In the *Spokesman-Review*, see February 25, March 22, 1895; March 2, 1899; February 23–24, October 23, 1904; August 28, September 3, 1905, October 15, November 5, December 28–29, 1907; January 12, 1908.

36. For other accounts of the home life and career choices of variety and vaudeville actresses, see Hill, "Variety-Vaudeville in Minneapolis," 261; Rodger, *Champagne Charlie and Pretty Jemima*, 27, 51–55, 87–91; Snyder, *Voice of the City*, 59–60.

37. McNamara, *New York Concert Saloon*, 84.

38. See "Considine Case," *Spokesman-Review*, December 12, 1895; Cochran, *Seven Frontier Women*, 50, 84, 197; Rettmann, "Business, Government, and Prostitution."

39. Council minutes record book E (WSAEB), 740, 748, 752.

40. Bederman, *Manliness and Civilization*, 12. See also Donovan, *White Slave Crusades*, 6.

41. *Spokesman-Review*, March 20, 25, April 20, 22–24, 1895; Jon C. Teaford, *The Unheralded Triumph: City Government in America, 1870–1900* (Baltimore: Johns Hopkins University Press, 1984), 9, 175.

42. "Broiled Belt," *Spokane Chronicle*, April 1, 1895. See also *Spokesman-Review*, March 30, April 1, 1895.

43. Reginald Horsman, *Race and Manifest Destiny: The Origins of American Racial Anglo-Saxonism* (Cambridge, Mass.: Harvard University Press, 1981); Matthew Frye Jacobson, *Whiteness of a Different Color: European Immigrants and the Alchemy of Race* (Cambridge, Mass.: Harvard University Press, 1999); Gareth Stedman Jones, *Outcast London: A Study in the Relationship between Classes in Victorian Society* (Oxford: Oxford University Press, 1971).

44. Bederman, *Manliness and Civilization*, 203; Hall, "Private Eyes, Public Women," 252; Matthew Frye Jacobson, *Barbarian Virtues: The United States Encounters Foreign Peoples at Home and Abroad, 1876–1917* (New York: Hill and Wang, 2001); Lears, *No Place of Grace*, 29–30.

45. "Hot Shot for Varieties," *Spokesman-Review*, March 25, 1895. Other ministers gave a racial, or at least emasculated, cast to the debate by describing male theatergoers as "enslaved" to the variety theaters.

46. Smilax, "The Varieties and Dance Halls," *Spokesman-Review*, March 23, 1895. Smilax was a household soap of the era.

47. Berglund, *San Francisco*, 68; Donovan, *White Slave Crusades*, 44–45; Neil Foley, *The White Scourge: Mexicans, Blacks, and Poor Whites in Texas Cotton Culture* (Berkeley: University of California Press, 1998), 6; Gilfoyle, *A Pickpocket's Tale*, 289; Horsman, *Race and Manifest Destiny*, 233; Jacobson, *Barbarian Virtues*, 125; Jones, *Outcast London*, 128–30; Ellen Ross, *Love and Toil: Motherhood in Outcast London* (Oxford: Oxford University Press, 1993), 206.

48. "Running the Gantlet," *Spokesman-Review*, April 1, 1895. See also "Rev. Euster on the True Citizen," *Spokesman-Review*, April 29, 1895.

49. "Mr. Belt's Position," *Spokesman-Review*, April 19, 1895.

50. Council minutes record book G (WSAEB), 667, 675, 676, 679. The September 19 votes concerned the licensing of Henry "Fisky" Barnett's Comique. The second series of votes concerned Gust Pearson's Stockholm and Goetz and Baer's Coeur d'Alene.

51. "Acuff Whips the Theaters," *Spokane Chronicle*, September 22, 1899; "Fiery Speech in the Council," *Spokesman-Review*, September 23, 1899; Bederman, *Manliness and Civilization*, 13.

52. "Bitter Words Were Spoken," *Spokesman-Review*, September 27, 1899. See also Council minutes record book G (WSAEB), 680–85.

53. "Omo Is in a Rage," *Spokesman-Review*, September 24, 1899.

54. A possible exception occurred in the summer of 1894, when the Women's Protective Association protested to the city government against the use of barmaids in variety theaters. Within a few weeks, the city began arresting barmaids at venues like the Louvre; the barmaids, in turn, petitioned the Women's Protective Association for relief. Like so many attempts to clean up the varieties, the 1894 effort failed: within one week of the raids, the "waiter girls" had returned to work. *Spokesman-Review*, May 16, 1894; Wasserman, "Early Theatre in Spokane," 376.

55. *Spokesman-Review*, March 14, 25, 27, 1895.

56. Engle, "Benefiting a City," 109, 121.

57. *Spokane Chronicle*, May 4, 1903.

58. Robert Charles Eckberg, "The Free Speech Fight of the Industrial Workers of the World, Spokane, Washington: 1909–1910" (master's thesis, Washington State University, 1967), 8; Kensel, "Economic History," 92.

59. John Ellingson, "Eighty-Five Years of Spokane Memories: The Recollections of Clarence Tesdahl," *Pacific Northwesterner: Westerners, Spokane Corral* 39, no. 1 (1995): 4–6; John Fahey, "Big Lumber in the Inland Empire: The Early Years, 1900–1930," *Pacific Northwest Quarterly* 76, no. 3 (1985): 97; Schwantes, *Pacific Northwest*, 219–21, 328, 333; Kensel, "Economic History," 145, 175–85; Wasserman, "Early Theatre in Spokane," 307.

60. "Theaters Work 278 Employes," *Spokesman-Review*, January 27, 1902; Durham, *History of the City of Spokane*, 1:511. The *Spokesman-Review*, which gathered these numbers, reported that the Coeur d'Alene employed 176 people, while the Comique employed 35 and had a yearly payroll of $36,400. The Auditorium, meanwhile, employed an average of 35 people and had an annual payroll of $16,470; the Spokane employed 32 souls and expended $12,250 annually. The Coeur d'Alene, despite its unsavory reputation, was clearly at the top of the local entertainment heap.

61. See "Spokane as It Is Today," *Spokane Chronicle*, May 2, 1903; *Spokesman-Review*, May 3, 1901, October 12, 1904.

62. See Abbott, *How Cities Won the West*, 143–45.

63. "No More Reforming," *Spokesman-Review*, January 17, 1900; "Rotten as Hell," *Spokesman-Review*, November 26, 1900.

64. *Spokane Chronicle*, April 30, 1901. See also *Spokane Chronicle*, April 15, 1901; "What Citizens' League Desires," *Spokesman-Review*, May 1, 1901.

65. "Roast for Spokane," *Spokesman-Review*, May 4, 1901; also Barber, *Reno's Big Gamble*.

66. "Say Stock Is Going Up," *Spokane Chronicle*, May 4, 1901; "Pastors Spoke on Politics," *Spokesman-Review*, May 6, 1901; Engle, "Benefiting a City," 126–27. According to Nancy Engle, local WCTU membership suffered during the late 1890s and then rebounded around 1901. It was at this point, with its endorsement of Anderson and the Citizens' League, that the WCTU began its first notable involvement with the drive to reform Spokane's variety theaters.

67. "Can You Trust Him," *Spokane Chronicle*, May 4, 1901; "The Autopsy," *Spokane Chronicle*, May 8, 1901; *Spokesman-Review*, November 11, 1901, May 3, 1903; Durham, *History of the City of Spokane*, 1:511, 515; Engle, "Benefiting a City," 127.

68. *Spokane Chronicle*, May 1–5, 1903; *Spokesman-Review*, May 2–6, 1903. The *Spokesman-Review* likewise supported Acuff but felt that Huber Rasher, the Democratic candidate, would also stand up to the so-called slum element.

69. See "Spokane as It Is Today," *Spokane Chronicle*, May 2, 1903.

70. "Spokane as It Is Today," *Spokane Chronicle*, May 4, 1903; "Brazen Vice in the Tenderloin," *Spokesman-Review*, May 3, 1903.

71. See *Spokesman-Review*, June 9, 1897, July 9, 1903, September 18, 1905.

72. *Spokane Chronicle*, May 2, 1903.

73. "Brazen Vice in the Tenderloin," *Spokesman-Review*, May 3, 1903.

74. "Spokane as It Is Today," *Spokane Chronicle*, May 4, 1903.

75. See "Pastors Spoke on Politics," *Spokesman-Review*, May 6, 1901.

76. "What Is the Price," *Spokane Chronicle*, May 2, 1903; "Acuff and Rasher Lead," *Spokesman-Review*, May 5, 1903; "It Was a Good Fight," *Spokane Chronicle*, May 6, 1903.

77. "Spokane's New Mission," *Spokane Chronicle*, May 2, 1903; "Politics in the Pulpits," *Spokesman-Review*, May 3, 1903.

78. "Shall It Remain Like This," *Spokane Chronicle*, May 4, 1903.

79. *Spokane Chronicle*, May 5, 6, 1903; *Spokesman-Review*, May 6, 1903; *Spokane Chronicle*, April 21–22, 24, 27, May 3, 1905; Durham, *History of the City of Spokane*, 1:528.

80. "Grateful Boy of 22 Gives $50 to Build Y.M.C.A. Home," *Spokesman-Review*, March 8, 1906.

81. Durham, *History of the City of Spokane*, 1:531; *Spokane Chronicle*, January 2, 12, February 2, 1906; "Colorado's Elected Executive Much Impressed with Beauty, Homelike Quality and Financial Strength of the City," *Spokesman-Review*, September 1, 1905.

82. "Denies Executive Right to Lift Lid," *Spokesman-Review*, December 23, 1907; Barber, *Reno's Big Gamble*, 45–46.

83. Henderson, "Mirror to the History," 104. In 1905, there were 75,000 people who lived in Spokane. The 150,000 Club was connected to the chamber of commerce and was especially promoted by the *Spokesman-Review*, though the *Chronicle* also supported it.

84. "Publicity Built Spokane," *Spokesman-Review*, September 14, 1905; "Spokane a Home City," *Spokane Chronicle*, January 1, 1906; *Spokesman-Review*, September 1, 3, 10, October 12, 1905.

85. "Do You Vote Yea or Nay," *Spokane Chronicle*, January 2, 1906.

86. Abbott, *How Cities Won the West*, 143–45; Paul Boyer, *Urban Masses and Moral Order in America, 1820–1920* (Cambridge, Mass.: Harvard University Press, 1978), 262–64; Greg Hise, *Magnetic Los Angeles: Planning the Twentieth-Century Metropolis* (Baltimore: Johns Hopkins University Press, 1997), 20; Issel and Cherny, *San Francisco*, 110–11; Starr, *California Dream*, 298–301; William H. Wilson, *The City Beautiful Movement* (Baltimore: Johns Hopkins University Press, 1994).

87. "Wider Scope of City Beautiful," *Spokesman-Review*, November 26, 1905.

88. "He Asks, 'Is There Graft in Spokane?'" *Spokane Chronicle*, January 12, 1906; *Spokesman-Review*, September 18, November 9, 1905, January 12, February 5, March 2, 1906.

89. "All Lines in the 150,000 Club," *Spokesman-Review*, September 3, 1905; *Spokesman-Review*, October 13, 15, 1905, January 14, March 4, 1906.

90. Boyer, *Urban Masses and Moral Order*, 113; *Spokesman-Review*, March 7, 1906.

91. "Shall the Varieties Go?" *Spokesman-Review*, March 25, 1895; *Spokesman-Review*, November 5, 1905, January 12, March 2, 1906; Morrissey, *Mental Territories*, 56; Wang, "Streetscape Evolution," 20. For the new establishments, see *Spokane Chronicle*, April 20, June 14, 1898, October 3, 1899, January 20, 1906; *Spokesman-Review*, March 25, 1895, November 11, 1896, June 15, 1897, January 16, 1909; Register of the city prison, July 1898–December 1899 (WSAEB); Rettmann, "Business, Government, and Prostitution," 74.

92. DePastino, *Citizen Hobo*, 130. See also "Ninety-Four Hotels Here," *Spokane Chronicle*, February 16, 1909; "For Home and City," *Spokesman-Review*, May 5, 1907; Abbott, *How Cities Won the West*, 135–36; DePastino, *Citizen Hobo*, xx, 61, 81, 91, 117, 129; Groth, *Living Downtown*, 131–51.

93. "Queer Scenes on Hoboes' Island," *Spokesman-Review*, November 26, 1905; Gilfoyle, *City of Eros*, 238–41; Lears, *No Place of Grace*, 29; DePastino, *Citizen Hobo*. "Hobohemia" was contemporary slang for a city's transient district.

94. "Sabbath Dawns on Dry Spokane," *Spokesman-Review*, January 12, 1908. See also *Spokesman-Review*, December 20, 23–24, 28–29, 1907;

Gilfoyle, *A Pickpocket's Tale*, 86, 110, 186; Hill, "Variety-Vaudeville in Minneapolis," 123. During the 1895 anti-vice drive, for instance, F. B. Cherington reported that, when a young man entered a variety theater box, a waitress taunted him with "'What kind of man are you if you won't buy a drink?' And a young man couldn't go there and uphold his standing . . . if he didn't." "Good Government," *Spokesman-Review*, March 20, 1895.

95. "Over Which Road Will You Send Your Boy," *Spokesman-Review*, March 7, 1906.

96. "Spokane's Boy Market," *Spokane Chronicle*, January 20, 1906; "Boys' Morals in the Balance," *Spokesman-Review*, January 22, 1906.

97. *Spokane Chronicle*, January 12, February 2, 6, 13, 1906; *Spokesman-Review*, March 11, April 21, 24, 26, 1907; R. L. Polk and Co., *Spokane City Directory*, 1907; Dyar, *News for an Empire*, 155; Edward R. Hodgson, "Early Spokane's 150,000 Club: Missed 1910 Population Goal by 31 Per Cent," *Pacific Northwesterner* 21, no. 2 (1977): 17.

98. "Danger in Overconfidence," *Spokesman-Review*, April 26, 1907. See also *Spokesman-Review*, April 21, 25, May 5, 1907; Berglund, *San Francisco*, 51; Dyar, *News for an Empire*, 55; Teaford, *Unheralded Triumph*, 6.

99. "Why They Support Moore," *Spokesman-Review*, April 28, 1907. For the constituencies reportedly behind Daggett and Moore, see *Spokesman-Review*, April 17–18, 20, 24, May 1, 3–4, 1907.

100. Barber, *Reno's Big Gamble*, 45.

101. *Spokesman-Review*, December 23, 28, 1907.

102. *Spokesman-Review*, May 21, 23–24, 29, December 20, 24, 1907.

103. *Spokesman-Review*, May 27, December 20, 23–24, 28–29, 1907. For more of the alleged victimizing of male variety theater patrons by box rustlers, see Dyar, *News for an Empire*, 55; *Spokesman-Review*, September 17, 1892, March 24, 1894, January 1, 1897.

104. "Unworthy of License," *Spokesman-Review*, December 24, 1907.

105. "Just a Few Wants," *Spokane Chronicle*, January 2, 1908; *Spokesman-Review*, January 4–6, 8–9, 1908.

106. *Spokesman-Review*, May 21, 29, 1907, January 4, 8, 1908.

107. "Theaters Can Wait," *Spokane Chronicle*, April 7, 1899; *Spokesman-Review*, May 2, December 23, 28, 1907; Engle, "Benefiting a City," ch. 4; Elizabeth Gurley Flynn, *The Rebel Girl: An Autobiography, My First Life (1906–1926)* (New York: International Publishers, 1973), 106–11.

108. *Spokesman-Review*, January 10, 11, 1908; Durham, *History of the City of Spokane*, 1:541.

109. "Comique Will Close," *Spokane Chronicle*, June 16, 1899; "Will Put Lid on Spokane May 31," *Spokesman-Review*, May 21, 1907.

110. "Sabbath Dawns on Dry Spokane," *Spokesman-Review*, January 12, 1908. For the connection of prohibition with New England, see Frick, *Theatre, Culture and Temperance Reform*, 42, 131. In 1909 Dr. E. Pittwood announced

his mayoral candidacy on a platform that included the reintroduction of free saloon lunches and variety theaters, which he claimed would bolster the city's population and prosperity. "Would Be Mayor of a Wild, Woolly Town," *Spokane Chronicle*, February 19, 1909.

111. Business Service Association, *The Coeur d'Alene of Spokane, Washington: "The Hotel with a Personality"* (Spokane: Business Service Association, 190–), 4, 10–11, 15; "Dutch Jake in Vaudeville," *Spokesman-Review*, March 17, 1908.

4. The Geography and Hierarchy of Show Business

1. "Come to Attend Show," *Spokesman-Review*, January 21, 1917. See also Donald W. Meinig, "American Wests: Preface to a Geographical Interpretation," in *Annals of the Association of American Geographers* 62, no. 2 (June 1972): 163; Snyder, *Voice of the City*, 82–83.

2. "Ballet Russe at Auditorium on Tour to Present Seven Ballets," *Spokesman-Review*, January 14, 1917.

3. *Spokesman-Review*, January 17, 1917.

4. *Spokesman-Review*, January 21, 1917, also January 14, 20, 1917.

5. Schwantes, *Pacific Northwest*, 148. See also Abbott, *Metropolitan Frontier*, xii; Kathleen A. Brosnan, *Uniting Mountain and Plain: Cities, Law, and Environmental Change along the Front Range* (Albuquerque: University of New Mexico Press, 2002), 20; Michael P. Conzen and Diane Dillon, eds., *Mapping Manifest Destiny: Chicago and the American West* (Chicago: University of Chicago Press, 2008), 94, 101; Cronon, *Nature's Metropolis*, 53; Lears, *No Place of Grace*, 34; Donald W. Meinig, *The Shaping of America: A Geographical Perspective on 500 Years of History*, vol. 2: *Continental America, 1800–1867* (New Haven: Yale University Press, 1993), ch. 10; Morse, *Nature of Gold*, 9–11.

6. Brosnan, *Uniting Mountain and Plain*, 10–13.

7. Meinig, "American Wests," 162–65.

8. Erenberg, *Steppin' Out*, preface; McArthur, *Actors and American Culture*, 8–9.

9. Allen, *Horrible Prettiness*; Ashby, *Amusement for All*; Halttunen, *Confidence Men and Painted Women*; Kasson, *Rudeness and Civility*; Levine, *Highbrow/Lowbrow*, Nasaw, *Going Out*.

10. Arthur Frank Wertheim, *Vaudeville Wars: How the Keith-Albee and Orpheum Circuits Controlled the Big-Time and Its Performers* (New York: Palgrave Macmillan, 2006), 44.

11. Fahey, *Inland Empire*, 3; Henderson, "Mirror to the History," 32–35; Kensel, "Economic History," 163–64, 200.

12. Eckberg, "Free Speech Fight," 8; Engle, "Benefiting a City," 9, 13; Wang, "Streetscape Evolution," 20; Matthews, "Kirtland Cutter: Spokane's Architect."

13. Kensel, "Economic History," 113–18, 153–56.

14. Morrissey, *Mental Territories*, 154–55; Schwantes, *Pacific Northwest*, 159–60, 141.

15. Londré, *Enchanted Years*, 33–34; *Spokesman-Review*, August 24, 1913, July 22, 1917; Fahey, "When the Dutch Owned Spokane," 3; Harry Hayward employment contracts, box 6, folder 26, Northwestern and Pacific Hypotheek Bank Records, Ms 46 (EWSHS).

16. For instance, May White Palmerston built the Spokane at the turn of the century for productions booked and controlled by the Northwest arm of the Klaw and Erlanger organization. Judge George Turner—one of the city's brightest lights—owned the Orpheum property, which was, for years, controlled by John Considine, respectable Spokane's erstwhile enemy. *Spokesman-Review*, March 5, 1910, February 18, August 17, 1915, December 9, 1917; Durham, *History of the City of Spokane*, 2:116–17.

17. McArthur, *Actors and American Culture*, 9–10.

18. Robert Grau, *The Business Man in the Amusement World: A Volume of Progress in the Field of the Theatre* (New York: Broadway Publishing, 1910), 2. See also Elliott, *Variety-Vaudeville in Seattle*, 45; *Spokesman-Review*, May 19, 1901.

19. Margaret Knapp, "Introductory Essay," in *Inventing Times Square: Commerce and Culture at the Crossroads of the World*, ed. William R. Taylor (New York: Russell Sage Foundation, 1991), 121–24.

20. Grau, *Business Man*, 8, 72, 76–83, 160, 185, 222–26; Brett Page, *Writing for Vaudeville* (Springfield, Mass.: Home Correspondence School, 1915), chs. 24, 25.

21. Julius Cahn, *Julius Cahn's Official Theatrical Guide, Containing Authentic Information of the Theatres and Attractions in the United States, Canada, Mexico and Cuba* (New York: Empire Theatre Building, 1908), 13:84, 249, 554, 768, 771; W. R. Dailey, ed., *Henry's Official Western Theatrical Guide, 1907–1908* (San Francisco, 1908), 83–90; Herbert Lloyd, *Vaudeville Trails thru the West: "By One Who Knows"* (Philadelphia: Herbert Lloyd, 1919), 9.

22. "Theatrical Syndicate Copy No. 1," box 1, Federal Theatre Project collection, acc. no. 5287-001, University of Washington Special Collections (hereafter UWSC), 2, 8; Jones, *Renegades*, 1; Nelson, "Road Shows in Seattle," 25, 40, 45. It was not until 1881, for instance, that eastern companies considered Washington populated and profitable enough to include in their tours.

23. *Spokane Chronicle*, June 14, 1893, July 6, 1900. For Spokane's growth, see *Spokane Chronicle*, August 30, 1916; *Spokesman-Review*, September 30, 1905, January 30, 1906, April 10, 1910, April 17, 1915; Kensel, "Economic History," 79–80, 88, 154, 160, 167. For New York, see Grau, *Business Man*, 160.

24. Peter A. Davis, "The Syndicate/Shubert War," in Taylor, *Inventing Times Square*, 150–52; Lippman, "Theatrical Syndicate"; Schwantes, *Radical Heritage*, 19; Wertheim, *Vaudeville Wars*, 97–98.

25. Wertheim, *Vaudeville Wars*, 51, 56–57; *Spokane Chronicle*, April 12, 1890, February 4, 1893, October 28, 1896; Booth, "Theatrical Boom in the

Kootenays," 42–43; Edwards, *Illustrated History*, 313; Jones, *Renegades*, 57–69; Wasserman, "Early Theatre in Spokane," 205, 324.

26. Berelson and Grant, "Pioneer Theatre in Washington," 128; Ernst, *Oregon Country*, 86, 130–40; "Theatrical Syndicate Copy No. 1" (UWSC), 11–13; Wertheim, *Vaudeville Wars*, 51, 56.

27. Davis, "Syndicate/Shubert War," 153–54; Grau, *Business Man*, 4–6; Lippman, "Theatrical Syndicate," 26.

28. Berelson and Grant, "Pioneer Theatre," 131; Ernst, *Oregon Country*, 139; Eric L. Flom, "Cort, John," HistoryLink.org Essay 3296, accessed February 3, 2011; "Theatrical Syndicate Copy No. 1" (UWSC), 22.

29. Jessica H. Kelly, "John Cort: The Frohman of the West," *The Coast* 8, no. 3 (March 1907): 144; "Theatrical Syndicate Copy No. 1" (UWSC), 22.

30. *Spokane Chronicle*, December 18, 1897, January 1, April 11, 13, 1898, July 22, 1899, June 15, August 3, 1900; Wasserman, "Early Theatre in Spokane," 324.

31. Margaret Bean, interview, December 8, 1958, pioneer voices series (OH 460, EWSHS); *Spokane Chronicle*, April 11, 29, 1901; A. C. Libby, Jr., "Stars Added Glamour to Old Auditorium," *Spokesman-Review*, June 13, 1943; "Theatrical Syndicate Copy No. 1" (UWSC), 22, 26; Wasserman, "Early Theatre in Spokane," 335, 338. The exact date of Hayward's rejection of the Syndicate is not extant. As late as March 9, 1901, Hayward had plans for his own "family" theater that would present "popular-priced" production, while he would reserve more expensive Syndicate-controlled shows for the Auditorium. By April 29, however, the *Chronicle* referred to a recent decision to build a new Syndicate house—not the Auditorium—in Spokane. In response to this Syndicate move, J. P. Howe announced his desire to create an independent northwestern circuit, in which Hayward's Auditorium would form a crucial link. By May 1901 the Syndicate and the NWTA had begun work on the Spokane Theater. *Spokane Chronicle*, March 9, April 29, 1901; *Spokesman-Review*, May 9, 1901.

32. When Henry Greenwall, the organizing force for regional theatrical circuits in Texas, refused to give into Syndicate demands, his prospects also darkened. At the turn of the century Greenwall's house in Fort Worth found it almost impossible to book a season of decent entertainment. Jones, *Renegades*, 71, 88.

33. *Spokesman-Review*, May 1, 9, 26, October 30, 1901, December 9, 1917. The Spokane was operated by the Spokane Theater Company, whose officers were John Cort of Seattle (president), Calvin Heilig of Portland (vice president), Sid Rosenhaupt of Spokane (secretary), and Dan Weaver of Spokane (assistant manager). The physical property was leased to Heilig, Cort, and Rosenhaupt. It was booked under the direction of Marc Klaw and Abraham Erlanger, of New York.

34. "New Spokane Theater," *Spokesman-Review*, May 1, 1901.

35. Kohlhauff, "Fifty Years of Theaters"; Bean, interview, December 8, 1958 (OH 460, EWSHS); *Spokesman-Review,* February 2, 1901, June 13, 1943; Wasserman, "Early Theatre in Spokane," 319.

36. Wasserman, "Early Theatre in Spokane," 324, 337; *Spokesman-Review,* February 2, May 25, June 7, 1902.

37. The *Argus* is cited from "Theatrical Syndicate Copy No. 1" (UWSC), 26–27.

38. See, for instance, *Spokesman-Review,* July 15, September 2, 1900. See Londré, *Enchanted Years,* 105, for an account of the civic role a similar theater played for the people of Kansas City.

39. *Spokesman-Review,* February 18, 1903, March 13, 1904.

40. See Durham, *History of the City of Spokane,* 1:560; Stratton, ed., *Spokane and the Inland Empire,* 180; Bean, interview, December 8, 1958 (OH 460, EWSHS); Horace Brown, interview by Louis Livingston, August 19, 1955 (OH 624, EWSHS); Libby, "Stars Added Glamour."

41. "Setting Forth the Reason of the Stars' Western Exodus," *Spokesman-Review,* January 23, 1910. See also Jones, *Renegades,* 88.

42. *Spokane Chronicle,* May 3, 1905; *Spokesman-Review,* May 27, 1900, September 18, 1904, October 22, 1905, January 23, May 8, 1910; Elliott, *Variety-Vaudeville in Seattle,* 46; Kelly, "Frohman of the West," 144; Lippman, "Theatrical Syndicate," 149.

43. "Theatrical Syndicate Copy No. 1" (UWSC), 32, 34, 35; *Spokane Chronicle,* January 4, August 26, 1909; *Spokesman-Review,* November 7, 1905, March 5, 1906; Elliott, *Variety-Vaudeville in Seattle,* 46; Ernst, *Oregon Country,* 130–31.

44. Davis, "Syndicate/Shubert War," 155–57; Grau, *Business Man,* 5–6; Lippman, "Theatrical Syndicate," 111, 133, 141.

45. "Theatrical Syndicate Copy No. 1" (UWSC), 32; Elliott, *Variety-Vaudeville in Seattle,* 46.

46. *New York Times,* May 1, 8, 11, 14, 16, 1910; *Spokesman-Review,* May 1, 8, 18, 22, 27, 1910; "Trust Is Busted," *Spokane Chronicle,* May 2, 1910; "Theatrical Syndicate Copy No. 1" (UWSC), 23; Ernst, *Oregon Country,* 139–40; Lippman, "Theatrical Syndicate," 149–52.

47. Grau, *Business Man,* 9. See also *New York Times,* May 11, 15, 27, 1910; Berelson and Grant, "Pioneer Theatre," 121n12.

48. *Spokesman-Review,* April 10, May 22 (quotation), 1910; Jones, *Renegades,* 48; Wertheim, *Vaudeville Wars,* 58–59, 62, 97.

49. *Spokane Chronicle,* April 3, 1906; *Spokesman-Review,* September 30, October 3, 6, 1905, January 30, 1906. See also *Spokesman-Review,* January 17, 1915, July 8, 1917; Jones, *Renegades,* 70; Nelson, "Road Shows in Seattle," 113.

50. Ida Estby, interview by Mary Avery, March 25, 1973 (OH 003, EWSHS), 4.

51. *Spokane Chronicle,* April 7, 1906; *Spokesman-Review,* February 18, 1903, September 18, 1904; Booth, "Theatrical Boom in the Kootenays," 43.

52. "Theatrical Truce in the Northwest," *New York Times*, November 2, 1910. See also "1,200 Theatres Are Now Independent," *New York Times*, May 8, 1910.

53. Allen, *Horrible Prettiness*, 74.

54. Snyder, *Voice of the City*, 12. See also Ashby, *Amusement for All*, ch. 4; Barth, *City People*, 192–201; Erdman, *Blue Vaudeville*, 8–13; Wertheim, *Vaudeville Wars*, ch. 1; Wilmeth, *Variety Entertainment*, 132–34.

55. Kibler, *Rank Ladies*, 18–19; Snyder, *Voice of the City*, ch. 5; Wertheim, *Vaudeville Wars*, 239; Wilmeth, *Variety Entertainment*, 132.

56. *Spokane Chronicle*, April 25, June 24, 1905, October 5, 1907, January 4, February 26, 1909; *Spokesman-Review*, May 3, 1902, February 29, 1904.

57. "Found Big Theater Trust," *Spokesman-Review*, February 5, 1908; Berelson and Grant, "Pioneer Theatre," 129; Ernst, *Oregon Country*, 145; Daniel Czitrom, "Underworlds and Underdogs: Big Tim Sullivan and Metropolitan Politics in New York, 1889–1913," *Journal of American History* 78, no. 2 (September 1991): 551; Flom, "Cort, John"; Kensel, "Economic History," 167; Morse, *Nature of Gold*; Schwantes, *Pacific Northwest*, 160; Theodore Saloutos, "Alexander Pantages, Theater Magnate of the West," *Pacific Northwest Quarterly* 57 (October 1966), 138–39; Dean Arthur Tarrach, "Alexander Pantages: The Seattle Pantages and His Vaudeville Circuit" (master's thesis, University of Washington, 1973), 51.

58. Berelson and Grant, "Pioneer Theatre," 117. John Cort and Alexander Pantages—the two other barons of northwestern show business—also advanced their careers by moving their theaters out of seedy Seattle neighborhoods and into more respectable areas of the city.

59. L. Carson, ed., *The Stage Year Book, 1914* (London: The Stage Offices, 1914), 70–72; "John Considine Sr., Veteran Showman," *New York Times*, February 13, 1943; Berelson and Grant, "Pioneer Theatre," 118, 131; Frank Cullen and Florence Hackman, *Vaudeville Old and New: An Encyclopedia of Variety Performers in America* (New York: Routledge, 2006), 263–65; Czitrom, "Underworlds and Underdogs," 551; Elliott, *Variety-Vaudeville in Seattle*, 53–57; Ernst, *Oregon Country*, 142–43; Robert Grau, *The Stage in the Twentieth Century* (New York: Broadway Publishing, 1912), 237–38; Grau, *Business Man*, 140–42; Laurie, *Vaudeville*, 411; Saloutos, "Alexander Pantages" 140; Oliver Simmons, "Passing of the Sullivan Dynasty," *Munsey's Magazine* 1, no. 3 (December 1913): 415; Tarrach, "Alexander Pantages," 41–43. The opening year of Sullivan and Considine's partnership is variously listed as 1901 and 1904.

60. *Spokane Chronicle*, December 5, 1905, January 19, 1906; *Spokesman-Review*, May 12, December 5, 1905; Grau, *Business Man*, 141; Tarrach, "Alexander Pantages," 43.

61. Morris Meyerfeld and Martin Beck headed the Orpheum circuit.

62. Helen Campbell, Diary, 1913–1917, box 1, folder 1, Helen Campbell papers, MsSC 224 (EWSHS); *Spokane Chronicle*, June 24, 1905, January 24, April 21, May 2, 1906, February 6, 1909; *Spokesman-Review*, May 1, 2, 1906. The Washington-Columbia theater company was composed of Spokane businessmen but was evidently connected to Considine as it operated (by lease) both the Washington and the Cineograph. This meant that by the second half of the 1900s Considine had a hand in three Spokane theaters. John Cordray represented S&C interests in Spokane and managed both the Washington and Orpheum. The Orpheum began life in 1906 as the Columbia, which played stock; this arrangement lasted only a short while. As the Orpheum "advanced vaudeville," seats for the two daily performances cost from fifteen to seventy-five cents in 1909.

63. Eric Flom, "Seattle's Orpheum Theatre Opens at 3rd Avenue and Madison Street on May 15, 1911," Essay 4247, HistoryLink.org, accessed February 17, 2011.

64. Carson, *Stage Year Book, 1914*, 66–67; Grau, *Business Man*, 273; Grau, *Twentieth Century*, 46–47, 158; Jones, *Renegades*, 95; Londré, *Enchanted Years*, 222–24; Wertheim, *Vaudeville Wars*, 152 (quotation). Evidence suggests that vaudeville moguls paid attention to well-connected regional capitals similar to Spokane, such as Kansas City, as they developed their networks. Like Spokanites, the residents of those provincial cities were subordinate in these relationships.

65. "Theatrical Syndicate Copy No. 1" (UWSC), 43; Ernst, *Oregon Country*, 143.

66. "Opening of Pantages," *Spokane Chronicle*, October 8, 1907; Berelson and Grant, "Pioneer Theatre," 129; Carson, *Stage Year Book, 1914*, xviii, 73; Grau, *Business Man*, 96 (globe-trotting), *Twentieth Century*, 150 (specialties); Saloutos, "Alexander Pantages," 137–42.

67. *Spokane Chronicle*, August 7, 1909.

68. "Uncle Sam Welcomes Spokane to the One Hundred Thousand League," *Spokesman-Review*, December 10, 1910; Durham, *History of the City of Spokane*, 1:553, 560–62; Henry Matthews, *Kirtland Cutter: Architect in the Land of Promise* (Seattle: University of Washington Press, 1998), 258–59; Morrissey, *Mental Territories*, 115–16; Schwantes, *Pacific Northwest*, 277; Wang, "Streetscape Evolution," 14. Boosters had pushed for Spokane to reach 150,000 by 1910 but Spokanites were still thrilled to join the "100,000 league" when that year's census counted 104,402 residents.

69. See *Spokane Chronicle*, February 13, 1909.

70. Schwantes, *Pacific Northwest*, 141. See also Schwantes, *Radical Heritage*, 19; Schwantes, "Wageworkers' Frontier," 128.

71. Fahey, *Inland Empire*, 3; Morrissey, *Mental Territories*, 161; Wang, "Streetscape Evolution," 22.

72. See Grau, *Business Man*, 139; Grau, *Twentieth Century*, 53; Page, *Writing for Vaudeville*, ch. 24.

73. "Syndicate to Have New Theatre Chain," *New York Times*, May 27, 1910; Jones, *Renegades*, 109–13, 121–23; Lippman, "Theatrical Syndicate," 178; Nelson, "Road Shows in Seattle," 142.

74. *Spokane Chronicle*, August 26, September 2, 1909; *Spokesman-Review*, September 22, 1909; *Official Gazette of the City of Spokane*, vol. 3, *January–December 1913* (Spokane, Wash.: Office of the City Clerk, 1913), 2428; Lippman, "Theatrical Syndicate," 133; George L. Lufkin, "American Theatre, Spokane, Wash.," *Marquee: The Journal of the Theatre Historical Society* 5, no. 2 (2nd quarter, 1973): 5.

75. *Spokesman-Review*, April 4 1910; see also April 10, 1910.

76. Cullen and Hackman, *Vaudeville Old and New*, 796–97; Grau, *Twentieth Century*, 45; Wertheim, *Vaudeville Wars*, 147.

77. *Spokesman-Review*, March 5, 1910. See also *Spokane Chronicle*, December 15, 26, 1910; *Spokesman-Review*, May 1, December 26, 1910, August 9, 1914; Durham, *History of the City of Spokane*, 3:613; *The Pacific Reporter* 121 (St. Paul: West Publishing, 1912), 46–47.

78. "Music Hall Gets No K. & E. Shows," *Spokane Chronicle*, November 29, 1910.

79. "Agreement with Theater Unbroken," *Spokane Chronicle*, November 30, 1910; *Spokesman-Review*, December 1, 1910, September 7, 1913, August 9, 1914.

80. *Spokane Chronicle*, December 13, 15, 1910; *Spokesman-Review*, December 10, 11, 13, 1910.

81. *Spokesman-Review*, December 26, 1910. See also *Spokane Chronicle*, December 24, 26, 1910; *Spokesman-Review*, December 18, 25, 1910, November 19, 1911; Durham, *History of the City of Spokane*, 1:553.

82. *Spokesman-Review*, May 28, 1916. See also *Spokesman-Review*, February 10, 26, 1911, September 7, October 3, 5, November 8, 1913, April 9, August 9, September 16, 1914.

83. Washington State, *Fourteenth Biennial Report of the Secretary of State, October 1, 1914, September 30, 1916* (Olympia, Wash.: Frank M. Lamborn, Public Printer, 1916), 61.

84. "Loew-Considine Agreement," *New York Times*, August 16, 1911; James Grant Thurston, "Managers Talk of Fight with Union," *Spokesman-Review*, August 27, 1911. See also *Spokane Chronicle*, November 13, 1909, May 13, 1911, September 7, 21, 1912.

85. Cullen and Hackman, *Vaudeville Old and New*, 264. See also ibid., 1074; Czitrom, "Underworlds and Underdogs," 557; Saloutos, "Alexander Pantages," 142.

86. "Loew in $4,000,000 Vaudeville Deal," *New York Times*, March 27, 1914; "Loew Buys Circuit," *Los Angeles Times*, March 28, 1914; *Spokane*

Chronicle, March 28, April 4, 1914; "Stars and Stardust," *Spokesman-Review*, April 5, 1914; Robert Grau, *The Theatre of Science* (New York: Broadway Publishing, 1914), 19, 192. The Spokane theater Marcus Loew briefly controlled was (in our period) first called the Columbia, then the Orpheum, then Loew's, and finally, the Hippodrome. George Turner built it in 1906, and John Considine operated it as both the Columbia and the Orpheum.

87. *Spokesman-Review*, August 2, 1914. See also Carson, *Stage Year Book, 1914*, 72–73; Cullen and Hackman, *Vaudeville Old and New*, 693; Grau, *Twentieth Century*, 45–47; *Spokesman-Review*, June 28, 1914.

88. Wilbur W. Hindley, "Return of Big Time Vaudeville Up to Spokane Theater-Goers," *Spokesman-Review*, May 17, 1914.

89. *Spokesman-Review*, May 10, 14, June 28, July 5, 26, August 2, 24, September 1, October 14, 1914.

90. *Spokane Chronicle*, July 31, August 21, 28, 30, September 4, 1915; *Spokesman-Review*, May 13, August 14, 17, September 5, 1915.

91. *Spokesman-Review*, August 21, 1915. See also *Spokane Chronicle*, July 10, 24, August 14, September 4, 1915; *Spokesman-Review*, August 17, 1915.

92. Londré, *Enchanted Years*, 222; Jones, *Renegades*, 125, 129; Nelson, "Road Shows in Seattle," 128–50; Jack Poggi, *Theater in America: The Impact of Economic Forces, 1870–1967* (Ithaca, N.Y.: Cornell University Press, 1966), ch. 2.

93. *Spokesman-Review*, August 16, 1914. See also *Spokane Chronicle*, September 4, 1915; *Spokesman-Review*, January 17, 1915.

94. L. Carson, ed., *The Stage Year Book, 1915* (London: The Stage Offices, 1915), 27, 33, 36; L. Carson, ed., *The Stage Year Book, 1916* (London: The Stage Offices, 1916), 40.

95. *Spokesman-Review*, July 4, 1915. See also *Spokane Chronicle*, January 4, 1913, July 17, September, 4, October 30, 1915; *Spokesman-Review*, August 22, 1913, March 11, June 24, October 7, 1917.

96. For coverage of stock productions in the *Spokane Chronicle*, see July 6, 17, November 4, 13, 22, 1915; May 27, September 2, 4, 1916. In the *Spokesman-Review*, see March 10, 1912; February 2, 1913; March 29, September 1, October 14, November 23, 1914; May 14, 1915; August 27, September 4, October 22, 30, 1916. See also Wasserman, "Early Theatre in Spokane," 314–16.

97. *Spokane Chronicle*, February 9, 1917; *Spokesman-Review*, February 11, 13, August 12, September 2, November 4, 1917; Abbott, *How Cities Won the West*, 52; Knapp, "Introductory Essay," 123.

98. Hannah Hinsdale, "'Very Good Eddie,' New York's Musical Comedy Hit, Is Coming," *Spokesman-Review*, August 5, 1917.

99. *Spokesman-Review*, November 4, 15, 1917. See also *Spokesman-Review*, September 10, October 14, November 11, 1917.

100. Margaret Bean, interview, April 23, 1984 (OH 366, EWSHS), 6.

101. Harry Hayward employment contracts, box 6, folder 26, Ms 46 (EWSHS).

5. The Respectable Stage and the Sources of Indecency

1. Helen Campbell, Diary, 1913–1917, box 1, folder 1, Helen Campbell Papers, MsSC 224 (EWSHS).

2. Lewis Erenberg, "Everybody's Doin' It: The Pre–World War I Dance Craze, the Castles, and the Modern Girl," *Feminist Studies* 3, nos. 1–2 (Autumn 1975): 159–60; Undeberg, "The Diary of Helen Campbell," 66, 71–73.

3. Many kinds of plays received local comment (positive or otherwise) during this era, but these types stand out for the frequency with which they were performed and the intense reactions—from anxious reviews to enormous audiences—that they generated.

4. Erdman, *Blue Vaudeville*, 7, 17; Snyder, *Voice of the City*; Sharon R. Ullman, *Sex Seen: The Emergence of Modern Sexuality in America* (Berkeley: University of California Press, 1997), 24–25; Wertheim. *Vaudeville Wars*, 166–67.

5. Allen, *Horrible Prettiness*, 49.

6. Barth, *City People*, 222–23; Dudden, *Women in the American Theatre*, ch. 7; Glenn, *Female Spectacle*, chs. 6, 7.

7. Johnson, *Sisters in Sin*, 51–60; *Spokesman-Review*, November 12, 1911.

8. For notices or reviews of problem plays in the *Spokane Chronicle*, see May 29, August 28, 1909; October 14–15, 1910. In the *Spokesman-Review*, see February 7–8, 10, 1904; October 22, November 26, December 2, 1905; November 18, 1906; February 4–6, November 10–11, 13, December 22, 1907; February 2–3, April 12, 19, 22–23, 1908; February 13, 20, May 1–2, 23, 29, October 9, 1910.

9. Annual Booklet 1911–1912, box 1, Women's Club of Spokane, Ms 199 (EWSHS). Anna Stratton Browne relished the opportunity to see Henrik Ibsen's *Peer Gynt* in Chicago, while a lecture on the work of Ibsen, George Bernard Shaw, and Hermann Sudermann in 1910 crowded the public library. Anna Stratton Browne to John J. Browne, November 24, 1906, box 1, folder 16, John J. Browne papers, Ms 21 (EWSHS); *Spokesman-Review*, October 11, 1910.

10. John Houchin, *Censorship of the American Theatre in the Twentieth Century* (Cambridge: Cambridge University Press, 2003), 41–51; Johnson, *Sisters in Sin*, ch. 2.

11. "In the Theaters," *Spokesman-Review*, February 5, 1907.

12. "Notable Show at Spokane," *Spokesman-Review*, January 20, 1907. A 1911 review of *Checkers* (a dramatization of the novel by Henry M. Blossom Jr.) presented the same argument: "*Checkers* is no novelty. It is merely a rugged, clean, interesting play of American life, with no problem, no suggestive line, no false sentiment, no 'smart set' and no woman with a past," *Spokesman-Review*, November 12, 1911.

13. Samuel Hopkins Adams, "The Indecent Stage," *American Magazine* 68 (October 1909): 41–47; Nelson, "Road Shows in Seattle," 115, 149. Apologists from other cities, including Seattle, also affected bucolic innocence when comparing their theatrical tastes with those of New Yorkers.

14. Houchin, *Censorship*, 51–60.

15. Throughout the first years of the twentieth century, Spokane's newspapers frequently discussed the propriety of stage productions. For a sampling of notices and commentary about daring plays in the *Spokane Chronicle*, see November 2, 28, December 14, 1900; October 3–4, 8, 1910; March 8, October 14, 1911; February 1, 8, 1913; July 15, August 28, 1915. For a more extensive sampling, see *Spokesman-Review*, March 13, 19, October 16, 1904; October 22, November 5, 13, 19, December 3, 1905; January 21, March 25, September 2, October 21, 1906; January 27, 1907; April 5, September 13, October 25, November 1, 8, 15, 18, 22, 1908; January 23, May 29, 30, October 2, 8, 9, 1910; January 23, March 5–6, October 22, November 5, 11, 1911; January 28, 30–31, February 4–5, March 17, April 7, 1912; September 21, October 26, November 2, December 19, 1913; January 16, April 19, May 3, 1914; January 25, 31, February 6, 1915.

16. Wasserman, "Early Theatre in Spokane," 316.

17. Jeffrey H. Huberman, *Late Victorian Farce* (Ann Arbor, Mich.: UMI Research Press, 1986), 2–3, ch. 2.

18. "A Stranger in a Strange Land," *Spokane Chronicle*, December 14, 1900; Ben Brewster, "The Circle: Lubitsch and the Theatrical Farce Tradition," *Film History* 13, no. 4 (2001): 372–73; Walter Prichard Eaton, "The Return of Farce," *American Magazine* 71 (December 1910): 264–73; Billy Budd Vermillion, "The Remarriage Plot in the 1910s," *Film History* 13, no. 4 (2001): 360–62.

19. See Adams, "The Indecent Stage."

20. Allen, *Horrible Prettiness*, 81; Erenberg, *Steppin' Out*, 206–8; Glenn, *Female Spectacle*, 156–57; Eve Golden, *Anna Held and the Birth of Ziegfeld's Broadway* (Lexington: University Press of Kentucky, 2000), 93; Michael Newbury, "Polite Gaiety: Cultural Hierarchy and Musical Comedy, 1893–1904," *Journal of the Gilded Age and Progressive Era* 4, no. 4 (October 2005): 381–407; Toll, *On with the Show*, 204–21.

21. "About a Rose Protected by Thorns and a Soldier Made of Chocolate," *Spokesman-Review*, March 3, 1912. See also Huberman, *Late Victorian Farce*, 42, 45, 64; William L. Chew III, "'Straight' Sam Meets 'Lewd' Louis: American Perceptions of French Sexuality, 1775–1815," in *Revolutions and Watersheds: Transatlantic Dialogues, 1775–1815*, ed. W. M. Verhoeven and Beth Dolan Kautz (Amsterdam: Rodopi, 1999), 61–86.

22. Harris, *Cultural Excursions*, 12.

23. Erenberg, *Steppin' Out*, xiv, 18, 40–56.

24. Howard Hindley, "Here and There in Stageland," *Spokesman-Review*, November 2, 1913.

232 NOTES TO PAGES 148–54

25. Adams, "The Indecent Stage," 45–47; Walter Prichard Eaton, "The Rise and Fall of the Theatrical Syndicate," *American Magazine* 70 (October 1910): 850–52.

26. "Gaby's Show Is Flesh and Fringe," *Spokesman-Review*, January 16, 1914.

27. Undeberg, "The Diary of Helen Campbell," 48, 56.

28. Helen Campbell, Diary, December 15, 1915 (EWSHS).

29. "Bankers to See *Miss Innocence*," *Spokesman-Review*, January 30, 1912. See also Margaret Bean, interview, December 8, 1958, pioneer voices series (OH 460, EWSHS), 3.

30. *Spokesman-Review*, December 19, 1913. For instances of Inland Northwesterners involved in show business see *Spokesman-Review*, October 22, 1905; August 19, 29, 1915; October 29, December 10, 1916; February 13, March 25, 26, May 6, June 20, August 19, 1917.

31. "Faint Traces of Beard Undoing of Man Who Was a Chorus Girl," *Spokane Chronicle*, September 17, 1915.

32. "It's a Proper Protest," *Spokane Chronicle*, June 5, 1909. The *Chronicle* here reprinted the protest of a theater critic from Buffalo, New York. See also the commentary about *Miss Innocence*, in the *Spokesman-Review*, January 31, February 4–5, March 17, 1912.

33. W. Kenneth Waters, Jr., "Baker Stock Company," in *American Theatre Companies, 1888–1930*, ed. Weldon B. Durham (New York: Greenwood Press, 1987), 43. This company was a satellite of George Baker's acclaimed Portland-based Baker Stock Company.

34. "Leading Lady Balks at Tights," *Spokesman-Review*, February 1, 1911. See also "Tights Tabooed by Leading Lady," *Spokane Chronicle*, February 1, 1911.

35. Allen, *Horrible Prettiness*, 116; Tracy C. Davis, *Actresses as Working Women: Their Social Identity in Victorian Culture* (London: Routledge, 1991), 134–35; Johnson, *Sisters in Sin*, 40, 58.

36. "Rails at Tights," *Spokane Chronicle*, October 14, 1911.

37. "Leading Lady Balks at Tights," *Spokesman-Review*, February 1, 1911.

38. McArthur, *Actors and American Culture*, 131, 143, 152; Dorothy Kolhauff Bartlett, interview, August 10, 1978 (OH 269, EWSHS), 7.

39. Justin Huntly McCarthy, *If I Were King* (New York: Samuel French, 1922), 45.

40. *Spokane Chronicle*, February 2, 6, 1911; *Spokesman-Review*, February 2, 5–6, 1911.

41. *Spokesman-Review*, March 6, 1911. See also *Spokane Chronicle*, March 8, 1911; *Spokesman-Review*, March 5, 8, 1911. Tickets for this production of *The Blue Mouse* cost from twenty-five to seventy-five cents; Wednesday and Saturday matinées cost from twenty-five to fifty cents.

42. See also *Spokane Chronicle*, October 3–4, 8, 1910; *Spokesman-Review*, October 2, 8–9, 1910.

43. For local recollections of Jessie Shirley and her company, see Glen Bankson, interview by Allegra Askman, August 26, 1975 (OH 055), Bartlett interview, August 10, 1978 (OH 269), Bean interview, December 8, 1958 (OH 460), Mary Brownell, interview by Randall Johnson, 1979 (OH 785), Ida Estby, interview by Mary Avery, March 25, 1973 (OH 003), all in EWSHS; Kohlhauff, "Fifty Years of Theaters."

44. Laurilyn J. Harris, "[Jessie] Shirley Stock Company," in *American Theatre Companies*, 408–41; McArthur, *Actors and American Culture*, 45, 254n55. In 1911 a reorganized Shirley company presented a seventeen-week season at the American.

45. See, for instance, May Arkwright Hutton papers, box 1, folder 3, box 3, folder 1, scrapbook 1, MsSC 55 (EWSHS); *Spokesman-Review*, December 18, 1913.

46. *Spokane Chronicle*, January 6, 8, 14, 20, 24–25, 27, 1909; *Spokesman-Review*, January 4, 7–17, 24, 1909; Dale Soden, "Billy Sunday in Spokane: Revivalism and Social Control," *Pacific Northwest Quarterly* 79, no. 1 (1988): 10–17.

47. *Spokane Chronicle*, January 25, 27, 1909; *Spokesman-Review*, January 17, 24, 1909.

48. "Miss Shirley Makes Protest," *Spokane Chronicle*, January 26, 1909.

49. Irving Lewis Allen, *The City in Slang: New York Life and Popular Speech* (New York: Oxford University Press, 1993), 3–4; Gilfoyle, *A Pickpocket's Tale*, 61; David W. Maurer and Ellesa Clay High, "New Words: Where Do They Come from and Where Do They Go?" *American Speech* 55, no. 3 (1980): 184–94.

50. "Actress Praised for Sunday Reply," *Spokesman-Review*, January 29, 1909. See also "'Good for You,' Says W. L. Bull," *Spokane Chronicle*, January 28, 1909.

51. Flynn, *Rebel Girl*, 106–13; Morrissey, *Mental Territories*, 100; Schwantes, *Pacific Northwest*, 340; Schwantes, *Radical Heritage*, 177, 186; Schwantes, "Wageworkers' Frontier," 134–35.

52. "'Good for You,' Says W. L. Bull," *Spokane Chronicle*, January 28, 1909. See also Harris, *Cultural Excursions*, 227; Singal, "Towards a Definition," 9–10.

53. "Actress Praised for Sunday Reply," *Spokesman-Review*, January 29, 1909.

54. Henry Brown, *War on the Theater*, 11, also 38–49; *Spokesman-Review*, October 18, 25, 1908.

55. McArthur, *Actors and American Culture*, chs. 5, 6.

56. Brown, *War on the Theater*, 51. See also ibid., also 62–63; "Actress Praised for Sunday Reply," *Spokesman-Review*, January 29, 1909; "Theater Bad, but Oh That Actress!" *Spokesman-Review*, March 8, 1909. Two years later, in a letter to the *Spokesman-Review*'s theater columnist, Jessie Shirley reemphasized her respect for the clergy, even as she dismissed Henry Brown as a crank, *Spokesman-Review*, January 15, 1911.

57. Erdman, *Blue Vaudeville*, 40. See also ibid., 25–27; Hamilton, *When I'm Bad, I'm Better*, 28–30, 36–37.

58. "Statistics in Holmes School Show Theaters Draw Scores of Pupils," *Spokesman-Review*, February 10, 1912; see also *Spokesman-Review*, July 26, 1915.

59. Lisa Tickner, "The Popular Culture of *Kermesse:* Lewis, Painting and Performance, 1912–13," in *In Visible Touch: Modernism and Masculinity*, ed. Terry Smith (Chicago: University of Chicago Press, 1997), 144–47. The exploits of the apaches filled European and American newspapers in the early twentieth century, even in such a remote place as Spokane. See *Spokesman-Review*, February 27, April 10, December 11, 1910.

60. Maurice Mouvet, *Maurice's Art of Dancing: An Autobiographical Sketch with Complete Descriptions of Modern Dances and Full Illustrations Showing the Various Steps and Positions* (New York: G. Schirmer, 1915), ch. 6.

61. Erdman, *Blue Vaudeville*, 125; Erenberg, *Steppin' Out*, 75; Mark Knowles, *The Wicked Waltz and Other Scandalous Dances: Outrage at Couple Dancing in the Nineteenth and Early Twentieth Centuries* (London: McFarland, 2009), 74; Joseph C. Smith, "Brought 'Tango' to America," *New York Times*, January 15, 1914.

62. *Spokane Chronicle*, March 4, 1910. See also ibid., 2–3, 1910, February 4, 6, 1911, February 1, 1913; *Spokesman-Review*, February 27–28, March 5, 1910, February 5, 9–12, November 19, 1911, February 28, 1912, May 11, 1914.

63. Erenberg, *Steppin' Out*, 12, 16–18, 151–55.

64. Hunter, *To 'Joy My Freedom*, ch. 8. Hunter makes a brilliant analysis of the role commercial dance halls and vernacular couple dances played in working-class black culture during the 1900s and 1910s.

65. Herbert Asbury, *The Barbary Coast: An Informal History of the San Francisco Underworld* (New York: Alfred A. Knopf, 1933), 293; Barbara S. Glass, *African American Dance: An Illustrated History* (London: McFarland, 2007), 168; Knowles, *Wicked Waltz*, 63–69; Marshall and Jean Stearns, *Jazz Dance: The Story of American Vernacular Dance* (New York: Macmillan, 1968), 96.

66. *Spokesman-Review*, February 16, 1913. See also ibid., October 18, 1912; Erenberg, "Everybody's Doin' It," 151; Knowles, *Wicked Waltz*, 67–69.

67. *Spokesman-Review*, January 22, 29, February 28, 1912, February 1, 1913.

68. "City Heads See Sensual Dances," *Spokesman-Review*, January 31, 1913.

69. *Spokane Chronicle*, October 14, 1909; *Spokesman-Review*, November 7, 1911, January 29, February 5, 1912, January 12, 1914; Erenberg, "Everybody's Doin' It," 156–57; Nasaw, *Going Out*, ch. 9; Peiss, *Cheap Amusements*, ch. 4.

70. *Spokesman-Review*, September 16, February 16, 1913; also ibid., February 9–12, 1911.

71. Knowles, *Wicked Waltz*, 93. Municipalities throughout the United States and Britain banned the animal dances.

72. *Official Gazette of the City of Spokane, Washington, Statement of City Business, Including a Summary of the Proceedings of the City Council during the Week Ending February 22, 1913*, vol. 3, no. 8 (Spokane, Wash.: Office of the City Clerk, 1913). See also *Spokane Chronicle*, February 1, 1913; *Spokesman-Review*, January 31, February 1, 3, 6, 8–12, 16, 21, 1913. The city defined public and quasi-public dances as those that charged admission fees. All dance hall owners or dance managers were required to obtain permits from the commissioner of public safety, who could deny their request. Those individuals who violated Ordinance No. C1233 could be fined up to one hundred dollars and jailed for up to thirty days. The city did not appoint an official dance censor. At this time, the local Masonic Temple association also barred all rag dances from its ballroom, while dancing teachers collectively drafted rules to protect their studios.

73. *Spokesman-Review*, December 19, 1913. See also Helen Campbell, Diary, May 31, 1913 (EWSHS); *Spokane Chronicle*, January 12–13, 15, March 14, 1914; *Spokesman-Review*, February 2, 8–9, 12, 22–23, April 20, December 17, 1913, January 11, 13, 16, 18, 1914.

74. Erenberg, *Steppin' Out*, 165. See also Knowles, *Wicked Waltz*, 107. Lewis Erenberg especially develops this argument.

75. Vernon and Irene Castle, *Modern Dancing* (New York: Harper and Brothers, 1914), 83; Erenberg, "Everybody's Doin' It," 157; Knowles, *Wicked Waltz*, 107–16.

76. *Spokesman-Review*, March 29, April 5, 12, 16–18, 20, September 12, 1914. In 1915 a performer at the Hippodrome vaudeville theater noted that in Spokane, as elsewhere, dance instructors had almost no occasion to teach the waltz and two-step, for their pupils only wanted the maxixe, fox trot, and other new dances. *Spokane Chronicle*, September 17, 1915.

77. Helen Campbell, Diary, May 31, December 15, 1913, February 22, November 2, 1915, January 26, 1916 (EWSHS).

78. Ullman, *Sex Seen*, 31.

Conclusion

1. In 1920 Peter's older siblings Raymond and Helen also worked at the candy factory. Their father, a carpenter, was a German immigrant; their mother was the child of Norwegian immigrants. U.S. Census 1920, Spokane, Spokane, Washington, p. 7b, image 935, Lloyd F. Peters, digital image, accessed August 1, 2015, ancestry.com.

2. Lloyd Peters, *Lionhead Lodge: Movieland of the Northwest*, 2nd ed. (Fairfield, Wash.: Ye Galleon Press, 1976), 2. See also ibid., 1, 5, 136–45; Dick Gentry, "Spokane's Film Industry: Who Says It Never Was?" *Spokane Daily Chronicle*, March 31, 1978.

3. See Holly George, "Municipal Film Censorship in Spokane, Washington, 1910–1916," *Pacific Northwest Quarterly* 103, no. 4 (2012): 176–89.

4. See Hubert Bartoo, interview with Allegra Askman, September 17, 1975 (OH 58, EWSHS), 16; Elizabeth Dilio Bedient, interview, March 11, 1978 (OH 249, EWSHS), 18. By the mid-1910s several Spokanites had achieved prominence in the world of film, notably Seena Owen. This was a source of pride in the city. See "'Beauty and Brains' Contest," *Photoplay* (June 1916): 101; James S. McQuade, "Chicago News Letter," *Moving Picture World*, September 30, 1916, 2119; *Spokane Chronicle*, October 9, 1916; *Spokesman-Review*, June 4, 1916, January 28, February 4, 8, 11, 1917.

5. Margaret Bean, *Spokane's Age of Elegance* (Spokane: Eastern Washington State Historical Society, 1960). See also Bean interviews, May 7, 1976, December 8, 1958, April 23, 1984 (OH 107, 108, 460, 366, EWSHS); Horace Brown, interview by Louis Livingston, August 19, 1955 (OH 624, EWSHS); Cochran, *Seven Frontier Women*, 83, 107; Kohlhauff, "Fifty Years of Theaters"; "J. J. Browne: The World's Largest Stage," vertical file, s.v. "Spokane–Theaters–Auditorium" (EWSHS); *Spokesman-Review*, June 13, 1943, February 11, 1945, July 28, 1957.

6. *Spokesman-Review*, December 19, 1926; see also Saloutos, "Alexander Pantages," 144.

7. *Spokesman-Review*, August 4, 1915, November 20, 1916, April 1, May 31, July 22, 1917.

8. The prevalence of western road and stock productions suggests that Spokanites frequented and enjoyed them. Such plays—often melodramas—included *The Tenderfoot, In Wyoming, Squaw Man,* and *The Girl of the Golden West.* For instances of these shows in the 1900s, see *Spokesman-Review*, October 29, 1905, September 30, November 11, 1906, October 27, 1907, November 1, 8, 22, December 6, 13, 17, 1908, January 31, 1909, March 27, April 24, June 6, 1910; *Spokane Chronicle*, January 23, 30, February 6, 13, May 1, June 30, December 4, 1909, November 26, December 19, 1910.

9. The disconnect between staged westerns and reality was evident, for instance, in January 1909. On the same pages that the *Spokane Chronicle* on January 30, 1909, discussed *The Alaskan, The King of Cowboys,* and a tableau of Frederick Remington paintings, there was a report that a knife fight had occurred downtown during the early morning hours. Similarly, the *Spokesman-Review* on December 7, 1912, remarked that too many hold-ups were occurring outside Spokane, which could no longer be considered acceptable in the year 1912. Earlier that year, a Jessie Shirley production of western "thriller" drew huge audiences remarkable for their "loud enthusiasm." *Spokesman-Review*, February 11, 1912.

10. The local newspapers reported extensively on these events, which were given the evocative names of the Diggin's (1912) and Dead Man's Gulch (1915). In the *Spokane Chronicle*, see November 29–30, December 2–4, 6, 1912; August 7, 1915. In the *Spokesman-Review*, see November 30, December 1–4, 6–7, 9, 1912; August 7, 1915.

11. For instances of western films playing at Spokane theaters, see the *Spokesman-Review* April 2, June 10, October 26, November 4, 19, December 2, 1917; January 21, February 11, 24, March 10–11, April 14–15, 17–18, 21, May 12, 19, 26, 31, June 9, August 12, 19, 31, September 2, 18, 1918.

12. "Washington Motion Picture Corporation," *Spokane Chronicle*, March 2, 1918.

13. Spokanites were not alone in their attempt to boost their city through motion picture production. The vice-president of a picture company in Ogden, Utah, for instance, remarked that his business decision "was prompted largely by a sense of civic pride." Likewise, his financial backers had an underlying hope that movies would get Ogden "placed on the map." And Utahns—like Washingtonians—learned that "wild cat" film studios were risky business. Richard Nelson, "Utah Filmmakers of the Silent Screen," *Utah Historical Quarterly* 43, no. 1 (1975): 16.

14. *Spokesman-Review*, August 20–21, 24, 1917; *Spokane Chronicle*, August 20, 25, 1917.

15. *Spokesman-Review*, February 17, 24, March 3, August 20, 1918; *Spokane Chronicle*, March 2, 1918. In early March 1918 the WMPC officers were W. W. Zent, Allen Meisenheimer, C. J. Ward, Harold Hooker, James Ramage, Thomas S. Griffith, Henri Crommelin, and Philip Harding. They were associated with the Spokane Bar Association, the National Apple Show, the local chamber of commerce, the Spokane Interstate Fair Association, and the Holland Bank, among other groups.

16. *Spokesman-Review*, August 24, 1917. See also *Spokane Chronicle*, August 25, 1917, March 2, 1918; *Spokesman-Review*, February 24, March 3, 1918.

17. "Washington Motion Picture Corporation," *Spokesman-Review*, February 24, March 3, 1918.

18. *The Editor: The Journal of Information for Literary Workers* 48, no. 8 (April 25, 1918): 279; *Spokesman-Review*, February 17, 24, March 3, April 7, 28, May 5, 12, 15–16, 1918.

19. "Shipman in Charge of Product," *Dramatic Mirror*, February 16, 1918, 24; *Spokesman-Review*, May 5, 1918.

20. *Spokesman-Review*, April 28, 1918; also April 7, May 5, 12, 1918.

21. *Spokesman-Review*, April 7, 1918. Nell Shipman, Ernest's fourth wife, described him as the kind of man who "made the '90's gay." Nell Shipman, *The Silent Screen and My Talking Heart: An Autobiography* (Boise, Idaho: Boise State University, 1987), 31.

22. "Shipman in Charge of Product," *Dramatic Mirror*, February 16, 1918, 24; *Spokesman-Review*, May 5, 1918. The Titan officers were J. Don Alexander, of a local electric company; Eugene de Smeth, the city engineer and a business owner; H. G. Twomey; R. E. Musser, who had a long association with the local Scotch Woolen Mills Stores; and C. L. Mayo, general manager of the local Allied Film Corporation. For information

on these men, see Tim Blevins, ed., *Film and Photography on the Front Range* (Colorado Springs: Pikes Peak Library District, 2012), 242; "The Store with the Motto," *Journal of Electricity* 42, no. 6 (March 15, 1919): 256; *Spokane Press*, September 30, 1910, 3.

23. "Titan Feature Photo-Play Company," *Spokesman-Review*, April 7, 1918.

24. *Spokesman-Review*, April 28, May 5, 1918; see also Ren H. Rice, "Contracts for Features," *Dramatic Mirror*, March 9, 1918, 26.

25. "Power Selects City for Filming Studio," *Spokane Chronicle*, August 25, 1917.

26. *Spokesman-Review*, March 10, 1918. See also ibid., May 26, June 23, 1918. These people included Laurence Trimble, Mitchell Lewis, Florence Turner, Evelyn Brent, William "Lone Star" Dietz, Sarah Truax, and of course, Tyrone Power. Dietz and Truax had strong connections to the Inland Northwest at this point.

27. A fire threatened the Titan studio in early May 1918, but although this could have affected its finances it did continue advertising after that point. The 1918 report of the Washington secretary of state listed the Titan studio as a new corporation and then as a stricken corporation by July 1918. The Allied Film Corporation, of which the Titan's C. L. Mayo was general manager, likewise began work in the late 1910s and was struck from the state records by 1921. However, a film company founded by the Titan's president, J. Don Alexander, went on to success, if outside of Spokane. I. M. Howell, *Fifteenth Biennial Report of the Secretary of State* (Olympia: Frank Lamborn, 1918), 26, 57, 90, 165; J. Grant Hinkle, *Seventeenth Biennial Report of the Secretary of State* (Olympia: Frank Lamborn, 1922), 13; *Official Gazette of the City of Spokane, Washington* 8, no. 21 (May 18, 1918): 4612; *Official Gazette of the City of Spokane, Washington* 8, no. 22 (May 29, 1918): 4618; Blevins, *Film and Photography*, 242; "Fire near Film Studio," *Spokesman-Review*, May 6, 1918.

28. Frederick A. Rowe, ed., "New Corporations," *National Corporation Reporter* 54, no. 19 (June 14, 1917): 794; Howell, *Fifteenth Biennial Report*, 47.

29. The "certain stockholders and trustees" were perhaps W. W. Zent and Harold Hooker. *George M. Barnes v. Washington Motion Picture Corporation*, March 1918, Spokane Superior Court, case 56364 (SCCA).

30. *C. R. Dixon, Receiver for Northwest Picture Corporation v. Fred K. McBroom, Receiver for Washington Motion Picture Corporation*, April 1919, Spokane Superior Court, case 58521 (SCCA); Howell, *Fifteenth Biennial Report*, 86.

31. *Spokane Chronicle*, August 27, 29, 31, 1918; *Spokesman-Review*, August 28, 29, 1918, August 3, 1980; Gene Fernett, *American Film Studios: An Historical Encyclopedia* (London: McFarland, 1988), 252–53; *Dixon v. McBroom* (SCCA); *E. W. Cole, Plaintiff, v. Washington Motion Picture Corporation, Respondent, Laurence Trimble, Appellant*, September 15, 1920, Supreme Court of Washington, no. 14901.

32. *Spokesman-Review*, August 21, 1919. See also J. Grant Hinkle, *Sixteenth Biennial Report of the Secretary of State* (Olympia: Frank Lamborn, 1920), 46; Motion Picture News, *Motion Picture Studio Directory and Trade Annual* (New York: Motion Picture News, 1921), 390.

33. For instance, the company's secretary-treasurer was John C. H. Reynolds, a Spokane businessman involved in insurance and lumber. Playter married Reynolds's daughter Dorothy, and at least for a time, the Reynolds and Playter families lived in the same suite of apartments. U.S. Federal Census, 1920, Spokane, Spokane, Washington, p. 3a, image 73, Wellington Playter, digital image, accessed August 1, 2015, ancestry.com; *Official Gazette of the City of Spokane* 11, no. 26 (June 29, 1921): 5775; "To Recruit Ex-Service Men for the Lumber Industry," *Lumber World Review*, November 25, 1919, 39; *The Insurance Year Book, 1921–1922: Fire and Marine*, vol. 49 (New York: Spectator Company, 1921), A-60; *Spokesman-Review*, August 24, 27, 1919.

34. *Official Gazette of the City of Spokane* 10 (1920): 5208, 5396, and 11 (1921): 5603, 5617, 5667, 6012; Peters, *Lionhead Lodge*, 9–10, 24.

35. Hinkle, *Seventeenth Biennial Report*, 97; J. Grant Hinkle, *Eighteenth Biennial Report of the Secretary of State* (Olympia, Wash: Frank M. Lamborn, 1924), 199.

36. Shipman, *The Silent Screen*, 30–31, 103, 114–15; Kay Armatage, *The Girl from God's Country: Nell Shipman and the Silent Cinema* (Toronto: University of Toronto Press, 2003), 14–22, 79, 161, 214, 356; Karen Ward Mahar, *Women Filmmakers in Early Hollywood* (Baltimore: Johns Hopkins University Press, 2006), 162–64; "Shoots 'Snow Stuff' in Summer," *American Cinematographer*, July 1, 1922, 6–7. Much has been written in academic, reference, and general-interest publications about Nell Shipman's filmmaking efforts. Boise State University has a significant collection of her papers and films. Likewise, in the late twentieth and early twenty-first centuries, Spokanites expressed pride and interest in the moviemaking ventures—however unsuccessful—at Minnehaha Park. See, for instance, Dick Gentry, "Spokane's Film Industry: Who Says It Never Was?" *Spokane Daily Chronicle*, March 31, 1978; "Filmmaking History Focuses on Minnehaha," *Spokesman-Review*, October 2, 1997; Dan Webster, "Striking It Rich with 'Fool's Gold,'" *Spokesman-Review*, July 13, 2002, D3.

37. "Hollywood North," *Pacific Northwest Inlander*, August 24–30, 2000.

38. For Wellington Playter's intended use of Spokane's setting, see *Spokesman-Review*, August 24, 27, 1919.

39. American Film Institute Catalog, s.v. *Fool's Gold*, accessed August 7, 2015, http://www.afi.com/members/catalog/. *Fool's Gold* was also known as *Undermined*.

40. Peters, *Lionhead Lodge*, 17, 22; Armatage, *Girl from God's Country*, 214–15.

41. "Why They Support Moore," *Spokesman-Review*, April 28, 1907.

42. Hook and McGuire, *Spokane Falls Illustrated*, 30.

43. Jones, *Renegades*; Londré, *Enchanted Years*.

44. Nelson, "Utah Filmmakers," 12, 22.

45. Willa Cather, *My Ántonia* (Boston: Houghton Mifflin, 1995).

46. Annie Pike Greenwood, *We Sagebrush Folks*, reprint ed. (Moscow, Idaho: University of Idaho Press, 1988), 90; also ibid., 28, 102, 362.

Epilogue

1. Schwantes, *Pacific Northwest*, 345–48; Timothy Egan, *Breaking Blue* (New York: Knopf, 1992); "State and County Quick Facts," U.S. Census Bureau, s.v., Spokane, Washington, accessed September 9, 2015, quick-facts.census.gov.

2. See, for instance, James Jarvis, Letter to the Editor, *Pacific Northwest Inlander*, May 15, 2003.

3. Mike Bookey, "Return to Glory," *Pacific Northwest Inlander*, July 10, 2012; KSPS documentary, *The Davenport Hotel: Grand Again*, aired April 2010.

4. "Spokane's Playhouse Beautiful," *Spokesman-Review*, September 3, 1931.

5. Jim Kershner, "Fox Theater (Spokane)," HistoryLink.org Essay 8631, accessed September 8, 2015, HistoryLink.org.

6. J. William T. Youngs, *The Fair and the Falls: Spokane's Expo '74: Transforming an American Environment* (Cheney: Eastern Washington University Press, 1996); Matthew W. Klingle, "Building Nature: Topics in the Environmental History of Seattle and Spokane," accessed September 9, 2015, at http://www.washington.edu/uwired/outreach/cspn/.

7. "Clemmer Theater," National Register of Historic Places, ID 88002758, accessed September 9, 2015, at http://www.focus.nps.gov/nrhp/.

8. "About the INB Performing Arts Center," INB Performing Arts Center, accessed September 8, 2015, at http://www.inbpac.com/about.php/.

9. "A Tragedy in Low Life," *Spokane Chronicle*, March 27, 1891.

10. Engle, "Benefiting a City," 19n89.

11. "Spokane a Home City," *Spokane Chronicle*, January 1, 1906.

Bibliography

Books, Articles, Interviews, Dissertations, and Other Sources

Abbott, Carl. *How Cities Won the West: Four Centuries of Urban Change in Western North America.* Albuquerque: University of New Mexico Press, 2008.

———. *The Metropolitan Frontier: Cities in the Modern American West.* Tucson: University of Arizona Press, 1993.

Adams, Samuel Hopkins. "The Indecent Stage." *American Magazine* 68 (1909): 41–47.

Allen, Irving Lewis. *The City in Slang: New York Life and Popular Speech.* New York: Oxford University Press, 1993.

Allen, Robert C. *Horrible Prettiness: Burlesque and American Culture.* Chapel Hill: University of North Carolina Press, 1991.

Appiah, Kwame Anthony, and Henry Louis Gates Jr., eds. *Africana, Arts and Letters: An A-to-Z Reference of Writers, Musicians, and Artists of the African American Experience.* Philadelphia: Running Press, 2004.

Armatage, Kay. *The Girl from God's Country: Nell Shipman and the Silent Cinema.* Toronto: University of Toronto Press, 2003.

Asbury, Herbert. *The Barbary Coast: An Informal History of the San Francisco Underworld.* New York: Alfred A. Knopf, 1933.

Ashby, LeRoy. *With Amusement for All: A History of American Popular Culture since 1830.* Lexington: University Press of Kentucky, 2006.

Baldwin, Edward Chauncey, ed. *The Lake English Classics: A Tale of Two Cities, by Charles Dickens.* New York: Scott, Foresman, 1919.

Bankson, Glen. Interview. August 26, 1975 (OH 055). Eastern Washington State Historical Society, Spokane, Washington.

Barber, Alicia. *Reno's Big Gamble: Image and Reputation in the Biggest Little City.* Lawrence: University Press of Kansas, 2008.

George M. Barnes v. Washington Motion Picture Corporation. March 1918. Spokane Superior Court, case 56364. Spokane County Courthouse Archives, Spokane, Washington.

Barth, Gunther. *City People: The Rise of Modern City Culture in Nineteenth-Century America.* New York: Oxford University Press, 1980.

———. *Instant Cities: Urbanization and the Rise of San Francisco and Denver.* New York: Oxford University Press, 1975.

Bartlett, Dorothy Kolhauff. Interview. August 10, 1978 (OH 269). Eastern Washington State Historical Society, Spokane, Washington.

Bartoo, Hubert. Interview. September 17, 1975 (OH 58). Eastern Washington State Historical Society, Spokane, Washington.

Bean, Margaret. Interviews. December 8, 1958 (OH 460), May 7, 1976 (OH 107, 108), April 23, 1984 (OH 366). Eastern Washington State Historical Society, Spokane, Washington.

———. *Spokane's Age of Elegance.* Spokane: Eastern Washington State Historical Society, 1960.

Bederman, Gail. *Manliness and Civilization: A Cultural History of Gender and Race in the United States, 1880–1917.* Chicago: University of Chicago Press, 1996.

Bedient, Elizabeth Dilio. Interview. March 11, 1978 (OH 249). Eastern Washington State Historical Society, Spokane, Washington.

Berelson, Bernard, and Howard Grant. "Pioneer Theatre in Washington." *Pacific Northwest Quarterly* 28, no. 2 (1934): 115–36.

Berglund, Barbara. *Making San Francisco American: Cultural Frontiers in the Urban West, 1846–1906.* Lawrence: University Press of Kansas, 2007.

Blevins, Tim, ed. *Film and Photography on the Front Range.* Colorado Springs: Pikes Peak Library District, 2012.

Blumin, Stuart M. *The Emergence of the Middle Class: Social Experience in the American City, 1760–1900.* New York: Cambridge University Press, 1989.

Booth, Michael R. "Theatrical Boom in the Kootenays." *The Beaver* 292 (1961): 42–46.

Boyer, Paul. *Urban Masses and Moral Order in America, 1820–1920.* Cambridge, Mass.: Harvard University Press, 1978.

Brady, William A. *Showman.* New York: E. P. Dutton, 1937.

Briscoe, Johnson. *The Actors' Birthday Book: An Authoritative Insight into the Lives of the Men and Women of the Stage Born between January First and December Thirty-First, Second Series.* New York: Moffat, Yard, 1908.

Brosnan, Kathleen A. *Uniting Mountain and Plain: Cities, Law, and Environmental Change along the Front Range.* Albuquerque: University of New Mexico Press, 2002.

Brown, Henry. *War on the Theater: A Discussion Which Grew Out of the "Billy Sunday" Meetings, Spokane, Washington: The Newspaper Articles Compiled, and the Argument Extended.* Spokane, Wash.: Dyer Printing Company, 1909.

Brown, Horace. Interview. August 19, 1955 (OH 624). Eastern Washington State Historical Society, Spokane, Washington.

Brownell, Mary. Interview. 1979 (OH 785). Eastern Washington State Historical Society, Spokane, Washington.

Brewster, Ben. "The Circle: Lubitsch and the Theatrical Farce Tradition." *Film History* 13, no. 4 (2001): 372–89.

Browne, John J., Papers. Ms 21. Eastern Washington State Historical Society, Spokane, Washington.

Business Service Association. *The Coeur d'Alene of Spokane, Washington: "The Hotel with a Personality."* Spokane: Business Service Association, 190–.

Cahn, Julius. *Julius Cahn's Official Theatrical Guide, Containing Authentic Information of the Theatres and Attractions in the United States, Canada, Mexico and Cuba.* Vol. 13. New York: Empire Theatre Building, 1908.

Campbell, Helen, Papers. MsSC 224. Eastern Washington State Historical Society, Spokane, Washington.

Carson, L. ed. *The Stage Year Book, 1914.* London: The Stage Offices, 1914.

———. *The Stage Year Book, 1915.* London: The Stage Offices, 1915.

———. *The Stage Year Book, 1916.* London: The Stage Offices, 1916.

Castle, Vernon, and Irene Castle. *Modern Dancing.* New York: Harper and Brothers, 1914.

Chew, William L., III. "'Straight' Sam Meets 'Lewd' Louis: American Perceptions of French Sexuality, 1775–1815." In *Revolutions and Watersheds: Transatlantic Dialogues, 1775–1815,* edited by W. M. Verhoeven and Beth Dolan Kautz, 61–86. Amsterdam: Rodopi, 1999.

Christensen, Bonnie. *Red Lodge and the Mythic West: Coal Miners to Cowboys.* Lawrence: University Press of Kansas, 2002.

Clarke, George S. Interview. June 17, 1958 (OH 459). Eastern Washington State Historical Society, Spokane, Washington.

Cloud, Barbara. *The Business of Newspapers on the Western Frontier.* Reno: University of Nevada Press, 1992.

Cobble, Dorothy Sue. *Dishing It Out: Waitresses and Their Unions in the Twentieth Century.* Urbana: University of Illinois Press, 1991.

Coben, Stanley. *Rebellion against Victorianism: The Impetus for Cultural Change in 1920s America.* New York: Oxford University Press, 1991.

Cochran, Barbara F. *Seven Frontier Women and the Founding of Spokane Falls.* Spokane, Wash.: Tornado Creek Publications, 2011.

Cody, Gabrielle H., and Evert Sprinchorn, eds. *The Columbia Encyclopedia of Modern Drama.* New York: Columbia University Press, 2007.

Conzen, Michael P., and Diane Dillon, eds. *Mapping Manifest Destiny: Chicago and the American West.* Chicago: University of Chicago Press, 2008.

Council minute record books (E, F, G). Spokane Municipal Government, EA598-3-7. Washington State Archives Eastern Regional Branch, Cheney, Washington.

Crommelin, Marinus. *Dear Mother: A Collection of Letters and Photographs describing Many Conditions in and around Spokane in 1901–1902.* Translated and edited by Patrick Serné. Summerland, B.C.: Valley Publishing, 1999.

Cronon, William. *Nature's Metropolis: Chicago and the Great West.* New York: W. W. Norton, 1991.

Cullen, Frank, and Florence Hackman. *Vaudeville Old and New: An Encyclopedia of Variety Performers in America.* New York: Routledge, 2006.

Czitrom, Daniel. "Underworlds and Underdogs: Big Tim Sullivan and Metropolitan Politics in New York, 1889–1913." *Journal of American History* 78, no. 2 (1991): 536–58.

Dailey, W. R., ed. *Henry's Official Western Theatrical Guide, 1907–1908.* San Francisco: 289 13th Street, 1908.

Davidoff, Leonore, and Catherine Hall. *Family Fortunes: Men and Women of the English Middle Class, 1780–1850.* New York: Routledge, 2002.

Davis, Peter A. "The Syndicate/Shubert War." In *Inventing Times Square: Commerce and Culture at the Crossroads of the World,* edited by William R. Taylor, 147–57. New York: Russell Sage Foundation, 1991.

Davis, Tracy C. *Actresses as Working Women: Their Social Identity in Victorian Culture.* London: Routledge, 1991.

DePastino, Todd. *Citizen Hobo: How a Century of Homelessness Shaped America.* Chicago: University of Chicago Press, 2003.

Dilgard, David. *Mill Town Footlights: The Theaters of Everett Washington.* Everett, Wash.: Everett Public Library, 2001.

C. R. Dixon, receiver for Northwest Picture Corporation v. Fred K. McBroom, receiver for Washington Motion Picture Corporation. April 1919. Spokane Superior Court, case 58521. Spokane County Courthouse Archives, Spokane, Washington.

Donovan, Brian. *White Slave Crusades: Race, Gender, and Anti-vice Activism, 1887–1917.* Champaign: University of Illinois Press, 2006.

Dudden, Faye E. *Women in the American Theatre: Audiences and Actresses, 1790–1870.* New Haven: Yale University Press, 1994.

Durham, Nelson W. *History of the City of Spokane and the Spokane Country: From Its Earliest Settlement to the Present Time.* 3 vols. Spokane, Wash.: S. J. Clark Publishing, 1912.

Durham, Weldon B., ed. *American Theatre Companies, 1888–1930.* New York: Greenwood Press, 1987.

Dyar, Ralph E. *News for an Empire: The Story of the* Spokesman-Review *of Spokane, Washington, and of the Field It Serves.* Caldwell, Idaho: Caxton Printers, 1952.

Eastern Washington Genealogical Society. *Spokane County Washington Marriage Licenses, 1891–1903.* Spokane: Eastern Washington Genealogical Society, 1993.

Eaton, Walter Prichard. "The Return of Farce." *American Magazine* 71 (1910): 264–73.

———. "The Rise and Fall of the Theatrical Syndicate." *American Magazine* 70 (1910): 832–42.

Eckberg, Robert Charles. "The Free Speech Fight of the Industrial Workers of the World, Spokane, Washington: 1909–1910." Master's thesis, Washington State University, 1967.

Edwards, Jonathan. *An Illustrated History of Spokane County, State of Washington.* San Francisco?: W. H. Lever, 1900.

Ellingson, John. "Eighty-Five Years of Spokane Memories: The Recollections of Clarence Tesdahl." *Pacific Northwesterner: Westerners, Spokane Corral* 39, no. 1 (1995): 1–15.

Elliott, Eugene Clinton. *A History of Variety-Vaudeville in Seattle: From the Beginning to 1914.* Seattle: University of Washington Press, 1944.

Engeman, Richard H. "The 'Seattle Spirit' Meets *The Alaskan:* A Story of Business, Boosterism, and the Arts." *Pacific Northwest Quarterly* 81, no.2 (1990): 54–66.

Engle, Nancy. "Benefiting a City: Women, Respectability and Reform in Spokane, Washington, 1886–1910." PhD diss., University of Florida, 2003.

Erdman, Andrew L. *Blue Vaudeville: Sex, Morals and the Mass Marketing of Amusement, 1895–1915.* London: McFarland, 2004.

Erenberg, Lewis A. "Everybody's Doin' It: The Pre–World War I Dance Craze, the Castles, and the Modern Girl." *Feminist Studies* 3, nos. 1/2 (1975): 155–70.

———. *Steppin' Out: New York Nightlife and the Transformation of American Culture, 1890–1930.* Westport, Conn.: Greenwood Press, 1981.

Ernst, Alice Henson. *Trouping in the Oregon Country.* Portland: Oregon Historical Society, 1961.

Estby, Ida. Interview. March 25, 1973 (OH 003). Eastern Washington State Historical Society, Spokane, Washington.

Etulain, Richard. *Re-imagining the Modern American West: A Century of Fiction, History, and Art.* Tucson: University of Arizona Press, 1996.

Fahey, John. *The Ballyhoo Bonanza: Charles Sweeney and the Idaho Mines.* Seattle: University of Washington Press, 1971.

———. "Big Lumber in the Inland Empire: The Early Years, 1900–1930." *Pacific Northwest Quarterly* 76, no. 3 (1985): 95–103.

———. *Inland Empire: D. C. Corbin and Spokane.* Seattle: University of Washington Press, 1965.

———. "When the Dutch Owned Spokane." *Pacific Northwest Quarterly* 72, no. 1 (1981): 2–10.

Fargo, Lucile F. *Spokane Story.* Minneapolis: Northwestern Press, 1957.

Federal Theatre Project collection. Acc. No. 5287-001. University of Washington Special Collections.

Fernett, Gene. *American Film Studios: An Historical Encyclopedia.* London: McFarland, 1988.

Ficken, Robert E., and Charles P. LeWarne. *Washington: A Centennial History.* Seattle: University of Washington Press, 1989.

Flom, Eric L. "Cort, John." HistoryLink.org Essay 3296. Accessed February 3, 2011.

———. "Seattle's Orpheum Theatre Opens at 3rd Avenue and Madison Street on May 15, 1911." HistoryLink.org Essay 4247. Accessed February 17, 2011.

Flynn, Elizabeth Gurley. *The Rebel Girl: An Autobiography, My First Life (1906–1926)*. New York: International Publishers, 1973.

Foley, Neil. *The White Scourge: Mexicans, Blacks, and Poor Whites in Texas Cotton Culture*. Berkeley: University of California Press, 1998.

Foner, Eric, and John Arthur Garraty, eds. *The Reader's Companion to American History*. New York: Houghton Mifflin Harcourt, 1991.

Frick, John W. *Theatre, Culture and Temperance Reform in Nineteenth-Century America*. Cambridge: Cambridge University Press, 2003.

Gallinger, Charles. Interview. January 30, 1976 (OH 072, 073, 074). Eastern Washington State Historical Society, Spokane, Washington.

Gassner, John, and Edward Quinn, eds. *The Reader's Encyclopedia of World Drama*. Toronto: Thomas Y. Cromwell, 1969.

George, Holly. "Municipal Film Censorship in Spokane, Washington, 1910–1916." *Pacific Northwest Quarterly* 103, no. 4 (2012): 176–89.

Gilbert, Adelaide Sutton. "The Letters of Adelaide Sutton Gilbert." *Pacific Northwest Forum*, 2d series, 5, no. 1 (1992): 3–96.

Gilfoyle, Timothy J. *City of Eros: New York City, Prostitution, and the Commercialization of Sex, 1790–1920*. New York: W. W. Norton, 1994.

———. *A Pickpocket's Tale: The Underworld of Nineteenth-Century New York*. New York: W. W. Norton, 2006.

Glass, Barbara S. *African American Dance: An Illustrated History*. London: McFarland, 2007.

Glenn, Susan A. *Female Spectacle: The Theatrical Roots of Modern Feminism*. Cambridge, Mass.: Harvard University Press, 2000.

Golden, Eve. *Anna Held and the Birth of Ziegfeld's Broadway*. Lexington: University Press of Kentucky, 2000.

Grau, Robert. *The Business Man in the Amusement World: A Volume of Progress in the Field of the Theatre*. New York: Broadway Publishing, 1910.

———. *The Stage in the Twentieth Century*. New York: Broadway Publishing, 1912.

———. *The Theatre of Science*. New York: Broadway Publishing, 1914.

Greenwood, Annie Pike. *We Sagebrush Folks*. Reprint edition. Moscow: University of Idaho Press, 1988.

Groth, Paul. *Living Downtown: The History of Residential Hotels in the United States*. Berkeley: University of California Press, 1994.

Halaas, David Fridtjof. *Boom Town Newspapers: Journalism on the Rocky Mountain Mining Frontier, 1859–1881*. Albuquerque: University of New Mexico Press, 1981.

Hall, Jacquelyn Dowd. "Private Eyes, Public Women: Images of Class and Sex in the Urban South, Atlanta, Georgia, 1913–1915." In *Work Engendered: Toward a New History of American Labor,* edited by Ava Baron, 243–72. Ithaca, N.Y.: Cornell University Press, 1991.

Halttunen, Karen. *Confidence Men and Painted Women: A Study of Middle-Class Culture in America, 1830–1870.* New Haven: Yale University Press, 1982.

Hamer, David A. *New Towns in the New World: Images and Perceptions of the Nineteenth-Century Urban Frontier.* New York: Columbia University Press, 1990.

Hamilton, Marybeth. *When I'm Bad, I'm Better: Mae West, Sex, and American Entertainment.* Berkeley: University of California Press, 1997.

Harris, Neil. *Cultural Excursions: Marketing Appetites and Cultural Tastes in Modern America.* Chicago: University of Chicago Press, 1990.

Heller, Adele, and Lois Rudnick, eds. *1915, the Cultural Moment: The New Politics, the New Woman, the New Psychology, the New Art, and the New Theatre in America.* New Brunswick, N.J.: Rutgers University Press, 1991.

Henderson, Robert Allen. "The *Spokesman-Review,* 1883–1900: A Mirror to the History of Spokane." PhD diss., Washington State University, 1967.

Herbes, Annika. "Rescuing the Destitute: The Salvation Army in Spokane, 1891–1920." *Columbia* 18, no. 3 (2004): 11–16.

Higham, John. "The Reorientation of American Culture in the 1890s." In *Writing American History: Essays on Modern Scholarship,* 73–102. Bloomington: Indiana University Press, 1970.

Hill, Lawrence James. "A History of Variety-Vaudeville in Minneapolis, Minnesota, from Its Beginnings to 1900." PhD diss., University of Minnesota, 1979.

Hinkle, J. Grant. *Sixteenth Biennial Report of the Secretary of State.* Olympia: Frank Lamborn, 1920.

———. *Seventeenth Biennial Report of the Secretary of State.* Olympia: Frank Lamborn, 1922.

———. *Eighteenth Biennial Report of the Secretary of State.* Olympia: Frank M. Lamborn, 1924.

Hise, Greg. *Magnetic Los Angeles: Planning the Twentieth-Century Metropolis.* Baltimore: Johns Hopkins University Press, 1997.

Hodgson, Edward R. "Early Spokane's 150,000 Club: Missed 1910 Population Goal by 31 Per Cent." *Pacific Northwesterner* 21, no. 2 (1977): 17–22, 24–32.

Hoemann, Thomas C., and Richard Nafziger. *Members of the Washington State Legislature, 1889–2005.* Olympia, Wash.: Secretary of the Senate, 2005.

Hook, Harry H., and Francis J. McGuire. *Spokane Falls Illustrated: the Metropolis of Eastern Washington; a History of the Early Settlement and the Spokane Falls of Today; Embracing the Commercial and Manufacturing Advantages of the City and Its Marvelous Growth, with Illustrations of Prominent Buildings,*

Beautiful Homes, and Portraits and Sketches of Leading Citizens. Minneapolis: F. L. Thresher, 1889.

Horsman, Reginald. *Race and Manifest Destiny: The Origins of American Racial Anglo-Saxonism.* Cambridge, Mass.: Harvard University Press, 1981.

Houchin, John. *Censorship of the American Theatre in the Twentieth Century.* Cambridge: Cambridge University Press, 2003.

Howell, I. M. *Fifteenth Biennial Report of the Secretary of State.* Olympia: Frank Lamborn, 1918.

Huberman, Jeffrey H. *Late Victorian Farce.* Ann Arbor, Mich.: UMI Research Press, 1986.

Hunter, Tera W. *To 'Joy My Freedom: Southern Black Women's Lives and Labors after the Civil War.* Cambridge, Mass.: Harvard University Press, 1995.

Hutton, May Arkwright, Papers. MsSC 55. Eastern Washington State Historical Society, Spokane, Washington.

Hyslop, Robert B. *Spokane's Building Blocks.* Spokane, Wash.: Standard Blue Prints, 1983.

In re Considine. Circuit Court, D. Washington, N.D. 83 F. 157, 1897 U.S. App.

Issel, William, and Robert W. Cherny. *San Francisco, 1865–1932: Politics, Power, and Urban Development.* Berkeley: University of California Press, 1986.

Jackson, Brenda K. *Domesticating the West: The Re-creation of the Nineteenth-Century American Middle Class.* Lincoln: University of Nebraska Press, 2005.

Jacobson, Matthew Frye. *Barbarian Virtues: The United States Encounters Foreign Peoples at Home and Abroad, 1876–1917.* New York: Hill and Wang, 2001.

———. *Whiteness of a Different Color: European Immigrants and the Alchemy of Race.* Cambridge, Mass.: Harvard University Press, 1999.

Johnson, Claudia D. "That Guilty Third Tier: Prostitution in Nineteenth-Century American Theaters." *American Quarterly* 27, no. 5 (1975): 575–84.

Johnson, Katie N. *Sisters in Sin: Brothel Drama in America, 1900–1920.* Cambridge: Cambridge University Press, 2006.

Johnson, Paul E. *A Shopkeeper's Millennium: Society and Revivals in Rochester, New York, 1815–1837.* New York: Hill and Wang, 1978.

Jones, Gareth Stedman. *Outcast London: A Study in the Relationship between Classes in Victorian Society.* Oxford: Oxford University Press, 1971.

Jones, Jan L. *Renegades, Showmen and Angels: A Theatrical History of Fort Worth, 1873–2001.* Fort Worth: Texas Christian University Press, 2006.

Kasson, John F. *Amusing the Million: Coney Island at the Turn of the Century.* New York: Hill and Wang, 1978.

———. *Houdini, Tarzan, and the Perfect Man: The White Male Body and the Challenge of Modernity in America.* New York: Hill and Wang, 2001.

———. *Rudeness and Civility: Manners in Nineteenth-Century Urban America.* New York: Hill and Wang, 1990.

Kaufman, Polly Welts. *Women Teachers on the Frontier.* New Haven: Yale University Press, 1984.

Kelly, Jessica H. "John Cort: The Frohman of the West." *The Coast* 8, no. 3 (1907): 144–47.

Kensel, William Hudson. "The Economic History of Spokane, Washington, 1881–1910." PhD diss., Washington State University, 1962.

Kibler, M. Alison. *Rank Ladies: Gender and Cultural Hierarchy in American Vaudeville.* Chapel Hill: University of North Carolina Press, 1999.

Kinzer, Donald L. *An Episode in Anti-Catholicism: The American Protective Association.* Seattle: University of Washington Press, 1964.

Kirkendall, Richard S. "The Manifest Destiny of Spokane." *Journal of the West* 42, no. 1 (2000): 3–7.

Knapp, Margaret. "Introductory Essay." In *Inventing Times Square: Commerce and Culture at the Crossroads of the World,* edited by William R. Taylor, 121–32. New York: Russell Sage Foundation, 1991.

Knowles, Mark. *The Wicked Waltz and Other Scandalous Dances: Outrage at Couple Dancing in the Nineteenth and Early Twentieth Centuries.* London: McFarland, 2009.

Kohlhauff, Edward, Sr. "Fifty Years of Theaters in Spokane." 1934. William Kohlhauff Papers, MsSc 29. Eastern Washington State Historical Society, Spokane, Washington.

Laurie, Joe. *Vaudeville: From the Honky-Tonks to the Palace.* New York: Holt, 1953.

Lears, T. J. Jackson. "From Salvation to Self-Realization." In *Culture of Consumption: Critical Essays in American History, 1880–1980,* edited by Richard Wightman and T. J. Jackson Lears, 1–38. New York: Pantheon, 1983.

———. *No Place of Grace: Antimodernism and the Transformation of American Culture, 1880–1920.* New York: Pantheon Books, 1981.

———. *Something for Nothing: Luck in America.* New York: Viking Press, 2003.

Lehuu, Isabelle. *Carnival on the Page: Popular Print Media in Antebellum America.* Chapel Hill: University of North Carolina Press, 2000.

Levine, Lawrence W. *Highbrow/Lowbrow: The Emergence of Cultural Hierarchy in America.* Cambridge, Mass.: Harvard University Press, 1988.

Libby, A. C., Jr. "Stars Added Glamour to Old Auditorium." *Spokesman-Review,* June 13, 1943.

Lippman, Monroe. "The History of the Theatrical Syndicate: Its Effect upon the Theatre in America." PhD diss., University of Michigan, 1937.

Lloyd, Herbert. *Vaudeville Trails thru the West: "By One Who Knows."* Philadelphia: Herbert Lloyd, 1919.

Londré, Felicia Hardison. *The Enchanted Years of the Stage: Kansas City at the Crossroads of American Theater, 1870–1930.* Columbia: University of Missouri Press, 2007.

Lotchin, Roger W. *San Francisco, 1846–1856*. Urbana: University of Illinois Press, 1974.

Lott, Eric. *Love and Theft: Blackface Minstrelsy and the American Working Class*. New York: Oxford University Press, 1993.

Lufkin, George L. "American Theatre, Spokane, Wash." *Marquee: The Journal of the Theatre Historical Society* 5, no. 2 (1973): 5–7.

———. "The Spokane Spectacle: A Study of Spokane, Washington, Theaters between 1883 and 1983." Rev. ed. Shelton, Wash.: Published privately, 1984.

Lukas, J. Anthony. *Big Trouble: A Murder in a Small Western Town Sets Off a Struggle for the Soul of America*. New York: Simon and Schuster, 1997.

Mahar, Karen Ward. *Women Filmmakers in Early Hollywood*. Baltimore: Johns Hopkins University Press, 2006.

Matthews, Henry. *Kirtland Cutter: Architect in the Land of Promise*. Seattle: University of Washington Press, 1998.

———. "Kirtland Cutter: Spokane's Architect." In *Spokane and the Inland Empire: An Interior Pacific Northwest Anthology*, edited by David H. Stratton, 142–77. Pullman: Washington State University Press, 1991.

Maurer, David W., and Ellesa Clay High. "New Words: Where Do They Come From and Where Do They Go?" *American Speech: A Quarterly of Linguistic Usage* 55, no. 3 (1980): 184–94.

McArthur, Benjamin. *Actors and American Culture, 1880–1920*. Philadelphia: Temple University Press, 1984.

McNamara, Brooks. *The New York Concert Saloon: The Devil's Own Nights*. Cambridge: Cambridge University Press, 2002.

Meinig, Donald W. "American Wests: Preface to a Geographical Interpretation." *Annals of the Association of American Geographers* 62, no. 2 (1972): 159–84.

———. *The Shaping of America: A Geographical Perspective on 500 Years of History*. Vol. 2: *Continental America, 1800–1867*. New Haven: Yale University Press, 1993.

———. *The Shaping of America: A Geographical Perspective on 500 Years of History*. Vol. 3: *Transcontinental America, 1850–1915*. New Haven: Yale University Press, 2000.

Meyerowitz, Joanne J. *Women Adrift: Independent Wage Earners in Chicago, 1880–1920*. Chicago: University of Chicago Press, 1988.

Morgan, Murray. *Skid Road: An Informal Portrait of Seattle*. Rev. ed. New York: Ballantine Books, 1971.

Morrissey, Katherine G. *Mental Territories: Mapping the Inland Empire*. Ithaca, N.Y.: Cornell University Press, 1997.

Morse, Kathryn G. *The Nature of Gold: An Environmental History of the Klondike Gold Rush*. Seattle: University of Washington Press, 2003.

Motion Picture News. *Motion Picture Studio Directory and Trade Annual.* New York: Motion Picture News, 1921.

Mouvet, Maurice. *Maurice's Art of Dancing: An Autobiographical Sketch with Complete Descriptions of Modern Dances and Full Illustrations Showing the Various Steps and Positions.* New York: G. Schirmer, 1915.

Myres, Sandra L. *Westering Women and the Frontier Experience, 1800–1915.* Albuquerque: University of New Mexico Press, 1982.

Nasaw, David. *Going Out: The Rise and Fall of Public Amusements.* New York: Basic Books, 1993.

Nelson, Edwin Leonard. "The History of Road Shows in Seattle, from Their Beginnings to 1914." Master's thesis, University of Washington, 1947.

Nelson, Richard. "Utah Filmmakers of the Silent Screen." *Utah Historical Quarterly* 43, no. 1 (1975): 4–25.

Newbury, Michael. "Polite Gaiety: Cultural Hierarchy and Musical Comedy, 1893–1904." *Journal of the Gilded Age and Progressive Era* 4, no. 4 (2005): 381–407.

Nord, David Paul. *Newspapers and New Politics: Midwestern Municipal Reform, 1890–1900.* Ann Arbor, Mich.: UMI Research Press, 1981.

Northwestern and Pacific Hypotheek Bank records. Ms 46. Eastern Washington State Historical Society, Spokane, Washington.

Official Gazette of the City of Spokane. Vols. 3, 8, 10, 11. Office of the City Clerk, Spokane, Washington.

Page, Brett. *Writing for Vaudeville.* Springfield, Mass.: Home Correspondence School, 1915.

Page, Michael. "Sarah Bernhardt's Visit to Spokane." *Pacific Northwest Forum,* 2nd series, 5, no. 1 (1992): 128–40.

Palmer, Colin A. *Encyclopedia of African-American Culture and History: The Black Experience in the Americas.* New York: Macmillan Reference, 2006.

Peiss, Kathy. *Cheap Amusements: Working Women and Leisure in Turn-of-the-Century New York.* Philadelphia: Temple University Press, 1986.

Peters, Lloyd. *Lionhead Lodge: Movieland of the Northwest.* 2nd ed. Fairfield, Wash.: Ye Galleon Press, 1976.

Poggi, Jack. *Theater in America: The Impact of Economic Forces, 1870–1967.* Ithaca, N.Y.: Cornell University Press, 1966.

Polk, R. L., and Co. *Spokane City Directory,* 1895–1899, 1905–1915.

Pomeroy, Earl S. *The Pacific Slope: A History of California, Oregon, Washington, Idaho, Utah, and Nevada.* New York: Knopf, 1965.

Pratt, George. "Early Stage and Screen: A Two-Way Street." *Cinema Journal* 14, no. 2 (1974–1975): 16–19.

Reams, Danny Ival. "Spokane Theatre, 1880–1892." Master's thesis, Washington State University, 1970.

Registers of the city prison, 1898–1901. Spokane Municipal Government, EA598-19-1. Washington State Archives Eastern Regional Branch, Cheney, Washington.

Reskin, Barbara F., and Patricia A. Roos. *Job Queues, Gender Queues: Explaining Women's Inroads into Male Occupations.* Philadelphia: Temple University Press, 1990.

Rettmann, Jef. "Business, Government, and Prostitution in Spokane, Washington, 1889–1910." *Pacific Northwest Quarterly* 89, no. 2 (1998): 77–83.

———. "Prostitution in Spokane, 1880–1910." Master's thesis, Eastern Washington University, 1995.

Richards, Jeffrey. *Sir Henry Irving: A Victorian Actor and His World.* New York: Palgrave Macmillan, 2005.

Riddle, Thomas. "The Old Radicalism in America: John R. Rogers and the Populist Movement in Washington, 1891–1900." PhD diss., Washington State University, 1976.

———. "Whitman County Populism and Washington State Politics, 1889–1902." Master's thesis, Washington State University, 1971.

Rodger, Gillian. *Champagne Charlie and Pretty Jemima: Variety Theater in the Nineteenth Century.* Urbana: University of Illinois Press, 2010.

Roediger, David. *The Wages of Whiteness: Race and the Making of the American Working Class.* New York: Verso, 1991.

Ross, Ellen. *Love and Toil: Motherhood in Outcast London.* Oxford: Oxford University Press, 1993.

Ryan, Mary P. *Cradle of the Middle Class: The Family in Oneida County, New York, 1790–1865.* New York: Cambridge University Press, 1981.

Saloutos, Theodore. "Alexander Pantages, Theater Magnate of the West." *Pacific Northwest Quarterly* 57 (October 1966): 137–47.

Saum, Lewis O. *The Popular Mood of America, 1860–1890.* Lincoln: University of Nebraska Press, 1990.

Schwantes, Carlos A. *Coxey's Army: An American Odyssey.* Moscow: University of Idaho Press, 1994.

———. *The Pacific Northwest: An Interpretive History.* Lincoln: University of Nebraska Press, 1989.

———. *Radical Heritage: Labor, Socialism, and Reform in Washington and British Columbia, 1885–1917.* Seattle: University of Washington Press, 1979.

———. "Spokane and the Wageworkers' Frontier: A Labor History to World War I." In *Spokane and the Inland Empire: An Interior Pacific Northwest Anthology,* edited by David H. Stratton, 122–41. Pullman: Washington State University Press, 1991.

Settlers' Guide to Homes in the Northwest, being a Handbook of Spokane Falls, W. T., the Queen City of the Pacific Its Matchless Water Power and Advantages as a Commercial Centre. Spokane Falls: Dallam, Ansell, and Edwards, 1885.

Shipman, Nell. *The Silent Screen and My Talking Heart: An Autobiography*. Boise, Idaho: Boise State University Press, 1987.

Simmons, Oliver. "Passing of the Sullivan Dynasty." *Munsey's Magazine* 1, no. 3 (1913): 407–16.

Singal, Daniel Joseph. "Towards a Definition of American Modernism." *American Quarterly* 39, no. 1 (1987): 7–26.

Snyder, Robert W. *Voice of the City: Vaudeville and Popular Culture in New York*. New York: Oxford University Press, 1989.

Soden, Dale. "Billy Sunday in Spokane: Revivalism and Social Control." *Pacific Northwest Quarterly* 79, no. 1 (1988): 10–17.

Stansell, Christine. *City of Women: Sex and Class in New York, 1789–1860*. Champaign: University of Illinois Press, 1982.

Starr, Kevin. *Americans and the California Dream, 1850–1915*. New York: Oxford University Press, 1973.

State of Washington, Plaintiff, v. John W. Considine, Defendant. November 1895, case 552, reel 6, criminal 68.7. Spokane County Courthouse Archives, Spokane, Washington.

State of Washington, Respondent, v. John W. Considine, Appellant. No. 2466. Supreme Court of Washington, 16 Wash. 358, 47 P. 755, 1897 Wash.

Stearns, Marshall, and Jean Stearns. *Jazz Dance: The Story of American Vernacular Dance*. New York: Macmillan, 1968.

Stilwell, Kristine. "'If You Don't Slip': The Hobo Life, 1911–1916." PhD diss., University of Missouri–Columbia, 2004.

Stratton, Anna M. Papers. MsSC 174. Eastern Washington State Historical Society, Spokane, Washington.

Stratton, David H., ed. *Spokane and the Inland Empire: An Interior Pacific Northwest Anthology*. Pullman: Washington State University Press, 2005.

Storms, A. D., ed. *The Players Blue Book*. Worcester, Mass.: Sutherland and Storms, 1901.

Tarrach, Dean Arthur. "Alexander Pantages: The Seattle Pantages and His Vaudeville Circuit." Master's thesis, University of Washington, 1973.

Taylor, William R., ed. *Inventing Times Square: Commerce and Culture at the Crossroads of the World*. New York: Russell Sage Foundation, 1991.

Teaford, Jon C. *The Unheralded Triumph: City Government in America, 1870–1900*. Baltimore: Johns Hopkins University Press, 1984.

"Theatrical Syndicate Copy No. 1." Box 1, Federal Theatre Project collection, Acc. No. 5287-001. University of Washington Special Collections.

Tickner, Lisa. "The Popular Culture of *Kermesse*: Lewis, Painting and Performance, 1912–13." In *In Visible Touch: Modernism and Masculinity*, edited by Terry Smith, 139–72. Chicago: University of Chicago Press, 1997.

Toll, Robert C. *On with the Show: The First Century of Show Business in America*. New York: Oxford University Press, 1976.

Tosh, John. *A Man's Place: Masculinity and the Middle-Class Home in Victorian England.* London: Yale University Press, 1999.

Trachtenberg, Alan. *The Incorporation of America: Culture and Society in the Gilded Age.* New York: Hill and Wang, 1982.

Trunk, Carl H. Interview. May 28, 1964 (OH 475). Eastern Washington State Historical Society, Spokane, Washington.

Ullman, Sharon R. *Sex Seen: The Emergence of Modern Sexuality in America.* Berkeley: University of California Press, 1997.

Undeberg, Krista Anette. "The Diary of Helen Campbell: Life during Spokane's Age of Elegance, 1913–1917." Master's thesis, Washington State University, 1997.

Vermillion, Billy Budd. "The Remarriage Plot in the 1910s." *Film History* 13, no. 4 (2001): 359–71.

Wade, Richard C. *The Urban Frontier: The Rise of Western Cities, 1790–1830.* Cambridge, Mass.: Harvard University Press, 1959.

Wang, Zhenyu. "A Study of Streetscape Evolution on Riverside Avenue in Downtown Spokane, 1881–1999." Master's thesis, Washington State University, 2001.

Washington State. *Fourteenth Biennial Report of the Secretary of State, October 1, 1914, September 30, 1916.* Olympia, Wash.: Frank M. Lamborn, Public Printer, 1916.

———. *House Journal of the Fourth Legislature of the State of Washington. Ellis Morrison, Speaker. January 14–March 15, 1895.* Olympia, Wash.: O. C. White, State Printer, 1895.

———. *Senate Journal of the Fourth Legislature of the State of Washington. January 14–March 15, 1895.* Olympia, Wash.: O. C. White, State Printer, 1895.

———. *Session Laws of the State of Washington, Session of 1895.* Olympia, Wash.: O. C. White, State Printer, 1895.

Wasserman, Bruce Martin. "Early Theatre in Spokane, Washington, 1889–1902." PhD diss., Washington State University, 1975.

Wertheim, Arthur Frank. *Vaudeville Wars: How the Keith-Albee and Orpheum Circuits Controlled the Big-Time and Its Performers.* New York: Palgrave Macmillan, 2006.

Wightman, Richard, and T. J. Jackson Lears, eds. *Culture of Consumption: Critical Essays in American History, 1880–1980.* New York: Pantheon, 1983.

Wilmeth, Don B. *Variety Entertainment and Outdoor Amusements: A Reference Guide.* London: Greenwood Press, 1982.

Wilson, William H. *The City Beautiful Movement.* Baltimore: Johns Hopkins University Press, 1994.

Wrobel, David M. *Promised Lands: Promotion, Memory, and the Creation of the American West.* Lawrence: University Press of Kansas, 2002.

Woman's Club of Spokane records. Ms 199. Eastern Washington State Historical Society, Spokane, Washington.

Woodward, Dorothy. Interview. April 30, 1984 (OH 364). Eastern Washington State Historical Society, Spokane, Washington.
Youngs, J. William T. *The Fair and the Falls: Spokane's Expo '74: Transforming an American Environment.* Cheney: Eastern Washington University Press, 1996.
———. "Spokane's Northwest Industrial Exposition of 1890." *Pacific Northwest Forum* 7, no. 1 (1994): 38–56.

Newspapers

American Cinematographer, 1922
Dramatic Mirror, 1918
Los Angeles Times, 1914
Moving Picture World, 1916
New York Times, 1895, 1897, 1901, 1910–1911, 1913–1914, 1918, 1943
Pacific Northwest Inlander, 2000, 2003, 2012
Photoplay, 1916
Seattle Post-Intelligencer, 1895
Seattle Post Times, 1895
Spokane Chronicle, 1890–1918
Spokane Daily Chronicle, 1978
Spokane Falls Daily Chronicle, 1890
Spokane Falls Review, 1889–1890, 1899
Spokane Press, 1910
Spokesman-Review, 1892–1919, 1926, 1931, 1943, 1945, 1957, 1980, 1997, 2002

Index